D1421339

THE THEORY OF PROFIT

THE THEORY
OF PROFIT

By

D. M. LAMBERTON

BASIL BLACKWELL
OXFORD
1965

Printed in Great Britain for BASIL BLACKWELL & MOTT, LTD.
by A. R. MOWBRAY & CO. LIMITED in the City of Oxford
and bound at the KEMP HALL BINDERY

PREFACE

CONCEPTS of profit and of profit maximization play a major role in economics. Nevertheless, theoretical discussion of profit as a form of income has for some considerable time shown confusion of concepts and of method. The theory has lacked empirical content and been widely regarded as an apologetic for business capitalism. In this book I have reconsidered the theory of profit in the light of empirical studies of business behaviour, especially of pricing and investment decisions under conditions of uncertainty.

In a dynamic setting, organization and information have considerable importance as factors in business behaviour. These factors provide the basis for a more general explanation of the phenomenon of profit which encompasses the traditional, rival explanations in terms of uncertainty, innovation and monopoly power. The implications of this emphasis upon organization and information for cost analysis, pricing and investment decisions, and the interpretation of profit statistics are discussed.

The organizational model of the firm which I have suggested raises serious issues for current controversy about the theory of the firm itself. I believe that future development should be away from the traditional static, welfare-oriented approach to business behaviour and toward a theory of the disequilibrium behaviour of the business firm.

I am indebted to the Trustees of the Services Canteens Trust Fund of Australia for the postgraduate scholarship which enabled me to work at Oxford on the thesis from which this book derives. I should like to thank the Warden and Fellows of Nuffield College who elected me a Student of the College, thereby greatly facilitating the conduct of my work. Participation in the Oxford Graduate Seminar in the Economics of Industries was of great assistance to me.

So many people have helped me in the development of the ideas expressed in this book that it is impossible to record them here by name. However, my special debt to Philip Andrews should be made explicit. Always approachable and ever ready to discuss and to encourage, he gave me invaluable assistance. Final responsibility for the book is, of course, my own.

For permission to use portions of some earlier material by the author, acknowledgements are due to the editors of *The Economic Journal* and *The Quarterly Journal of Economics*. Hart, Schaffner & Marx kindly granted permission to quote from Frank H. Knight, *Risk, Uncertainty and Profit*.

D. McL. LAMBERTON

March, 1965

CONTENTS

CHAPTER I

EXTENSIONS TO THE THEORY OF THE FIRM

THERE is small need to defend the theory of profit as a subject of study, for few if any fields in economics can disclaim concern with profit. As the assumed objective of business behaviour, as a source of income, and as a dominant element in the supply of capital, a profit variable finds its place in most micro- and macro-economic models. Policy questions such as the fostering of growth and stability, taxation, and the control of monopoly, reveal the same preoccupation with profit. On what grounds is reconsideration of the theory of profit justified? The detailed answer to this question will emerge in the following pages; it suffices here to offer two brief comments. For some considerable time the theory of profit has been in a confused and tangled state;[1] and, a connected point, the theory has lacked empirical content. To clear away all these confusions and impart empirical content to theory is a task of considerable magnitude. This chapter points to the source of difficulty; namely, the over-abstraction which has led to neglect of the firm, its nature, policy criteria and even its activities. Such neglect is open to interpretation as the use of an outmoded model of social and economic organization; or, alternatively but somewhat superficially, as a consequence of the traditional theory of the firm being a theory of markets rather than a theory of the behaviour of the firm.

For the theorist caught in the profit confusion, the solution is to take account explicitly of the nature of the firm; by which is meant the firm's essential qualities: its structure, objectives, modes of decision-making, and activities directed to the attainment of its objectives. This can lead to a theory of the behaviour of the firm which is not merely an adjunct to or building block for a theory of markets, although ultimately it may enable improvements in aggregative analysis. Much work done since the Cost Controversy and the early contributions of Joan Robinson and E. H. Chamberlin might be interpreted as a move towards such a theory of the firm. Acceptance of this interpretation has been inhibited by a compelling

---

[1] See, for example, the multiplicity of theories and definitions classified by J. Fred Weston, 'The Profit Concept and Theory: A Restatement', *Journal of Political Economy*, LXII (April 1954), pp. 152–170; G. L. S. Shackle, *Decision, Order and Time in Human Affairs* (Cambridge at the University Press, 1961), Chapter XXVIII.

need to fit new facts into the old theoretical framework, which has a normative bias. By abandoning this impossible task it becomes possible to proceed with study of the behaviour of the firm which can throw much needed light upon the nature of profit, the meaning of profit maximization under conditions of uncertainty, the significance of information, and the role of organization. Unless attention is directed to the nature of the firm it is necessary to adopt the tactic of either ignoring uncertainty or assigning a key role to expectations which are themselves unexplained. Neither of these two latter courses does more than reveal the poverty of thought on this important subject.

NEGLECT OF THE NATURE OF THE FIRM

It is difficult to characterize unambiguously traditional or orthodox theory of the firm. Perhaps its most widely accepted meaning is a theory of the behaviour of competitive markets; to which might be added theories of monopoly and imperfect or monopolistic competition. Such a view excludes the elusive theory of oligopoly, full and normal cost theories of pricing, growth maximization, profit satisficing,[1] information and organization theory, and activity analysis. It is not implied that these are, or could be, independent elements in a new 'theory of the firm'. It can be argued, for example, that organizational aspects of the firm are linked with the theory of oligopoly, growth maximization, and profit satisficing; and that taken together some of these elements provide an improved, a more general explanation of the observed behaviour that has been the foundation stone of the full and normal cost theories. However, these excluded items have been regarded frequently as radical departures motivated by a misguided search for realism which stems from a lack of understanding of the purposes of the traditional theory.

What are these purposes? Using the maximization postulate the traditional theory has sought to provide an explanation of price determination and resource allocation through markets; a conceptual scheme to serve as a basis for aggregative analysis. The firm itself is unimportant: 'all the economist needs for his models is that in economic matters the firm should behave as he postulates, and it

---

[1] Profit satisficing is perhaps the least known of these developments. It relates to the attempt to formulate the objective of the firm as 'satisfactory' rather than maximum profit. The concept bears an affinity to the normal, ordinary and fair profits discussed by Marshall, Chamberlin and Andrews and will be dealt with in detail in Chapters IV and VII.

has not yet been shown that non-economic factors enter so strongly and so perversely into firms' decisions that all economic reasoning about them must be invalid'.[1] This view savours of protest that the effects of such non-economic factors as status and craftsmanship are negligible. It fails to perceive that the fundamental problem concerns not the non-economic factors, although in aggregate their effect may merit attention, but the meaning of profit maximization in relation to decisions taken outside an equilibrium state of perfect competition and under conditions of uncertainty. It is against this background that the neglect of the nature of the firm can be illustrated by considering briefly definition of the firm and its production function and the treatment of behaviour of organizations and expectations.

Definitions of the firm support the view that the firm, the decision-making unit, is treated as given. As an example consider the following statement:

The concept of a firm is simple, a matter of definition; it is the effective decision-taking unit in whatever production activity is considered. In practice, this may be what is called an establishment or plant, or it may be a company. On the other hand, it may be a group of establishments or companies organised in some unit of effective control, an organisation like Unilevers or a nationalised industry. Whatever the organisation, however, it is assumed here that there is a decision-taking unit—for the particular activity and time period (short or long) considered—and the unit is called the firm as a matter of convenience.[2]

This simple concept of the firm is supposed to be adequate in both short and long period analysis. Likewise Hicks in his discussion of the equilibrium conditions for the firm treats the organizational unit as given.[3]

The closely allied definition of the firm's production function further illustrates the neglect of the nature of the firm. For example, Samuelson suggested 'that only "inputs" be explicitly included in the production function, and that this term be confined to denote measurable quantitative economic goods and services. The production function must be associated with a particular institution (accounting, decision-making unit, etc.), and must be drawn up as of any unique circumstances pertaining to this unit.'[4] The implications

[1] N. H. Leyland. Review of R. Ells, *The Meaning of Modern Business. An Introduction to the Philosophy of Large Corporate Enterprise* (New York: Columbia University Press, 1960), *Economic Journal*, LXXI (September 1961), p. 618.

[2] R. G. D. Allen, *Mathematical Economics* (London: Macmillan & Co., Ltd., 1956), p. 608.

[3] J. R. Hicks, *Value and Capital* (Oxford at the Clarendon Press, 1939), Chapter VI.

[4] P. A. Samuelson, *Foundations of Economic Analysis* (Cambridge: Harvard University Press, 1947), p. 84.

of such a definition need to be explored. If the objective is prediction of the behaviour of the firm it is necessary to specify the nature of the 'particular institution'. In a sense its history and organization will be unique and difficult to treat as measurable quantitative services.[1] If the production function is defined in relation to a given decision-making unit the nature of that unit or institution, its complex of policies is excluded from the analysis and must be the subject of supplementary studies. Inter-firm differences will be acknowledged and may lead to a profit residual even under conditions of competition.[2] The explanation of profit should take account of the nature of the unit; profit accrues to the firm as it is the socially approved institution of business organization. This is far removed from the level of abstraction at which Wicksell was suggesting that either the labourer or the capitalist could become the entrepreneur.[3]

Further confirmation of the neglect of the nature of the firm is provided by an examination of the treatment of the behaviour of such an institution as the cartel; for the cartel, being an aggregate of firms, had to be treated as an organization. The firms participating in a cartel relinquish their freedom of action in certain areas to the organization. Knowledge of the organizational objective(s) is a prerequisite for a theory of the behaviour of the organization; but there are no simple norms such as maximization of utility or maximization of profit available.[4] The cartel may have political associations and its objectives may be changing through time. It is convenient to regard the aims of the organization as having the nature of an end-index which permits the stressing of different goals, or elements of policy, at different times. Such an end-index would not be independent of change internal to the organization. However, 'There is within economic theory, no general theory of the behaviour of organizations corresponding to the theory of the behaviour of households and firms. Whether such a general theory could be created remains to be seen; perhaps the problem is a sociological one.'[5]

---

[1] Measurement of capital and labour likewise encounters major obstacles.

[2] Cf. Samuelson, *op. cit.*, p. 87. J. A. Schumpeter has criticized Samuelson's treatment, stating that there is no justification 'at all for his statement . . . that "net revenue"—if this means "pure profits"—does not tend to be zero even in (perfect equilibrium of) pure competition'. (*History of Economic Analysis* (New York: Oxford University Press, 1954), p. 1053, n. 72.) However, Schumpeter's view requires that all activities of the firm, all aspects of its existence as an organizational unit be included as inputs in the production function.

[3] K. Wicksell, *Lectures on Political Economy*, trans. E. Classen (London: George Routledge & Sons, 1934), I, p. 109. Wicksell was dealing with 'a logical construction without any counterpart in reality'. Subsequent contributors have not always made this distinction.

[4] See Bent Hansen, *The Economic Theory of Fiscal Policy* (London: Allen & Unwin, 1958), Chapters I, XI. [5] *Ibid.*, p. 211.

This is a sound view; it is clearly desirable to have a theory of organizational behaviour. However, the problem has to be faced in its full generality. Firms, and for that matter households too, are organizations. If it is unsatisfactory to assume that trade associations and cartels do nothing, at least in the long-run, that would not have resulted from the operation of a market mechanism,[1] it should be equally unsatisfactory to make a similar assumption about the organization called a firm. The units which go to make up a firm have relinquished certain action parameters. To assume that the organization is equivalent to the functioning of the price mechanism is to dismiss the question why firms exist at all.

The remaining illustration of the neglect of the nature of the firm relates to expectations. The trend of thought about the dominant influences on prices has been described as follows: 'The prices of all goods could be deduced if we knew with sufficient detail for each person in the market the answers to the questions "What does he like?" and "What does he possess?" It did not occur to most of those who built the beautiful neoclassical structure of static value theory to put upon the same footing as those questions a third kind of question: "What does he know?" or "What does he believe?" '[2] This third kind of question leads directly to the problem of formulating a theory of expectations. But to answer this question it is necessary to first ask 'What is the nature of the possessor of the knowledge, the holder of the beliefs?' Of course, it is possible to argue that Shackle's and this further question are subsumed by the neoclassical questions: a statement of preferences, provided some reasonable measure of stability attaches to them, renders the knowledge and belief question unnecessary if 'rational' behaviour is assumed; and knowledge and belief, the capacity to add to the store of information, the whole complex organization of the firm, could be treated as possessions.

Some consequences of this neglect of the nature of the firm are of special interest to the theorist concerned with profit. The result of limiting the range of inputs included in the production function in the Samuelson fashion is that the theory of the firm, like the theory of consumer behaviour based upon given preferences, is applicable only to short-run conditions and to marginal changes in

---

[1] *Ibid.*, pp. 209–210. Hansen rightly rejects this interpretation of the role of the cartel.
[2] G. L. S. Shackle, 'The Nature of the Bargaining Process', J. T. Dunlop, ed., *The Theory of Wage Determination* (London: Macmillan & Co., Ltd., 1957), p. 298.

institutions.[1] It excludes the forces of change that arise from within the firm or through its interaction with the social framework. Over-abstraction, coupled with or occasioned by the longstanding pre-occupation with equilibrium states, has produced what is essentially a 'pre-firm' theory of the firm. This defect can be remedied by extending the range of inputs. Conceptually, this might be treated as modification of the concept of capital; for capital, contrary to practice but perhaps in accord with the underlying idea, would then include organization and information. It could be argued that at both macro- and microeconomic levels such a revision of the concept of capital would be quite logical but that disaggregation of capital in this broader sense, a more detailed classification of the factors of production, is preferable in order to develop a theory of the behaviour of the firm. Such disaggregation has significant implications for productivity analysis and the theory of income distribution.

Adoption of the firm as the fundamental unit, the aims and methods of which are not themselves a subject of study but are incorporated in theory by means of conventional assumptions, has yielded a theory of the firm which has limited scope. It has not assisted with the problems of behaviour under conditions of un-certainty; only by ignoring the complex relationships between uncertainty, information, and business organization has it been able to link profit and uncertainty, but in a way that is neither useful theoretically nor applicable empirically. Nor has the theory acknowledged the fact and consequences of decisions made under disequilibrium conditions; disequilibrium may give rise to market imperfections, influence the organization and information-collecting activities of the firm, and modify the firm's policy criteria.

Why have economists persisted with such a concept of the firm? There are, no doubt, many reasons. There may be an inevitable time lag before economic models reflect existing conditions; the obstacle may have been intellectual vested interests in a tidy equili-brium theory which was threatened by a widening of the concept of factor of production to include 'resources' such as organization and information which seemed not only difficult to quantify but also not so obviously subject, at least in known ways, to the penetrative powers of the price mechanism. No doubt reluctance to move

[1] For some comment to this effect in the context of the theory of consumer behaviour see T. Surányi-Unger, 'Individual and Collective Wants', *Journal of Political Economy*, LVI (February 1948), pp. 1–22; M. Abramovitz, 'The Welfare Interpretation of Secular Trends in National Income and Product', M. Abramovitz *et al.*, *The Allocation of Economic Resources* (Stanford: Stanford University Press, 1959), pp. 1–22.

beyond the boundaries of the economist's traditional field of inquiry played some part, especially when the subject matter included the practical problems of business and the more recent developments known as 'management science'. However, the dominant reasons are much the same as those that have led economists to avoid the role and measurement of human capital. 'Free men are first and foremost the end to be served by economic endeavour; they are not property or marketable assets.'[1] Admirable as this attitude may be, it should not cause the contribution of human capital to productivity and economic growth to be ignored. How is this related to the concept of the firm? For study of the individual firm it must be recognized that the firm possesses a stock of capital,[2] an organization, and a stock of information which will be modified by the firm's own endeavours and not merely as an automatic result of the operation of the market. It is tempting to regard the need for such recognition as a consequence of the abandonment of the perfect competition model; but even in that model the assumptions have not wholly excluded problems of information and expectations.[3]

SOME COMMENTS ON METHOD AND METHODOLOGY

More than ten years ago Wilson argued that a revolt against orthodoxy would be premature;[4] in the intervening period much has been written and little conceded, except that more emphasis is being placed upon long-run profit maximization. Today revolt might still be premature; or, alternatively, it might be lacking in purpose. Consequently, this book examines the firm's major areas of decision, pricing and investment, in an attempt to establish the relationship between the nature of the firm and profit. In the course of this examination it explores defects of the traditional scheme: for example, the limited concepts of capital and the cost-output relationship, and the problems of defining and testing the profit

[1] T. W. Schultz, 'Investment in Human Capital', *American Economic Review*, LI (March 1961), p. 2.

[2] 'This initial stock of goods is neither homogeneous nor an amorphous heap. Its various parts complement each other in a way that we readily understand as soon as we hear of buildings, equipment, raw materials and consumers' goods. Some of these parts must be available before we can operate others; and various sequences or lags between economic actions impose themselves and further restrict our choices; and they do this in ways that differ greatly according to the composition of the stock we have to work on' (J. A. Schumpeter, *op. cit.*, p. 631).

[3] Cf. K. J. Arrow, 'Toward a Theory of Price Adjustment', M. Abramovitz *et al.*, *The Allocation of Economic Resources* (Stanford: Stanford University Press, 1959), pp. 41–51.

[4] T. Wilson, 'The Inadequacy of the Theory of the Firm as a Branch of Welfare Economics', *Oxford Economic Papers*, N.S., 4 (February 1952), p. 19.

maximization hypothesis. This is not an exhaustive list and is intended merely to indicate the mode of approach. This study concentrates attention upon the firm's decisions in a dynamic setting rather than the fruitless task of reconciliation of dynamic patterns with static analysis,[1] for it is doubtful whether the traditional theory furnishes a basis for a theory of profit in view of its neglect of both the nature of the firm and the determinants of uncertainty and its lack of interest in the growth of the firm.

The theory of the firm was characterized earlier in this chapter as fundamentally a theory of competitive markets which neglects the nature of the firm. How then should a theory of the behaviour of the firm be developed? The response will depend upon the individual theorist's methodological predilections; some will undoubtedly continue to deny the existence of the problem. Can this negative point of view be refuted? In short, is it possible to establish the methodological respectability of the emergent solution to the problem: to take account explicitly of the nature of the decision-making unit?

The recently enlivened interest in methodological issues has centred upon the testing of implications as opposed to the testing of assumptions.[2] There has been a growing tendency to condemn inquiry directed to assumptions rather than implications; in its extreme this leads to the view that realism is irrelevant, on the grounds that successful prediction is the criterion by which economic models are to be judged. Three intertwined strands of criticism of this methodology can be advanced and are of interest for this study of the theory of profit.

---

[1] 'There is little exaggeration in saying that apart from the work of a few pioneers like Schumpeter, the study of the firm in a dynamic setting has scarcely been begun, and it will be further delayed if we are now to devote our energies to showing that, provided the terms are properly defined, the static marginal analysis can be defended on purely formal grounds against some of its critics' (Wilson, *op. cit.*, p. 44).

[2] See Richard Ruggles, 'Methodological Developments', B. F. Haley, ed., *A Survey of Contemporary Economics* (Homewood, Illinois: Richard D. Irwin, 1952), pp. 408–457. Milton Friedman, 'The Methodology of Positive Economics', *Essays in Positive Economics* (Chicago: University of Chicago Press, 1953), pp. 3–43; Fritz Machlup, 'The Problem of Verification in Economics', *Southern Economic Journal*, XXII (July 1955), pp. 1–21; T. C. Koopmans, *Three Essays on the State of Economic Science* (New York: McGraw-Hill Book Company, Inc., 1957); K. Klappholz and J. Agassi, 'Methodological Prescriptions in Economics', *Economica*, N.S., XXVI (February 1959), pp. 60–74; Eugene Rotwein, 'On "The Methodology of Positive Economics"', *Quarterly Journal of Economics*, LXXIII (November 1959), pp. 554–575; Bengt-Christer Ysander, 'Truth and Meaning of Economic Postulates'; Hugo Hegeland, ed., *Money, Growth and Methodology and other Essays in Economics in Honor of Johan Åkerman* (Lund, Sweden: CWK Gleerup, 1961), pp. 323–334; G. C. Archibald, 'Chamberlin *versus* Chicago', *Review of Economic Studies*, XXIX (October 1961), pp. 2–28.

Predictive power may not be a sufficient guide in the process of constructing economic knowledge. A model may, initially or after a period of success, be found to lack predictive power; in which case an attempt is made to improve the model. 'It is the evaluation of axioms which gives investigators some of their best clues as to how to improve on existing inadequacies since the alternative direct testing of implications cannot easily do this for us. Each direct confirmation of the model as a whole tests, indeed, the model as a whole. It cannot localize the culpable portion.'[1] This point gains greater force if the scope of the model is, as it must be to be useful for theorizing about profit phenomena, such as to bring up the conflicts and omissions that result from differences or changes in the nature of the firm and the underlying structure and organization of the economy; that is, if the use of the model depends upon its accord with such a changing reality.

The second strand concerns interpretation of the terms introduced into economic analysis.[2] Consider such terms as *entrepreneur* and *firm*. For some purposes the definitions adopted may be merely a matter of convenience; but for any purpose the interpretation of the terms must be understood clearly. Such understanding is needed both for theoretical discourse and for the practical task of testing theory by reference to the behaviour of the units for which the terms are symbols. For example, lack of clarity of interpretation and the resultant confusion of production process, plant, single-product firm, and multi-product firm have been serious obstacles to the testing of hypotheses about the behaviour of the firm. This is a problem of identification. If the theory does not require identification of the units it has no use for observation and measurement.

The third strand can be indicated by reference to the problem of causal relationship and spurious correlation. It is recognized that the same statistical evidence of correlation will in one case be rejected as spurious while in another case it will be accepted as indicative of a causal relationship.[3] Willingness to differentiate between the two cases rests not upon the statistical evidence but upon implicit empirical assumptions that form part of the interpretation of the terms; or alternatively upon time sequence considerations.[4] Here is an answer to the 'prediction alone matters' school of

---

[1] Jerome Rothenberg, *The Measurement of Social Welfare* (Englewood Cliffs, N.J.: Prentice-Hall, 1961), p. 225, n. 12.   [2] Cf. Koopmans, *op. cit.*, pp. 132–133.

[3] See H. A. Simon, 'Spurious Correlation: a Causal Interpretation', *Models of Man* (New York: John Wiley and Sons, Inc., 1957), pp. 38–39.

[4] Time sequence considerations become more involved when expected values are introduced.

thought; correlation coefficients are on the threshold of the realm of science. What is needed is explanation to serve as a basis for prediction, and this requires specification of the interpretations of terms and rules about time sequences.

Examinations of assumptions, interpretation of terms, and specification of implicit assumptions about causal relationships are integral parts of economic inquiry; in each case they require consideration of the nature of the firm. For example, expectations play an important role in investment decisions; a role that merits emphasis because there has been a tendency to treat the acceleration principle as a purely technological matter deriving from a fixed capital-output ratio. Hicks, criticized for constructing a machine which required neither human judgement nor decision, replied that the inducement to invest is 'not a mere matter of technical necessity; it works through the state of mind of entrepreneurs, having a close connection with . . . the "elasticity of expectations" '.[1] He had sought to work with 'a standard form of entrepreneurial reaction, the form which looks like being typical, though it is certainly not necessary'.[2] Investment motivation may be so complex, so dependent upon learning processes, industry structure and age, and growth paths, as to make it extremely difficult to select such a standard form of reaction without detailed study of the nature of the firm.[3]

The importance of the nature of the firm for interpretation of terms needs no further comment in the light of the foregoing remarks. The specification of assumptions about causal relationships can be illustrated by an aspect of price flexibility. Discussion of price flexibility sometimes proceeds on the assumption that price changes are lagged responses to changes in costs that have occurred already.[4] An implicit assumption is that there is no causal relationship between price changes and expected changes in costs. Clarification is needed and requires examination of the information available to the firm, the determinants of the firm's expectations, and the decision-making procedures employed by the firm.

Does this emphasis upon the nature of the firm amount to a return to institutional economics? The heated controversy between

---

[1] J. R. Hicks, *A Contribution to the Theory of the Trade Cycle* (Oxford at the Clarendon Press, 1950), Preface to the Third Impression.   [2] *Ibid.*
[3] The absence of a standard form of reaction leads to difficult problems of aggregation in this area.
[4] For example, J. V. Yance, 'A Model of Price Flexibility', *American Economic Review*, L (June 1960), pp. 401–418. Yance's model is applicable to a series of cost changes only on the assumption of zero elasticity of cost expectations.

theorist and institutionalist has died away. 'In the last twenty years the spirit of the institutionalist has permeated the whole of economic analysis and has become more or less integrated with the other approaches.'[1] The approach to the study of the behaviour of the firm suggested in this book does not lack theory; it attempts to impart greater significance to theory. It might be objected that such an approach does not permit quantification. For several reasons it is difficult to evaluate this criticism: firstly, there is a tendency to overrate the traditional theory of the firm in this respect; secondly, theory may be important without quantification if it contributes to the understanding of economic processes; and thirdly, lack of quantification may be a merely temporary disability—theory may have outstripped measurement.

A further objection might be that this treatment of the subject is merely apologetics, a label which has been placed upon much writing on the theory of profit. Although organization and information are emphasized this is not seen as apologetics; as yet another endeavour to furnish a function for which profit is the reward. The problems of organization and information encountered by the business firm are shared with the public sector; they have their counterparts in collectivized economies. This generality is one of the features which distinguishes the approach here from that of the historico-economic entrepreneurship school of thought, which has stressed the role of the individual rather than the organizational unit.[2]

EXTENSIONS TO THE THEORY OF THE FIRM

The additional aspects of reality to be incorporated in a theory of the firm have been mentioned earlier. Organization and information are to be treated as resources of the firm, which is regarded as retaining its identity despite changes in the co-ordinating mechanism, production technique, and expectations. In elucidating the nature of the firm the concept of policy will be helpful. For example, Andrews commends the use of the concept of policy because 'such a concept makes it possible to eschew the rigid distinction between

[1] Richard Ruggles, op. cit., p. 427.

[2] There is adequate justification for the historians' complaints about the entrepreneur concept in economic theory. G. Herberton Evans points out that economists have tended to emphasize now one and now another aspect of entrepreneurship: uncertainty bearing, innovation, superintendence, management ('Business Entrepreneurs Their Major Functions and Related Tenets', Journal of Economic History, XIX (June 1959), p. 250). Perhaps the chief critic has been Arthur H. Cole; for an expression of his views see Business Enterprise in its Social Setting (Cambridge: Harvard University Press, 1959).

centralized authority and member groups; it also makes it possible to understand the sense in which such and such a business is *a* firm from the abstract economic point of view'.[1] There is, however, grave danger in invariably attributing policy-making wholly to top-level management. The sequential nature of business decision-making inevitably means that a great deal of policy is formulated in the course of day-to-day decisions. Here formulation does not mean the act of voting at an executive meeting, but rather the process of reduction culminating in a definite and systematic statement, the process of narrowing the range of practical possibilities, of focusing attention on some of the alternative courses of action to the exclusion of others.

From the point of view of short period study of the behaviour of the firm it is possible to specify a number of policies in combination equivalent, but not necessarily in any precise way, to profit maximization:[2] preservation of a market share within minimum and maximum limits; selling through particular distributive outlets; opposing (or encouraging) labour organization; limitation of the number of products; maintenance of a high level of liquidity; reliance upon internal finance for all replacement investment. In a long period the policies might be concerned with such matters as the selection of the most profitable fields for investment; alternating growth and consolidation; and survival.

Policy is reflected in certain behaviour patterns which persist provided profits are considered by the decision-makers to be satisfactory. It depends in part upon the legal rules and the interpretations of them under which the firm operates and the stability of the relationships between management and various groups such as shareholders, bankers, unions, and trade associations which have an interest in the firm's activities and some ability to influence its decision-making.[3] More generally, however, the firm as an organizational unit supersedes the price mechanism because it is profitable to do so. 'The main reason why it is profitable to establish a firm would seem to be that there is a cost of using the price mechanism. The most obvious cost of "organising" production through the price

---

[1] P. W. S. Andrews, Review of H. R. Bowen, *The Business Enterprise as a Subject for Research* (New York: Social Science Research Council, 1955), *Kyklos*, X (1957, Fasc. 1), p. 71.

[2] Cf. R. A. Gordon, 'Short-Period Price Determination', *American Economic Review* XXXVIII (June 1948), pp. 267–271, where such policies were regarded as *additional* to profit maximization.

[3] See Neil W. Chamberlain, *The Union Challenge to Management Control* (New York: Harpers, 1948), pp. 66–73, for a discussion of influences on managerial decisions.

mechanism is that of discovering what the relevant prices are.'[1] So the persistent behaviour patterns are substitutes for information which is unobtainable, at least sufficiently quickly, or obtainable only at a high cost. This complex of persistent behaviour patterns which is identified as the firm's 'policy', rather than the simple equality of marginal cost and marginal revenue, furnishes the 'equilibria' in the sequential process of decision-making under conditions of uncertainty.

This book attempts to reconsider the theory of profit in the light of empirical studies; the meaning of 'empirical studies' being bound up closely with the search for these additional significant aspects of the firm. This study incorporates a critical analysis of the conceptual apparatus that has been employed in recent times in the study of profit phenomena. It is critical and selective, seeking both to evaluate errors of reasoning and also, more importantly, to examine the empirical aspects of theory. For the most part theorizing about profit has attempted to escape conceptual difficulties by the adoption of new definitions of profit. However, there has been too little effort directed towards the empirical testing of theory. For this there is a twofold explanation. Theorizing has sought to indicate a single cause such as exploitation, innovation, disequilibrium, monopoly or uncertainty, whereas the net revenue customarily observed as profit is a fascinating compound produced by these and other forces; and the model of the firm did not lend itself to empirical inquiry. It was this apparent gap between theory and testing that stimulated this study and it has been pursued in the belief that when concerned with a dynamic and constantly changing economy it is desirable and necessary to inform theory by empirical observation and so reduce in number, and render useful, some of the 'myriad deductive possibilities'. The word 'empirical' was interpreted initially in a very narrow sense; it was hoped to reconcile recent developments in the theory of the firm and the results of statistical studies of business profits. However, as work progressed it was found necessary to widen the interpretation to include qualitative information about business expectations and behaviour. Out of this process grew the belief that the model of the production unit so widely used in the theory of the firm was inappropriate because it neglected aspects of reality that are significant for the theory of profit.

[1] R. H. Coase, 'The Nature of The Firm', *Economica*, N.S., IV (November 1937), pp. 386–405, reprinted in American Economic Association, *Readings in Price Theory* (London: George Allen and Unwin, 1953), p. 336.

Empirical studies thus came to mean work of a quantitative or qualitative type which contributed to the judgement about which aspects are significant for the theory of profit.

A theory of profit should do more than define profit; it should describe the workings and interrelations of the various aspects of the profit phenomenon; it should provide a systematic explanation of profit. Measured against this standard many if not most contributions to the literature on the theory of profit must be classed as definitional only, the principal reason for this state of affairs being neglect of the nature of the firm. The relevance of the nature of the firm for a more adequate theory of profit arises from its bearing upon the firm's resources and selection of profit criteria, activities, and techniques. This selection process is based upon expectations held by the firm, which are in turn dependent in important respects upon the information available during the decision process. The firm can, through its information-collecting activities, modify the information stock at its disposal and through its internal organization can affect the use made of this stock, and hence can change the degree of uncertainty involved in decisions. Treatment of the firm as a given unit has nullified efforts to develop a theory of profit because the essential links between profit and uncertainty were ignored. This situation calls for integration of the theories of pricing and investment; a development foreshadowed by some recent treatments of non-price competition and stability in oligopoly. When the development of organization and active collection of information are viewed as part of the process of growth and capital formation, it can be seen that investment strategy may be the firm's primary means of competing.

It may be helpful to relate this approach to the theory of profit to the current fashionable interest in economic growth and growth theories. The durability and structure of capital and technical progress are the factors to be taken into account when examining changes in aggregate capital coefficients. A short-run theory can ignore these factors and concentrate on the (expected) demand-capacity relationship; in the long-run these factors, especially technical progress, become dominant. The effect of changing organization and information is part of the residual attributed to technical progress. However, technical progress needs to be broken down into its component parts for several reasons: it embraces too much; one component, organization and information, is of special interest for the theory of profit; and disaggregation may clarify the extent to which technical progress should be regarded as autonomous. The view that technical progress is almost wholly an autonomous influence becomes less tenable the longer the period of the analysis; and the nature of the investment decision process suggests the possibility that a significant proportion of technical progress may not be autonomous. For example, changes in organization and information involved in and following from the establishment by a firm of a research and development department are not entirely, or perhaps even largely, random; they arise from the (multi-product) firm's planning activities.

PLAN OF THE INQUIRY

The procedure is as follows. Chapter II examines the current state of the theory of profit. Chapters III-VI review modern contributions in the areas of uncertainty, alternative profit criteria, the investment decision, and the interpretation of profit statistics to support the contention that the nature of the firm has been neglected and to bring out some consequences of this neglect. What is meant by modern? While it will be necessary to point to the line of development down to the contribution of Marshall, the main emphasis will be upon Knight's *Risk, Uncertainty and Profit*[1] (published in 1921) and subsequent contributions in British and American literature. Chapter VII comprises new developments and shows how a number of aspects of the behaviour of the firm can best be rationalized in the frame of reference developed here. These aspects include the production function and cost conditions, pricing decisions, profit criteria, information and uncertainty, investment decisions, and the measurement of profit. In the concluding chapter the workings and interrelations of the various aspects of the profit phenomenon dealt with in the earlier sections are summarized and the theory of profit based upon the new model of the firm is expounded. Profit is defined as the income accruing to the firm, in part as a result of the firm's organization and planning activities.[2] This permits a fusing of the leading types of theories of profit: uncertainty, monopoly, disequilibrium, entrepreneurship. This is an important step towards 'a scheme of things in which all

---

[1] Frank H. Knight, *Risk, Uncertainty and Profit* (New York: Houghton Mifflin Company, 1921: No. 16 in The London School of Economics and Political Science Series of Reprints of Scarce Tracts in Economics and Political Science).

[2] Precise definition depends upon fixing the boundary between interest and profit. Much of the recent advance in interest theory appears to have been at the expense of the theory of profit.

the various aspects and meanings of profit arise simultaneously from a single essential vision'.[1] The final sections of the concluding chapter touch upon such questions as the boundary between profit and interest, profit differentials and fluctuations, the significance of this treatment of profit for distribution theory, and the prospects for further empirical study.

Review and criticism have their value; they have been a necessary part of this study of the theory of profit. It would be foolish and unscholarly to deny or ignore the points of departure from the work of other contributors for those points of departure emerge from a study of contemporary economic thought. What further contributions have been made by this reconsideration of the theory of profit? The most important contribution is the point of view, the judgement about the significant features of reality to be incorporated in a theory of the firm. A consideration of the nature of the firm, especially organization and information, has achieved a synthesis which yields an improved theory of profit. Other more specific contributions follow from this point of view: clarification of the concepts of capital, 'satisfactory' profit, and policy; generalization of the gambler indifference map treatment of the investment decision; furthering of the integration of pricing and investment theories; and a modification of the method of measuring profit has been formulated. These are contributions to the study of the firm in a dynamic setting, to the economics of disequilibrium.

Two points about the relationship in which these contributions stand to received economic theory might be emphasized. First, economists have begun to show a rudimentary awareness of the importance of organization and information but hitherto there has been no attempt to probe the significance of these resources of the firm for the theory of profit. Second, criticism of the traditional theory of the firm has been incidental to the task of showing the connection between the nature of the firm and profit; it is not intended as destructive criticism. It has been necessary to extend the theory of the firm because traditional theory, despite its elegance, its supposed logical completeness, and its considerable value for many purposes, does not furnish an adequate basis for an understanding of the nature and role of profit.

[1] G. L. S. Shackle, 'Expectation, Income and Profit', *Ekonomisk Tidskrift*, LVII (December 1955), p. 215.

CHAPTER II

A VIEW OF THE STATE OF THE THEORY OF PROFIT

THE purpose of this chapter is to elaborate the view of the state of the theory of profit introduced in earlier pages: abstraction from the nature of the firm has prevented the development of a general theory of profit possessing empirical content. The generations of essays in this area of economic theory have bequeathed many terminological difficulties. Because of these difficulties it is convenient to follow historical precedent and take the zero profit condition of the perfectly competitive state of equilibrium as a starting point. This choice does not imply agreement that all clear thinking starts from the proposition that, with perfect competition prevailing, firms would break even in an equilibrium state.[1] Thought may start from this point; but unless it comprehends the nature of the firm, and hence the requirement that all activities of the firm, all aspects of its existence as an organizational (decision-making) unit be included as inputs in the production function, it cannot yield more than a fragmented explanation of the profit phenomenon.[2]

TERMINOLOGICAL DIFFICULTIES

Profit has been assigned many definitions even in contemporary writings. There are echoes of the mercantilist identification of profit with trade;[3] and a slightly less all-embracing usage in distribution theory where profit is contrasted with wages and comprises the income of property owners generally. As the difference between expected and actual income, profit, positive or negative, may be a component of all income categories. If this divergence of *ex post* from *ex ante* values is attributed to economic change and change

[1] J. A. Schumpeter, *History of Economic Analysis* (New York: Oxford University Press, 1954), p. 893.

[2] A further reason to be wary of the zero profit condition is that welfare implications are deduced from it only too easily.

[3] It is, of course, dangerous to sum up 'mercantilist' theory of profit in this brief way. The diversity of outlook of mercantilist writers and the evolution of mercantilist thought must be acknowledged. However, the emphasis upon foreign trade appears to be a common element. For discussion of mercantilist theory of profit see J. A. Schumpeter, *op. cit.*, Chapter 7; H. B. Ehrlich, 'British Mercantilist Theories of Profit', *American Journal of Economics and Sociology*, 14 (July 1955), pp. 377–386; Charles Wilson, *Profit and Power* (London: Longmans, Green, 1957); G. S. L. Tucker, *Progress and Profits in British Economic Thought 1650–1850* (Cambridge at the University Press, 1960), Chapters III–IV.

arises from the process of innovation, profit becomes the reward of the innovator. Or the term may be applied to the remuneration of selling power rather than the remuneration of production. As if this multiplicity of definitions were not problem enough there are also frequent cases of inadequate definition and of failure to define at all. Illustrations may be drawn from discussion of economic policy, industry investigations and historical studies. For example, the wages policy debate has raised questions concerning the uniformity of profit levels in different industries and the general level of profits but has given inadequate attention to problems of definition and measurement. It might make considerable difference were profit measured as a gross margin rather than as a rate of return on capital employed. Industry investigations often imply that profit is the test of successful innovation but some provide neither definition nor measures of profits achieved. Some interesting and otherwise valuable historical studies emphasize the role of profit and quote profit statistics but fail to indicate how these statistics have been computed. Nor is any purpose served by merely emphasizing the differences between accounting and economic concepts of profit.

In any case the definitions usually have had a strong emotional connotation. It might be asked if it is worthwhile persevering with the term. Would it not be better to recognize that it has only a limited value for communication in theoretical discussion and replace it with some new and neutral label? Attractive as this proposal seems the idea of profit still has considerable significance and theory must take it into account when seeking to explain business behaviour. Furthermore, the alternatives advanced have not been free from this defect. It is questionable, for example, whether the language of the theory of games with its pay-off matrices does provide a solution to this problem.

The multiplicity of definitions and related theories makes it impossible to give an outline of the 'conventional' theory of profit; little more could be done than to select the work of some contributors of obvious quality or to adopt the eclectic approach which characterizes the chapter on the theory of profit in so many textbooks. The historical development of theory indicates a way out of this difficulty; for that development can be viewed as a subtraction process, a stripping away of capital charges and wage elements to reach a core of pure profit. By way of illustration Marshallian profit may be compared with the profit concept of recent contributions to the uncertainty theory.[1] 'Marshall as a rule considered the profit item of the balance sheet of business practice—and especially the balance sheets of owner-managed firms—rather than anything that has any claim to be called "pure profit", and he considered this item as it is rather than as it would be in (static) equilibrium of a stationary process.'[2] Such a profit is complex in origin, dependent upon institutional arrangements, the financial structure of the firm, and business expectations: but it can be identified with observable magnitudes. Nevertheless, Schumpeter's warning that this may be 'a schema that is Ulysses' bow to less powerful minds' should be remembered.

Because competitive equilibrium entails zero pure profit levels, uncertainty has been regarded as the necessary and sufficient condition for a residual. If uncertainty causes the divergence of actual from expected returns, profit as the result of uncertainty should be defined, according to the uncertainty theorists, as the difference between *ex post* and *ex ante* income. Profit in this sense is not a functional return; rather it is a measure of forecasting error applicable to all income categories. Such a profit can be observed only in so far as budget data can be compared with realized income and is irrelevant to business behaviour because it cannot be an objective of the firm's planning and activity. It may, however, retain significance as a means to action if the assumption of a perfectly competitive capital market is abandoned.

THE ZERO PROFIT CONDITION

The method of the uncertainty theorists can be adopted; the zero profit condition can serve as a starting point, but without accepting the explanatory value of uncertainty by itself. In this way it will be possible to approach the problems of defining profit and entrepreneurship and of distinguishing the bases of the various theories of profit. In doing so it must be clearly understood that the changing (disequilibrium) conditions of the real world in no way disprove the zero profit of perfect equilibrium because the reality and the equilibrium state that is never reached are not comparable.

The complex differences between the Marshallian and uncertainty theories—and these are two only from many theories—make the

[1] See, for example, J. Fred Weston, 'A Generalized Uncertainty Theory of Profit', *American Economic Review*, XL (March 1950), pp. 40–60; 'The Profit Concept and Theory: A Restatement', *Journal of Political Economy*, LXII (April 1954), pp. 152–170.
[2] J. A. Schumpeter, *op. cit.*, pp. 1048–1049.

seeming simplicity of the zero profit condition attractive as a starting point. This chosen starting point leads immediately to the marginal analysis of production which derives first- and second-order equilibrium conditions for the firm, assuming technology to be such that there is a single-valued maximum output for each set of factor inputs. This is the relationship known as the production function and written, in the case of the multi-product firm,

$$f(x_1, x_2, \ldots, x_r, y_1, y_2 \ldots, y_s) = 0,$$

where r inputs are used in the production of s outputs. These equilibrium conditions are well known.[1] So too are the various propositions about the distribution of the product amongst the factors.[2]

Several features of this analysis merit attention. Firstly, the assumption of a single-valued maximum output is far removed from the practical problems of business decision-making which involve both limited knowledge of alternatives and also recognition of the costs of information and the importance of learning processes. Unless complete knowledge of the technology is assumed for purposes of theory, the analysis should consider the implications of this kind of uncertainty and attempt to explain how the firm responds. This is difficult, to say the least, where the analysis treats the firm as a given decision-making unit and endeavours to use the profit maximization hypothesis to furnish a full statement of the firm's mode of action; for the choice of the mode of action cannot be divorced from the available, though incompletely known, technology.[3] And if the firm is not to be treated as a given decision-making unit, if organizational change may occur and influence the

[1] See J. R. Hicks, *Value and Capital* (Oxford at the Clarendon Press, 1939), Chapter VI; P. A. Samuelson, *Foundations of Economic Analysis* (Cambridge: Harvard University Press, 1947), Chapter IV; R. G. D. Allen, *Mathematical Economics* (London: Macmillan & Co., Ltd., 1956), Chapter 18.

[2] See American Economic Association, *Readings in the Theory of Income Distribution* (Philadelphia: The Blakiston Company, 1946), pp. 103–217; B. F. Haley, 'Value and Distribution', H. S. Ellis, ed., *A Survey of Contemporary Economics* (Philadelphia: The Blakiston Company, 1949), Chapter I; B. S. Keirstead, *An Essay in the Theory of Profits and Income Distribution* (Oxford: Basil Blackwell, 1953) and *Capital, Interest and Profits* (Oxford: Basil Blackwell, 1959); Sidney Weintraub, *An Approach to the Theory of Income Distribution* (Philadelphia: Chilton Company, 1958).

[3] T. C. Koopmans suggests that 'economics has suffered from looking on the production function as a boundary of its domain of competence. Without a more thorough analysis of the choices open to the productive establishment, the economist's prescriptions for profit maximization are non-operational and his descriptive assumption of profit maximization is not subject to direct empirical test' (*Three Essays on the State of Economic Science* (New York: McGraw-Hill Book Company, Inc., 1957), p. 70).

firm's policy, the question arises whether such organizational change differs fundamentally from technological change.

Secondly, exact exhaustion of the product amongst the factors is simply another way of stating that price equals average cost and that the maximized profit is zero. This point deserves emphasis because it makes apparent that exact exhaustion of the revenue product depends not only upon the conditions summarized in the production function but also upon the nature of the input and output price functions. Furthermore, it demonstrates that no profit residual remains and hence profit is not a distinct distributive share, unless there is some factor input to which profit can be attributed; a conclusion which followed from the application of Euler's theorem and was interpreted as destroying the theory of pure profit.[1] This study suggests that a more useful response would have been re-examination of the nature and classification of factor inputs, in particular of the role of organization and information.

Thirdly, actual industry situations may involve conditions other than those of perfect competition and, as already mentioned, may be disequilibrium states. One approach which follows from this is to examine the nature of the deviations from competitive equilibrium. But to catalogue the ways in which conditions deviate does not tell very much about the overall results because there is no simple way of summing the effects of deviations. An alternative approach has been to select a single criterion of performance and attempt to measure the extent of its deviation from a competitive standard. Because competitive equilibrium implies zero profit, profit has been used as one such criterion; another has been the number of firms as used in studies of industrial concentration. The Lerner-Kalecki measure of the degree of monopoly power[2] illustrates the use of the profit criterion. This measure is derived from the marginal cost pricing formula and has been adapted for empirical investigations on the basis of the margin between an adjusted rate of profit and an interest rate for industrial capital.[3] Such a procedure has been criticized because it measures the degree of monopoly power along with the effects of barriers to entry,

---

[1] Originally confined to the production function which was homogeneous of order one, this conclusion was later extended to long-run competitive equilibrium whatever the form of the production function.

[2] See M. Kalecki, 'The Distribution of the National Income', *Essays in the Theory of Economic Fluctuations* (London: Allen & Unwin, 1939), pp. 13–41.

[3] For example, Joe S. Bain, 'The Profit Rate as a Measure of Monopoly Power', *Quarterly Journal of Economics*, LV (February 1941), pp. 271–293.

monopsony, imperfect knowledge, and uncertainty.[1] Nevertheless, the conceptual background is shared with linear programming; both are closely related to welfare economics and both utilize the zero profit condition.[2]

TYPES OF THEORY OF PROFIT

For the same reasons that difficulty has been encountered in applying the standard of competitive equilibrium, diverse theories of profit have developed. These theories have been presented as alternative explanations of profit phenomena when in reality each has tended to emphasize one or other of the necessary elements for a general theory of profit: no synthesis of these various theories has emerged. It is true that the uncertainty theory dominates contemporary thought but one suspects that it has won acceptance through its seeming generality. Hicks stated that Knight's *Risk, Uncertainty and Profit* (published in 1921) 'has laid securely the first foundation on which any future theory of profits must rest—the dependence of profits on uncertainty. That is a service whose importance can hardly be over-estimated. It commits us finally to one and one only of the various roads that earlier economists had explored. It puts us on the right track.'[3] However, examination of Knight's work reveals that uncertainty was treated as the most important way in which, *apart from monopoly considerations*, the conditions which theory is compelled to assume, and those which exist in fact, differ.[4] The interrelationships between uncertainty and monopoly considerations remained to be explored. Nor is this problem solved by stressing 'that monopolistic profit is not an additional profit, but part of the global profit in an economy that tends to secure an equilibrium between the demand and supply of uncertainty-bearing'.[5] For this proposition involves a return to the treatment of uncertainty-bearing as a factor input and needs to be supplemented by examination of the determinants of the firm's

---

[1] See K. W. Rothschild, 'A Further Note on the Degree of Monopoly', *Economica*, N.S., X (February 1943), p. 69. However, Rothschild failed to give due attention to the carefully worded qualifications inserted by Bain.
[2] There are, of course, important differences. As inputs must be increased proportionately under linear programming conditions there can be no concept corresponding to marginal productivity of a factor input.
[3] J. R. Hicks, 'The Theory of Uncertainty and Profit', *Economica*, II (May 1931), p. 170.
[4] Frank H. Knight, *Risk, Uncertainty and Profit* (New York: Houghton Mifflin Company, 1921: No. 16 in The London School of Economics and Political Science Series of Reprints of Scarce Tracts in Economic and Political Science), p. 51.
[5] R. F. Harrod, *Economic Essays* (London: Macmillan & Co., Ltd., 1952), p. 188.

uncertainty-bearing capacity and of the firm's willingness to bear uncertainty.

As implied above, the chief types of theory of profit can be distinguished in terms of the nature of the deviation from the zero profit condition which the particular theorist or group of theorists has chosen to emphasize.[1] Profits could arise from market imperfections, uncertainty, and disequilibria. An entrepreneurship theory may then be developed by defining an entrepreneurial function of uncertainty-bearing or by linking innovation as the prime activity of the entrepreneur with uncertainty, disequilibria, and economic change. Clearly there is a need to give precise meaning to the entrepreneurial input. The following comments focus attention on some of the many facets of this problem:

The usual marginal analysis treats the firm as if it had nothing but an income account; it has no balance sheet, no capital problems, and no dynamics; it maximizes an odd variable called 'net revenue', of which no accountant ever heard, and presumably lives happily every after.[2]

Marginal-productivity analysis commonly concluded that wages, rent, and interest would exhaust the total income of the firm, with the profit share conspicuous by its omission. Silence reigned not because of any deprecation of the importance of the entrepreneur, but rather as a logical inference from the premises of a model in which entrepreneurial functions had vanished. In a world in which today is a replica of yesterday and an exact image of tomorrow, then with activity and resource organization invariant entrepreneurial energies are stilled, with neither scope nor space for maneuver. Routine eliminates the need for decisions; risk taking, organization, and co-ordination, usually pictured as the entrepreneurial burden, atrophy in this environment and the entrepreneur is at least transformed into a special type of wage earner or capitalist. Stationariness is thus a stultifying hypothesis, for it excludes the characteristic managerial actions and also precludes the emergence of a profit share.[3]

The introduction of change through time . . ., and particularly of the agent most productive of change, threatens to upset traditional theory in a far-reaching manner. When the tempo of the theory is altered from that of short-run 'adjustment', the entrepreneur with his living enterprise, his 'creative' responses, his capacity to alter the course of economic development by idiosyncratic performances—these all enter the picture and must be taken care of by the theorists.[4]

Reflection upon these statements suggests the reason why much discussion of profit has proved barren. Profit is bound up essentially

[1] For a comprehensive classification of contributions see J. Fred Weston, 'The Profit Concept and Theory: A Restatement', *Journal of Political Economy*, LXII (April 1954), pp. 152–170.

[2] K. E. Boulding, *A Reconstruction of Economics* (New York: John Wiley and Sons, Inc., 1950), p. viii.   [3] Sidney Weintraub, *op. cit.*, p. 18⁹.

[4] Arthur H. Cole, *Business Enterprise in its Social Setting* (Cambridge: Harvard University Press, 1959), p. 49.

with the nature of the firm; with the firm's organizational capacity, information flows, and activities. These are not only interrelated but are also understandable only in an historical sense; accordingly they have been excluded from the usual type of analysis. Attempted developments of the theory of the firm have added to the considerations taken into account: selling costs, product variation, liquidity, retention of control through ownership, and the determinants of expectations. However, theorizing about profit has not kept pace with this development. The entrepreneur, once thought of as a special kind of labour or even bracketed with capital, became a fourth factor of production, personified and possessing all the dynamic qualities of the firm, but was not a major subject of study for the economist. There is a real need to break through the shackles of contemporaneity and ask whether the productive factors usually considered by the economist is an exhaustive list.

The nature of the market situation tends to limit the decision-making possibilities. In the limiting case of pure or perfect competition the market pressures so constrain the behaviour of the firm that it is not obliged to make any real decisions for no genuine alternatives are open. In such circumstances there can be no entrepreneur for the unit of production activity has neither asset structure nor organization and yet, although its history is irrelevant, knows the future. It is not surprising that doubts have been raised about the consistency of expectations with the information assumed to be available to the firm under conditions of perfect competition; nor that it has been suggested that perfect competition can prevail only in equilibrium. Considering the degree of abstraction involved in the model of perfect competition, it appears advisable to reconsider the realism of the assumptions before pursuing too far these doubts and suggestions.

In this connection consideration of the 'unique circumstances' pertaining to the firm, the given accounting, decision-making unit, might prove helpful. Unless these unique circumstances can be identified and their importance assessed, any attempt at comparative study of the behaviour of firms must come back to the simple admission that the firms are not identical units; that some, in brief, are more efficient than others. This problem lies in a field where measurement is extremely difficult and perhaps impossible. Also, it might be suggested that the unique circumstances are not significant for economic analysis. For example, it has been said that these problems need not be investigated if the theory of the firm is simply an under-pinning for propositions about aggregates for the economy as a whole. But it seems advisable to be cautious about aggregate relationships which require that firms behave in ways that are inconsistent with observed behaviour. Furthermore, the detail of circumstances of firms must be studied if the analysis concerns itself with the growth of the individual firm and with inter-firm comparison.

These difficulties associated with the concept of an entrepreneurial input cast serious doubt upon the desirability of an eclectic approach to the theory of profit. Monopolistic power may be based upon the firm's organization and information collecting capacity; it may be conferred by the uncertainty inherent in disequilibrium positions; or it may follow in Schumpeterian fashion from innovatory activities. Likewise, exercise of the entrepreneurial function, unnecessary in the stationary situation, may require modification of the firm's organization with the changing impact of uncertainty and changes in the firm's competitive position. And uncertainty itself lacks explanatory value if it leads to changes in the nature of the firm that are excluded from the analysis. Just as the marginal analysis of production assumed that the firm had been successful in solving the physical problems of production methods, so there has been a tendency in dealing with the role of profit to assume that the firm has solved the problems of decision-making; that it possesses appropriate information and a decision-making mechanism which makes optimum use of that information. If this latter assumption is unwarranted, changing degrees of uncertainty are inconsistent with treatment of the firm as a given decision-making unit; and the information that the firm requires to guide its responses to changes in degrees of uncertainty involves costs. For the firm operating under such conditions of uncertainty it is doubtful whether the profit maximization hypothesis yields any definite plan of action. This problem will be taken up in greater detail in Chapter IV which deals with alternative profit criteria.

The majority of contributions to the theory of profit have followed from the eclectic approach and consequently the interdependence between the various factors that have been regarded as causes of profit has tended to remain in the background. Such a procedure stemmed from the treatment of the firm as a given decision-making unit; and it was this very assumption that stood in the way and prevented the study of the firm itself. This assumption restricted the range of variable inputs. Variations in internal resources such as organization and information were not considered; there was a tendency to regard uncertainty as the key explanatory factor; and the development of profit criteria alternative to profit maximization was hampered. Perhaps the difficulties of giving a precise meaning to profit maximization can be overcome and the conventional rules of behaviour, or elements of policy, of business firms rationalized through examination of the firm, its organization, and its information. For changes internal to the firm as well as those that are external and involve the activities of other institutions—even the creation of new institutions—may be important in the process of consolidation of risk and uncertainty.

CLASSIFICATION OF FACTORS OF PRODUCTION

The complex nature of the task of defining and classifying factors of production can be clarified by considering some aspects of the production function

$$f(x_1, x_2, \ldots, x_r, y_1, y_2, \ldots, y_s) = 0$$

and the accompanying price functions. The inputs may not be homogeneous; and there may be some measure of interdependence between inputs, between products, and between input and output. Some influences or conditions necessary for production may not have been included at all. To these must be added the dynamic considerations and problems of expectations that enter into the firm's policy. Marginal productivity theory has lent a spurious precision to discussion of increasing production by neglecting many of these aspects; they have been summarized as shifts of the production function. At the microeconomic level the aspects neglected include improved technology, the spread of technological knowledge, learning processes within firms, and industrial relations.

It is not sufficient to confine attention to static equilibrium conditions because this procedure may omit much that is important. Rather situations as they are found in the real economy should be considered. There industries can be expected to show differential rates of growth and earnings, reflecting changes in income, consumer preferences, technology, and population. This pattern of development becomes even more likely if the economy operates at full employment level because pressure against a ceiling may lead to competition for resources and the industries with higher rates of profits and superior prospects may tend to be more successful in obtaining resources than those less well favoured. This tendency will be reinforced by any differential impact of credit restrictions and other policy measures that may be introduced to deal with inflationary pressures arising from excess demand. Within the individual industries, the size distribution of firms will be determined by managerial objectives, profitability, the rate of innovation, conditions of capital supply, and the level of merger activity. Some firms may be more willing than others to spread their activities into new fields, which may be technologically similar to their existing activities or related through a marketing system, but which are probably distinguished from them by their demand flexibility[1] and growth prospects. Even if the industry were to achieve some high degree of stability in terms of price, output, and the range of products, its component firms may still be changing in relative size in the way Marshall suggested in his 'trees of the forest' analogy.

It was pointed out above that factor inputs may not be homogeneous. This is commonly recognized in the case of labour and somewhat less frequently in discussions of capital. This problem arises with management, organization, and information. If the managerial personnel of the firm is fixed in number and of given capacity, and if the rule of profit maximization is applied, technological conditions determine a maximum relationship between inputs and outputs, provided always that the influence of uncertainty is ignored. Managerial activity can be defined as actions performed without a definite set of instructions or rules; and discussion can be limited to 'top' management, subject to the qualification that actions at lower levels are contributing continuously to the formulation of policy especially through the search for alternatives and the provision of information.

Variation in the size of the managerial personnel involves a change in the size and structure of an integrated organization; and adaptation of the additional personnel to the existing decision-making unit will require time. While it is true that management functions as a team,[2] the team quality should not be overemphasized. Conflict

---

[1] The shift of the demand curve with changes in the income level.

[2] Cf. J. Marschak, 'Elements for a Theory of Teams', *Management Science*, 1 (1955), pp. 127–137; E. T. Penrose, *The Theory of Growth of the Firm* (Oxford: Basil Blackwell, 1959), pp. 45–49.

may arise through the use of inconsistent criteria which result from uncertainty and inadequate integration, or because component units have conflicting objectives. Such conflict should not be treated as evidence of failure to minimize costs and so to fulfil one of the conditions necessary for profit maximization. For example, internal competitiveness,[1] given an appropriate decision-making system, may be conducive to cost minimization and to speedier, more wide-ranging, and more farsighted perception of business conditions, encompassing the firm's whole environment and not merely the behaviour of competitors and investment opportunities. These are aspects of the more general question of learning processes to which reference will be made later. Corresponding to each of the several time periods which follow a change in managerial personnel there would be a different production function. A similar result follows from relaxation of the assumption of a given capacity of an existing managerial team, even in the absence of learning processes. If management has objectives other than profit maximization, as seems plausible where ownership and management are separated, and these objectives conflict with profit maximization, there can be levels of managerial activity, changes in which could be more or less systematic or random, each yielding a different production function.

As regards interdependence between inputs, it is unsatisfactory to treat the factors as passive. There is an element of joint decision-making to be taken into account over and above the market forces that are summarized in the costs of the factor inputs. Banks and other sources of finance may play an important part in the formulation of the firm's policy.[2] Less spectacular but perhaps more important are the cases where a condition of supply of finance is representation on the Board of Directors and therefore direct participation in the firm's decision-making. In principle, such representation of suppliers of capital does not differ from representation of firms supplying raw materials and equipment. Both may be treated as participation in decision-making and as partial integration of business organizations. Similarly labour exercises an important influence in the firm's decision-making, not only in those cases in which joint consultation schemes have been put into operation,

[1] See P. W. S. Andrews, 'Competition in the Modern Economy', *Competitive Aspects of Oil Operations* (London: Institute of Petroleum, 1958), p. 3.

[2] For example, Charles Wilson records how a British bank to which Lever Brothers were indebted, forced surrender of control over business policy. (*The History of Unilever: A Study in Economic Growth and Social Change* (London: Cassell & Co., 1954), Vol. 1, p. 258.)

but also where negotiations occur and union influence is extended to activities usually regarded as of a managerial nature. Such 'penetration' has been recorded into the areas of finance, personnel, procurement, production, distribution, and miscellaneous matters such as product mix and quality, location, and research and development.[1]

Interdependence between products has received a good deal of attention both in terms of joint production and marketing costs and in terms of complementarity and substitution. Even so, tardy recognition has been accorded the significance of the multi- as opposed to the single-product establishment. But consideration of this point leads into the conventional field of inquiry in terms of number, cross elasticities, etc., into inter-firm relationships. Although primarily concerned so far with matters which are in a sense internal to the individual firm, it is necessary to note the problem of evaluating the whole relationship of a firm with its environment; so it is worthwhile drawing attention to two aspects of market structure that are commonly neglected. Within the industry group 'the chief cause of monopoly (in a broad sense) is obviously competition. . . . An industry which is strongly competitive must be in the course of tending towards a condition of oligopoly; competition can be permanent only when it is hampered by highly imperfect markets or softened by a spirit of live and let live among the entrepreneurs concerned.'[2] But concentration of market power, either as monopoly or oligopoly, 'at one stage in an industrial structure fosters competition at other stages'[3] by its effects upon the condition of entry. A second possibility is that reciprocal relationships may develop when one firm not only sells to another firm but also acquires factor inputs from that same firm.[4]

Moving to a somewhat different level, inputs and outputs may not be independent, at least in value terms. Price functions associated with each factor input and each product output are customarily assumed without taking into account possible interdependence. If propositions about aggregates are to be built upon marginal productivity analysis, allowance must be made for such interdependence as arises, for example, with general wage increases. This

---

[1] N. W. Chamberlain, *The Union Challenge to Management Control* (New York: Harper & Brothers, 1948), Chapter 4; Seymour Melman, *Decision-Making and Productivity* (Oxford: Basil Blackwell, 1958), Chapter VII.

[2] Joan Robinson, 'Imperfect Competition Revisited', *Economic Journal*, LXIII (September 1953), p. 692.   [3] *Ibid.*

[4] Cf. G. W. Stocking and W. F. Mueller, 'Business Reciprocity and the Size of Firms', *Journal of Business of the University of Chicago*, XXX (April, 1957), pp. 73–95.

amounts to a recognition of the partial equilibrium limitation of the marginal analysis. But can analysis ignore this limitation when concerned with the individual firm? Clearly, in some cases, cost changes might not lead to demand changes; but the firm may fail to differentiate between cases of this type and cases where interdependence is a warranted assumption. There is some evidence which points to a belief on the part of firms that increased costs will be accompanied by increased selling prices and increased profits, provided the changes in costs are moderate. However, this evidence relates to investment plans.[1]

Examination of the influences which find no place in classification of factors of production involves consideration of the benefit derived from the environment, as it was discussed by Marshall in relation to consumer's and producer's surplus. Marshall felt that there was no satisfactory equivalent to the German *Conjunctur* and quoted with approval Wagner's statement that this implied '. . . the sum total of the technical, economic, social and legal conditions; which in a mode of national life (*Volkswirthschaft*) resting upon division of labour and private property, —especially private property in land and other material means of production—determine the demand for and supply of goods, and therefore their exchange value: this determination being as a rule, or at least in the main, *independent* of the will of the owner, of his activity and his remissness'.[2] This leads on to Marshallian external economies or 'those dependent on the general development of the industry';[3] they were benefits that accrued to the individual firm as the industry's output expanded and were independent of the individual firm's output.[4] What then were these external economies? Marshall indicated[5] the following: improvements in transport, production methods, machinery, and organization accessible to the whole industry; benefits arising from the growth of subsidiary industries; and advances in knowledge as reflected in trade publications.

---

[1] See Robert Eisner, *Determinants of Capital Expenditures. An Interview Study* (Urbana: University of Illinois, 1956), pp. 26–27.

[2] Alfred Marshall, *Principles of Economics*, 8th ed. (London: Macmillan & Co., Ltd., 1925), p. 125, n. 1.

[3] *Ibid.*, p. 266. Marshall's discussion of external economies was largely confined to partial equilibrium analysis.

[4] Cf. J. Viner, 'Cost Curves and Supply Curves', reprinted from *Zeitschrift für National Ökonomie*, III (1931), pp. 23–46, American Economic Association, *Readings in Price Theory* (London: George Allen & Unwin Ltd., 1953), p. 217.

[5] *Op. cit.*, pp. 266, 271, 284, 317–318, 615, 808.

Recognition of internal economies made it necessary to explain why monopoly conditions did not inevitably emerge. The answer appears to be that Marshall regarded the operation of increasing returns as very long run: 'but for goods, of which the cost of transportation is low and which are under the law of Increasing Return, there might have seemed to be nothing to prevent the concentration in the hands of a single firm of the whole production of the world, except in so far as it was closed by tariff barriers. The reason why this result did not follow was simply that no firm ever had a sufficiently long life of unabated energy and power of initiative for the purpose.'[1] In contrast external economies were believed to present no such problem. These accrued to the individual firm independently of the size of its own output. Cost reductions of this type, which might become available to a single industry or to several industries simultaneously, if they outweighed any external diseconomies, brought about a lower level of cost of production for the Marshallian 'representative firm'. Now this proposition differs in a significant way from some more recent formulations. Consider, for example, Haberler's statement that 'External economies, cost reductions accruing to one or several industries from causes outside the individual enterprise, result in a downward shift of the marginal cost curve for *each* firm when the industry as a whole expands'.[2] This view seems to aim at consistency with the zero profit equilibrium situation; it seems to require not only that the external economies be equally accessible to all firms in the industry but also that all firms possess the same degree of responsiveness to changing conditions.

If allowance is made for the possibility that the firms have different histories, different organizational and asset structures, and hence different response patterns as well as standing in different relationships with the old and new organizations outside their industry which are changing and so giving rise to the external economies, it can be expected that the impact of these external economies on

---

[1] Alfred Marshall, *Industry and Trade* (London: Macmillan & Co. Ltd., 1919), pp. 315–316. For a discussion of this point see D. C. Hague, 'Alfred Marshall and the Competitive Firm', *Economic Journal*, LXVIII (December 1958), pp. 673–690; J. A. Maxwell, 'Some Marshallian Concepts, Especially the Representative Firm', *Economic Journal*, LXVIII (December 1958), pp. 691–698. This statement by Marshall merits consideration because it embodies an assertion that there had been no exceptions to the life cycle hypothesis and because it is free from the qualifications that appear in the passages cited by Hague. Furthermore, it is as concise as any other statement by Marshall of the theoretical limit case of absolute monopoly.

[2] Gottfried Haberler, *A Survey of International Trade Theory* (International Finance Section, Department of Economics and Sociology, Princeton University, 1955), p. 53. Italics added.

the firms' marginal cost curves would be by no means a uniform one. In these circumstances the definition of profit which allows varying rates to emerge is to be preferred. The concept of an industry equilibrium for which all the individual firms are required to be in equilibrium, may be of value for some purposes but not for the study of the behaviour of the individual firm. In this connection there is an interesting suggestion for treating the representative firm 'as an abbreviated notation for the size distribution of firms' and making 'this size distribution the result of a process of chance'.[1]

There are also problems of drawing the line between internal and external economies. The immediate effect of a reduction in price of an input brought about by growth of the industry is clear enough. But suppose this reduction leads to factor substitution which in turn permits modification of production techniques and subsequently of organizational structure; at what point does the external economy end and the internal one begin? Then, too, some internal economies are transformed into external economies; for example, in the development of trade journal.

Even more difficult problems arise if it is suggested that Marshall's category of external economies failed to include any type of advantage accruing from 'the general development of industry',[2] because the external category is residual. For example, Cole has discussed the importance of circular and cumulative interactions between firms and management advisory units, advertising agencies, credit reporting services, industrial research bureaus, and educational institutions, and between company executives and specialists and their professional organizations. He argues that such interactions are built-in to the entrepreneurial system and states: 'This aspect of the matter seems . . . theoretically important. If these concepts are valid, there is here a variable acting through time which is not encompassed in the economist's "productive factors" as usually elaborated.'[3] Such influences do find a place in the Marshallian analysis; they enter into the category of institutional external economies. But it seems reasonable to say that these matters have been neglected because the theory of the firm has not really been concerned with the behaviour of the individual firm. Away from

---

[1] J. N. Wolfe, 'Some Marshallian Concepts: A Comment', *Economic Journal*, LXIX (December 1959), p. 809. See also H. A. Simon and C. P. Bonini, 'The Size Distribution of Business Firms', *American Economic Review*, XLVIII (September 1958), pp. 607–617.
[2] Marshall, *Principles of Economics*, p. 314.   [3] Arthur H. Cole, *op. cit.*, p. 83.

the competitive model, and recognizing that the growth of the individual firm, in, say, an oligopolistic situation, may imply a simultaneous and significant growth of the industry, it is no longer possible to preserve the distinction between internal and external economies. The initiating firm may derive strategic advantages.

Although external economies were a residual category for Marshall, and so with internal economies exhausted all the advantages of large scale production, it is nevertheless necessary to consider some influences which seem to be independent of scale, both of the individual firm and of the industry. At the level of the individual firm there may be consultation between the members of groups making decisions. This is only an aspect of decision-making by an organization. But consultation may occur between the firm and other firms, or at least between individuals or committees in different firms. The existence of such an informal consulting service has rarely been recognized.[1] When it is recognized, it is grouped with external economies.

At a different level there is the conceptual difficulty that arises because the firm operates in an environment that is largely shaped by government action—both as a direct participant in production and consumption and as the body responsible for economic policy. Of course, firms, individually or as groups, may enter into formulation of economic policy. Modification of the legal rules, and the interpretations of them, and of economic policy measures is an important way in which firms seek to maximize profits. But in fact the influence of economic policy will extend in varying degrees beyond the mere provision of a monetary standard compatible with growth. The significance of this is that economic policy constitutes part of the firm's environment and must not be regarded as given independently of the behaviour of the firms.

The concept of external economies is really relevant to a process of cost reduction through time; it brings up questions of dynamics. In fact many of the foregoing points only acquire their full significance in a dynamic context. This is so, for example, with some changes in economic policy. Depending upon preceding events, some firms may perceive the implications of the change of policy

---

[1] Paul F. Lazarsfeld draws attention to a report in a Harvard symposium by the owner of a small company who systematically sought out the advice of business friends all over the country ('Reflections on Business', *The American Journal of Sociology*, LXV (July 1959), p. 17). Lazarsfeld expressed surprise that this point was not touched upon by the representatives of large firms but they may have felt that they had adequate consultation facilities within their firms.

more quickly and be more prepared for action. Once the dynamic nature of the economy is recognized all decisions must be treated as based on expectations and due allowance made for uncertainty.

Turning to some other dynamic aspects of the firm's behaviour, Marshall regarded the tendency towards increasing returns as a long-run phenomenon. Harrod narrowed this down when he stated that 'The entrepreneur avers that he could in principle and indeed hopes in practice to produce twice (or ten times) his present output at a substantially lower cost per unit, but cannot do so immediately. His enterprise is a delicate organism with complicated labour relations and managerial relations. There is an optimum rate at which labour can be diluted and management formalized in the way required for larger scale; to accelerate beyond this rate would not yield increasing returns.'[1] More recently Penrose pointed out that 'Since the services from "inherited" managerial resources control the amount of new managerial resources that can be absorbed, they create a fundamental and inescapable limit to the amount of expansion a firm can undertake at any time'.[2] This latter statement almost implies a homogeneous management resource; it fails to recognize the considerable flexibility that exists and the way in which factor costs may rise through managerial inefficiency. The limit to the amount of expansion that can be undertaken at any time, is fixed if the time period during which the expansion must be completed and a minimum level of managerial productivity are specified. But these remarks have been concerned with the adaptation of new to 'inherited' managerial resources.

Equally important are the learning processes involved in the activities of both labour and management. These need to be extricated from the box labelled *division of labour* because they may bear directly upon costs independently of scale of output. Costs may vary with an irreversible change in technical knowledge as distinct from a change in technical organization.[3] If a cost function permits changes in technical knowledge and if this change is a cumulative process, the cost function should display a progressive lowering. Thus Hirsch discusses and attempts to measure progress functions applicable to direct labour, management, engineering departments, and material suppliers. As a first approximation the learning process

---

[1] *Op. cit.*, pp. 184–185.   [2] *Op. cit.*, p. 48.
[3] Cf. Werner Z. Hirsch, 'Manufacturing Progress Functions', *The Review of Economics and Statistics*, XXXIV (May 1952), p. 143; Sune Carlson, *A Study of the Pure Theory of Production* (Stockholm: Stockholm Economic Studies, No. 9, 1939), pp. 15–16.

of direct labour might be regarded as a once-for-all adaptation of a factor input; but then direct labour might continue to be a source of new ideas about production activities. Even if the importance of the process for direct labour is minimized, it is extremely difficult to argue that there are any absolute limits for management. If the managerial function is restricted to making decisions in the face of uncertainty, a given managerial team might be expected to show continuous improvement. This would not be so if each decision were truly unique;[1] but decision-making would seem to involve a learning-process which probably rests more upon repetitive action by the decision-maker than similarity of the choices being made.

Just as the learning process for direct labour might be interrupted by strikes, holidays, changes of attitude, etc., so with management. But in the latter case it is difficult to think of a normally continuous process subject to interruptions; the criteria being employed, themselves substitutes for more complete information, may change. Lazarsfeld had noted that a lack of appropriate criteria may initially lead to greater uncertainty and delay but that other irrelevant criteria may be adopted and lead to greater self-assurance and speed in decision-making.[2] Only empirical studies can show how much the businessman learns from experience of decision-making. In so far as the criteria are inapplicable, inappropriate, or subject to change, the management learning process may be intermittent and need not yield increasing managerial productivity. These points are concerned with economies of growth as distinct from economies of scale.[3] Unfortunately, there is little to be gained by examining the age distribution of firms, even in a particular industry, because the hypothesis that age and maturation in the management learning process are associated does not argue for a strong association. There may be radical reorganizations and in any case differences in the qualities of other factors and market forces will be at work. Little more can be suggested than that given the personnel, the information system, and the criteria, a management team will be more proficient the longer it has been a going unit. While some time limit has to be recognized it is not necessary to go as far as the Marshallian life cycle hypothesis. There is, however, the possibility that the individual member of a management team will, with age and success, be obliged to divert abilities away from the firm.[4]

[1] This raises important questions about the use of the theory of probability in economics.
[2] *Op. cit.*, p. 15.   [3] Cf. Penrose, *op. cit.*, Chapter VI.
[4] Cf. P. W. S. Andrews, *Manufacturing Business* (London: Macmillan & Co., Ltd., 1949), p. 140.

To recapitulate briefly, these considerations suggest that some of the causes giving rise to movements of the production function may need to be brought more explicitly within the scope of economics. On the one hand there are decisions leading to the selection of techniques of production; on the other, there is the area of business administration.[1] The second line of development has obvious implications for the profit maximization hypothesis. In conventional terminology these activities can be embodied in the entrepreneurial input. For example, Penrose states that 'Entrepreneurial services are those contributions to the operations of a firm which relate to the introduction and acceptance on behalf of the firm of new ideas, particularly with respect to products, location, and significant changes in technology, to the acquisition of new managerial personnel, to fundamental changes in the administrative organization of the firm, to the raising of capital, and to the making of plans for expansion, including the choice of method of expansion'.[2] Changes in the ability to perform these functions and those that might be classified as managerial, lead to shifts of the firm's production function, so creating a problem similar to that of technological change. In fact, technological change is commonly defined as a shift in the production function such that for some combination of inputs a greater output is obtained than formerly. But while changes of an organizational and institutional character can achieve this result they have not usually been explicitly treated as a form of technological change.[3]

In purely competitive models, inter-firm relationships could be ignored and factors other than the entrepreneur were regarded as passive. Even the entrepreneur's role bore little resemblance to the activities of a modern business organization. This passivity assumption, which paved the way for exploitation theories, led to a shifting emphasis on various entrepreneurial functions rather than an attempt to assess fully the role and functions of the business undertaking. In addition there seems to have been a tendency to take the

---

[1] Cf. G. F. Thirlby: 'To students of business administration, it may seem . . . odd that, so far, little has been done to integrate into the body of pure economics any developed theory of the functioning of the administrative organization' ('Notes on the Maximization Process in Company Administration', *Economica*, N.S., XVII (August 1950), p. 266). Obviously a change in the traditional definition of economics is implied.   [2] *Op. cit.*, p. 31, n. 1.

[3] See, for example, H. A. Simon, 'Effects of Technological Change in a Linear Model', T. C. Koopmans, ed., *Activity Analysis of Production and Allocation* (New York: John Wiley & Sons, Inc., 1951), pp. 260–281. As Andrews points out 'Business has developed techniques of management and systems of organization, and the existence of these is well recognized in practical life as facilitating the growth of the business and *extending* the capacity of the business man' (*op. cit.*, p. 130).

institutional structure in a particular type of economy for granted. An awareness of this is apparent in discussions of wage theory[1] but not in discussions of the theory of profit. Comparative study of management[2] in a variety of economic systems so emphasizes the need to allow for institutional factors that it is surprising to find Koopmans suggesting that because 'In the modern world largely the same fund of technological knowledge is utilized under an amazing variety of institutional arrangements, ranging all the way from American corporate and individual enterprise to Soviet communism . . ., it may help to start from models that formalize nothing but the range of technological alternatives open to a producing organization, whether an individual, a plant, a firm, a governmental agency, or society as a whole. In this way the character and range of the possible decisions are clarified before the decision-makers, their functions and their incentives enter upon the stage of the analysis.'[3]

If the techniques and organization are complementary and if the latter is achieved through a process of growth, then the institutional conditions may impose severe constraints upon the choice of technique. For example, Granick argues that Soviet metalworking could not copy the most recent Western technology and production organization because technology and production organization are 'inseparably linked, and because matured, intricate organizational methods cannot be "adopted". They must to a considerable extent be developed anew in each country, with the requisite bases for them being established over an extended time-period.'[4] Technological possibilities and institutional conditions should be put on an equal footing when model building.

It is not surprising, therefore, that so little progress has been made in the problem of defining the firm as a unit. But the problem must be solved both for the study of the behaviour of the individual firm and for attempts to make predictions which will hold for at least the majority of firms. To define the firm as a given decision-making unit is unsatisfactory as any change in the unit means that there is a new firm. Such a definition also ignores internal structure; presumably all internal processes of change have worked themselves out. It is no more satisfactory really than definition in terms of

[1] See J. T. Dunlop, ed., *The Theory of Wage Determination* (London: Macmillan & Co., Ltd., 1957), p. x.
[2] For example, F. H. Harbison and C. A. Myers, *Management in the Industrial World* (New York: McGraw-Hill Book Company, Inc., 1959).   [3] *Op. cit.*, p. 71.
[4] David Granick, 'Economic Development and Productivity Analysis: The Case of Soviet Metalworking', *Quarterly Journal of Economics*, LXXI (May 1957), p. 232.

product. Penrose has reviewed the literature on this topic—surprisingly without reference to the contribution of Coase.[1] Various possibilities were posed.[2] For Kaldor the firm had been a 'productive combination possessing a given unit of co-ordinating ability'; it could become a different firm when that given unit changed. Triffin thought that a new firm emerged when the producer's appraisal of cost and revenue conditions was revised. To Penrose the way out of this difficulty is to have many theories of the firm, changing the theory as the problem to be investigated changes. Plausible as this may seem, it does not fully justify the view that recent developments on the empirical front are devoid of implications for the conventional theory of the firm even though that theory was designed as a theory of price determination and resource allocation. Penrose rejects Papandreou's proposal that the conventional theory can be integrated with organizational theory through the introduction of organizational techniques side by side with technological techniques as data.[3]

It does seem convenient to keep organization and technology apart despite the increasing mechanization of communication and analysis of data. Nevertheless it seems unnecessary to rule out the possibility that the conventional theory can benefit from the new developments. Even if the firm is simply a price and output decision-maker, organization is relevant to the firm's long-run cost curves; and furthermore the study of organization may help to clarify the meaning of profit. There is also the possibility that management science will help with problems of the economy as a whole. Marginal cost equals marginal revenue is a gross oversimplification and management science may provide more realistic hypotheses about business behaviour. As Koopmans points out 'In those situations in which the complications of the problem have so far prevented business from approximating optimal policies, the advice of management science if heeded may help bring theory and practice closer together and thus make the economy more understandable and possibly more predictable than it would otherwise have been'.[4]

[1] R. H. Coase, 'The Nature of the Firm', *Economica*, N.S., IV (November 1937), pp. 386–405, reprinted in American Economic Association, *Readings in Price Theory* (London: George Allen & Unwin, 1953), pp. 331–351.

[2] Penrose, *op. cit.*, pp. 13–14.

[3] Penrose, *op. cit.*, p. 14; A. G. Papandreou, 'Some Basic Problems in the Theory of the Firm', B. F. Haley, ed., *A Survey of Contemporary Economics* (Homewood, Illinois: Richard D. Irwin, 1952), pp. 187–188.

[4] Koopmans, *op. cit.*, p. 186.

The Entrepreneur and Business Policy

One attempt to solve the problems of the nature and classification of factor inputs raised in the preceding section, together with the associated problem of the definition of profit, merits more attention than it has received. Stauss suggested that the firm itself as a working organization might be regarded as the entrepreneur.[1] This approach has distinct merits. Firstly, it is consistent with the view of the firm as an organization; a unit but with problems of internal structure, conflict, and learning processes, and with complex ties with other firms in the same and in different industries, with factor markets, and with the entire fabric of the modern economy. Not all of these conditions can be reduced and compressed within cost and revenue curves relating to the scale of output. Rather they act upon information flows, perception, and decision-making in ways that strike at the usefulness of these functions. To take this view of the firm is more than seeking simply to identify an entrepreneurial service for which profit is the reward; a type of explanation of profit which has been described as 'a relic of subjective cost theory parallel to the use of the disutility of labour and no more essential to profit theory than that concept is to wage theory'.[2] For the theory of profit, even though the firm is substituted for the entrepreneur, disutility and incentives of the persons comprising the firm remain to be incorporated into a fuller account of the circumstances which lead to the emergence of profit residuals.

Secondly, Stauss's approach is consistent with abandonment of the passivity view of the non-entrepreneurial factors. Once this has been done and the firm is visualized in its institutional setting, it is possible to give real meaning to Schumpeter's distinction between the creation of profit and the receiving of profit. Consider the following statement:

Profit, in our sense, is a functional return—its peculiarities and especially its temporary character constitute a justifiable reason for hesitating to call it an income —but it would not always be safe to locate the entrepreneurial function according

[1] J. H. Stauss, 'The Entrepreneur: The Firm', *Journal of Political Economy*, LII (June 1944), pp. 112–127. This attempt was dismissed by Haley as 'not altogether satisfactory' and criticized by Bronfenbrenner on the grounds that it 'gives no clue to the allocation or distribution of profit among the natural persons of the firm's ownership and control groups, and leaves this whole issue to the indeterminacy of corporate infighting'. See Haley, *op. cit.*, p. 47; M. Bronfenbrenner, 'A Reformulation of Naive Profit Theory', *Southern Economic Journal*, XXVI (April 1960), p. 302.

[2] J. K. Eastham, 'A Redefinition of the Boundary between Interest and Profit Theories', *Dundee Economic Essays* (Dundee: The School of Economics, 1955), p. 45.

D

to the criterion of accrual. Whether it accrues to entrepreneurs or not is a matter of institutional pattern. . . . In corporate industry profits accrue to the firm as such, and their distribution ceases to be automatic and becomes a matter of policy —shareholders, executives (whether entrepreneurs or not), and employees receiving, in the most varied forms . . . indeterminate shares in it or contractual equivalents for shares in it.[1]

Schumpeter was, of course, stressing the temporary nature of profit income. There is a tendency for this form of income to be eroded but the emphasis upon organization and information developed in this chapter suggests that there may be limits to the rate of erosion. Marshall, for example, wrote of the profits of 'capital and business power'. There is a further ground for disagreement with Schumpeter. Entrepreneurial activity is not confined neatly within the firm; in part it is a matter of interaction between the firm, or its component parts, and its environment, so that the shifting of profit through bargaining might not involve any eroding of entreprenurial gains.

It will be argued in subsequent chapters that this view of the firm eliminates some of the difficulties that have bedevilled the concept of profit maximization. Some objectives which cannot be reconciled with profit maximization in the conventional treatment of the firm's behaviour now find their place; for example, conflict in the form of internal competitiveness to which reference has already been made. Or again cost differences between firms in the same industry, which might appear to be failures to reach minimum cost levels even when allowance is made for scale differences, may be explicable in terms of learning processes. A consideration of organizational structure and institutional relationships suggests that the firm operating under conditions of uncertainty may seek to formulate policies or adopt fixed behaviour patterns that are consistent with profit objectives other than maximization. However, it should be noted that the wider the view of the firm, the more difficult it becomes to hold to the assumption that the opportunities facing one firm are independent of the choices actually made by other firms.

A further consequence of recognition of the organizational nature of the firm is that the concept of policy can be employed. This concept permits full scope for interfirm differences; it looks to the character of the firm as a stage in an evolutionary process. It would seem to go some considerable way to meet the historians' criticism of the entrepreneur concept. But there is the danger that

[1] J. A. Schumpeter, *Business Cycles* (New York: McGraw-Hill Book Company, Inc., 1939), Vol. 1, p. 106.

while providing a method for the study of the history of the individual firm,[1] it may not further economic analysis in the sense of making it possible to make predictions about the behaviour of firms. Considerable development of the concept is needed. When persistent behaviour patterns have been detected it becomes necessary to inquire into the events which cause changes in those patterns. If policy is interpreted as a substitute for information and as a reflection of objectives that compete with profit maximization, it is possible to explore the effects on profit of the influence of non-pecuniary elements of output, price, and cost procedures.[2] These aspects of the firm's behaviour can be studied in a static equilibrium sense but a dynamic approach is also possible. It can be asked whether the efficiency of policy or the importance of non-pecuniary considerations change in any systematic way with the size of firm, its maturity, and the stability of its relationships with factor markets, sales outlets, and its environment generally. It may be, for example, that rigidities appear; that rules of behaviour are worked out and applied during a phase of the firm's development but are not adapted quickly to changing circumstances.

An Alternative Approach

In the final section of this chapter an alternative approach to the formulation of a theory of profit is indicated. This approach goes beyond the substitution of firm for entrepreneur and calls for consideration of the resources which constitute the firm as opposed to those which are purchased by the firm; in particular emphasis is placed upon organization and information.[3] The firm's input of the services of such resources will be treated as variable but subject to limits determined by the structure of the firm, its market position, and its stage and rate of growth. A consideration of these inputs is needed to complement the customary analysis of production because the firm lacks knowledge of the optimum combination of inputs, and because the inputs of organizational resources and

[1] Andrews suggests that the crucial training for the economist in this field may be that of the historian. See his review of H. R. Bowen, *The Business Enterprise as Subject for Research* (New York: Social Science Research Council, 1955) *Kyklos*, X (1957, Fasc. 1), p. 71.

[2] Cf. J. H. Dunning, 'Non-Pecuniary Elements and Business Behaviour', *Oxford Economic Papers*, N.S., 11 (October 1959), pp. 229–241.

[3] This is not to say that the services of such resources cannot be purchased. Management consultants can be hired and research findings can be purchased. Available empirical material is inadequate to establish the relative importance of purchased services and services generated within the firm.

information are associated closely with the formation of expectations. Expectations, in turn, are of vital importance because of their influence in investment decisions, irrespective of the attainment of equilibrium positions.

Several consequences follow from the adoption of this approach. As already mentioned it is difficult to preserve the distinction between the technological and economic; once uncertainty in both these areas is assumed and it is recognized that the reduction of uncertainty involves costs—both when achieved internally by reorganization and externally by purchase of managerial services and information or by changed relationships with the suppliers of other factors—the firm may have to decide which area affords the most profitable risk reduction. Nor can a sharp distinction between technological and organizational influences be upheld; both lead to shifts of the production function once the assumption of an optimum solution to the technological problems of production is relaxed.

A second consequence is that firms may resort to conventional procedures, such as pricing by means of a fixed margin over direct costs, as a substitute for information which if it were immediately available would be too costly, or for information which although relatively inexpensive can be developed only with a considerable lapse of time. In such circumstances profit criteria alternative to profit maximization become meaningful. Which of the criteria from the large range of possibilities the firm actually adopts will depend upon conditions both internal and external to the firm; nor will this selection be independent of historical influences such as the stage of growth of the firm, its current rate of growth, and expected future rate of growth.

A third consequence is that uncertainty can be viewed in a new light. It remains true that uncertainty moulds the organization of market and firm; but the firm can seek actively to reduce uncertainty in ways that are not necessarily amenable to probability analysis. For example, the oligopolistic firm may be willing to forego price competition and resort to product research, market research and advertising, and restrictive practices. Such measures reduce uncertainty; and in doing so they may require the collection of information, modification of the firm's organization, and changes in its relationship to its environment. This view of uncertainty requires consideration of the accumulated stock of information, the activities which are adding currently to that stock, and the policy rules which serve as substitutes for information.

The central problem may be viewed in another manner. The theory of the firm aims at predicting the firm's price, output and investment decisions,[1] using the profit maximization postulate. Consequently the definition of profit needs to be such that the firm can direct its efforts towards maximization, perhaps subject to some constraints—unless profit-making is placed in the constraint category and pride of place given to some other objective, such as sales revenue maximization. The approach suggested above must then be seen as bearing upon the firm's choice of resource inputs and also upon the firm's policy criteria. As yet there is no general theory of decision-making under conditions of uncertainty but recent work supports the view that the firm's decisions are made by abstracting from the total situation confronting it.[2] This process of abstraction is related to the sources and uses of information. For example, it is important to ask in what ways the firm makes use of accounting data. In appropriate form, such data could be used to measure the results from existing factor combinations, to evaluate proposals for the acquisition of additional factors, and, within the firm, to focus attention on managerial problems.[3] This question will be taken up in Chapter VI, but it should be noted that it has a bearing upon the study of investment behaviour. For example, Eisner has reported the results of estimating parameters of distributed lag investment functions on the basis of a cross-section of accounts of 200-odd large non-financial companies. Profit variables did not generally reveal significant coefficients in multiple regressions including sales change variables. 'These results appear to be consistent with the theory that past profits *per se* have little or no bearing on capital expenditures and that the positive relation observed in some past investigations stemmed from the role of profits as a "proxy

[1] Cf. M. J. Farrell, 'Deductive Systems and Empirical Generalizations in the Theory of The Firm', *Oxford Economic Papers*, N.S., 4 (February 1952), p. 45. Farrell adds that it need say nothing about the psychological processes by which the decision is reached and that it need predict only 'the policy which successful businessmen will tend to follow'. This view rests upon the survival thesis and is of limited usefulness where adjustment processes are slow.

[2] 'Thus it might be agreed that what matters to a decision-maker is not the whole of the facts and expectations which might bear on his decision, but the simplified model of these facts and expectations which he forms in his mind. . . . Simplification is essential to decisions about complex matters; that at once suggests that attention should be given to the nature of the simplifying process' (C. F. Carter, Review of M. J. Bowman, ed., *Expectations, Uncertainty, and Business Behavior* (New York: Social Science Research Council, 1958), *Kyklos*, XII (1959, Fasc. 1), pp. 83–84.)

[3] See J. G. March and H. A. Simon, *Organizations* (New York: John Wiley & Sons, Inc., 1958); Wesley Mitchell, Introduction to R. C. Epstein, *Industrial Profits in the United States* (New York: National Bureau of Economic Research, Inc., 1934).

variable" for other factors, in particular past sales changes which had brought pressure on capacity.'[1]

It might also be pointed out that the alternative approach suggested in this chapter bears an affinity to some recent developments in organization theory.[2] Furthermore, it might help to meet the growing criticism[3] of the traditional distribution categories, provided it can be adapted to the needs of empirical inquiry. For example, Bowman has argued that there is a 'need for an inductive approach that will start with easily identifiable empirical categories of income receivers such as wage-earners, independent proprietors, corporate officials, moneylenders, investors in corporate securites, and rent receivers (in the lay sense)'.[4] When the identification of the entrepreneur and firm is pressed further as suggested above, it might be useful to treat interest and dividends as transfer payments. This idea has been developed in connection with national income accounting but its implications for the theory of profit have not yet been explored.

When the failure to take account explicitly of the nature of the firm is viewed against the background sketched in this chapter it is apparent that that failure has led to a diversity of theories of profit, has prevented a thorough analysis of information and uncertainty, and consequently has clouded the understanding of the nature and role of profit. Furthermore, that failure has hampered the development of positive economics and left the initiative with managerial studies or what is essentially normative economics of the behaviour of the firm. In the previous chapter some of the reasons for this failure were suggested. To conclude this chapter it might be asked why and from what point of view it is inadequate to merely acknowledge uncertainty and speak of its 'inevitable connection'

---

[1] Robert Eisner, 'A Distributed Lag Investment Function', Abstract, *Econometrica*, 27 (April 1959), p. 308. This paper was subsequently published in full; see *Econometrica*, 28 (January 1960), pp. 1–29. The investment decision is examined in detail in Chapter V.

[2] See, for example, March and Simon, *op. cit.*

[3] For example, B. R. Williams, 'The Impact of Uncertainty in Economic Theory, with Special Reference to the Theory of Profits', C. F. Carter, G. P. Meredith, and G. L. S. Shackle, eds, *Uncertainty and Business Decisions* (Liverpool: Liverpool University Press, 1957), p. 74; B. S. Keirstead, 'The Structure and Accumulation of Capital', *Canadian Journal of Economics and Political Science*, XXIII (November 1957), pp. 557–558; K. W. Rothschild, 'Some Recent Contributions to a Macro-economic Theory of Income Distribution', *Scottish Journal of Political Economy*, VIII (October 1961), pp. 173–199.

[4] M. J. Bowman, 'Theories of Income Distribution: Where do We Stand?', *Journal of Political Economy*, LVI (December 1958), pp. 537. The work of Marchal and Lecaillon represents a venture in this direction. They have sought to replace the conventional categories by the following groups: salariés, titulaires de profits, exploitants agricoles, prêteurs, bénéficiaries de transferts. See Jean Marchal and J. Lecaillon, *La répartition du revenue national*. Part 1, Les participants. Vol. 1, Les salariés; Vol. 2, Les non-salariés. (Paris: Ed. Genin, 1958.)

with profit? An answer may be given along the following lines: the firm is not passive; it can respond to uncertainty (or create uncertainty for others) by modification of its activities, resources, and policy criteria. The firm's efforts in these directions will normally require some allocation of resources to be devoted to the reduction of uncertainty. An understanding of the firm's decision processes is consequently necessary to the full explanation of the allocation of resources in the economy. The firm's decisions in this area may lead to inter-firm differences and thus have a bearing— which may not be unimportant—upon market structure and the nature of competition.[1] The allocation of resources to the collection of information and the reduction of uncertainty, and the effects of such an allocation upon not only market structure but also productivity and economic growth, have general economic policy implications. Taken together these considerations seem sufficient to justify treatment of these aspects of the behaviour of the firm as significant; as aspects to be incorporated in a model of the firm for use in the theory of profit.

[1] This does not imply any precise relationship between market structure as measured, say, by concentration ratios, and behaviour.

CHAPTER III

'THE INEVITABLE CONNECTION BETWEEN PROFIT AND UNCERTAINTY'

THE history of the theory of profit indicates that while profits tended to be regarded originally as a residual return to the owner, more recently a functional distinction has been drawn between the capitalist and the entrepreneur. But for various reasons the problem was not to be solved simply by treating interest as the income going to the capitalist and profit as the income going to the entrepreneur. Recognition of the institutional changes taking place, lack of progress with the entrepreneurship theory, the underlying clash of an ideological nature on the functions of profit, and generally a changing economic and social climate combined to produce essentially two types of theory of profit.[1] The first treats profit as a residual from a process of imputation; the second seeks to implement the simple division between interest and profit, the latter accruing to entrepreneurship. The dismal situation Hicks saw existing prior to 1931 has not changed significantly. Knight's *Risk, Uncertainty and Profit* may have appeared to commit economists to the uncertainty theory of profit. Nevertheless, while the connection between profit and uncertainty has tended to dominate discussion, some other tracks have been followed. There are good reasons for the dominance of the uncertainty theory. Firstly, the residual in the imputation process can be attributed to uncertainty. If profit is attributed to monopoly there is the problem that the creation and maintenance of a monopoly situation can be regarded as a response to uncertainty. Secondly, however the function of entrepreneurship is interpreted—organizing, adapting, innovating, or more generally, decision-making—it is occasioned by the basic fact of uncertainty about the future.

Knight's book was if not the first, then the most significant elaborate statement of the connection between profit and uncertainty. A number of earlier writers had commented upon this aspect. Without going back to the classical economists, there are such

[1] Cf. F. H. Hahn, 'A Note on Profit and Uncertainty', *Economica*, N.S., XIV (August, 1947), p. 211.

contributors as Hawley,[1] J. B. Clark,[2] Willett,[3] and Pigou.[4] Amongst Knight's immediate contemporaries Hardy[5] is a neglected contributor. On the whole it is plausible to see Knight's work as completing a picture already sketched by Clark and Hawley. The former had viewed profit as a dynamic residual emerging from the process of economic change; the latter saw this residual as the inducement to the entrepreneur or the enterprise to assume all the risks. So at this juncture, thought had not really departed from the classical tradition which found the rationale of pure profit in the need for incentives or savings.

KNIGHT'S CONTRIBUTION

Examination of 'the inevitable connection between profit and uncertainty' can begin by reviewing Knight's contribution. This seems warranted on several grounds: no other writer has developed such a scholarly and comprehensive treatment of the theory of profit; his theory has had, and still has, considerable influence upon thought on this subject. And as sometimes happens, a condensed and somewhat distorted version of an important theory is handed down with some important elements receding into obscurity. For example, Knight is sometimes held to state that the only function for which profit can be regarded as a reward is uncertainty bearing. Discussion in the following pages will show the inadequacy of such an assertion.

Knight's essay attacked the problem of profit through 'an inquiry into the causes of the failure of ideal competition to be fully realized in fact'.[6] To this end he sought to define the assumptions necessary to the state of ideal or perfect competition. These

[1] F. B. Hawley, 'Profits and the Residual Theory', Quarterly Journal of Economics, IV (July 1890), pp. 387–396; 'The Risk Theory of Profit', Quarterly Journal of Economics, VII (July 1893), pp. 459–479; 'Enterprise and Profit', Quarterly Journal of Economics, XV (November 1900), pp. 75–105; 'Reply to Final Objections to the Risk Theory of Profit', Quarterly Journal of Economics, XV (August 1901), pp. 603–620; Enterprise and the Productive Process (New York: G. P. Putnam's Sons, 1907); 'The Orientation of Economics on Enterprise', American Economic Review, XVII (September 1927), pp. 409–428.

[2] J. B. Clark, 'Distribution as Determined by a Law of Rent', Quarterly Journal of Economics, V (April 1891), pp. 289–318; 'The Statics and the Dynamics of Distribution', Quarterly Journal of Economics, VI (October 1891), pp. 111–119; 'Insurance and Business Profit', Quarterly Journal of Economics, VII (October 1892), pp. 40–54; The Distribution of Wealth (New York: The Macmillan Company, 1899).

[3] A. H. Willett, The Economic Theory of Risk and Insurance (Columbia University Studies in History, Economics and Public Law, XIX, 1901–1902. New York: Longmans, Green & Co.).

[4] A. C. Pigou, The Economics of Welfare, 4th ed. (London: Macmillan & Co., Ltd., 1932), pp. 771–781.

[5] C. O. Hardy, Risk and Risk-Bearing (Chicago: University of Chicago Press, 1923).

[6] Frank H. Knight, Risk, Uncertainty and Profit (New York: Houghton Mifflin Company, 1921), p. 22.

assumptions were important because they formed ' . . . the limiting tendency of actual economic processes. . . . The key to the whole tangle will be found to lie in the notion of risk or uncertainty and the ambiguities concealed therein. . . . Uncertainty must be taken in a sense radically distinct from the familiar notion of Risk, from which it has never been properly separated.'[1] The link between uncertainty and profit is then postulated. Uncertainty is 'the most important underlying difference, [, outside of monopoly considerations,] between the conditions which theory is compelled to assume and those which exist in fact'.[2] The absence of profit is 'the essential distinction between theoretical and actual economic society'.[3]

The nature of this uncertainty theory and its relationship to the less subtle dynamic view of Clark is brought out in the following statement:

Dynamic changes give rise to a peculiar form of income only in so far as the changes and their consequences are unpredictable in character.

It cannot, then, be change, which is the cause of profit, since *if the law of the change is known*, as in fact is largely the case, no profits can arise. The connection between change and profit is uncertain and always indirect. Change *may* cause a situation out of which profit will be made, *if* it brings about ignorance of the future. Without change of some sort there would, it is true, be no profits, for if everything moved along in an absolutely uniform way, the future would be completely foreknown in the present and competition would certainly adjust things to the ideal state where all prices would equal costs. It is this fact that change is a necessary condition of our being ignorant of the future (though ignorance need not follow from the fact of change and only to a limited extent does so) that has given rise to the error that change is the cause of profit.

Not only may change take place without occasioning profit, but profit may also arise in the entire absence of any 'dynamic' or progressive changes of the kind enumerated by Professor Clark. If the conditions are subject to unpredictable fluctuations, ignorance of the future will result in the same way and inaccuracies in the competitive adjustment and profits will be the inevitable consequence. And the failure of an anticipated change to occur is the same in effect as the occurrence of an unanticipated one. It is not dynamic change, nor any change, as such, which causes profit, but the divergence of actual conditions from those which have been expected and on the basis of which business arrangements have been made. For a satisfactory explanation of profit we seem to be thrown back from the 'dynamic' theory to the *Uncertainty of the Future*, a condition of affairs loosely designated by the term 'risk' in ordinary langauge and in business parlance.[4]

What of the distinction between risk and uncertainty? For Knight, risk was simply measurable uncertainty which could then

[1] *Ibid.*, pp. 18–19.
[2] *Ibid.*, p. 51. The qualifying phrase appeared as a footnote in the original.
[3] *Ibid.*   [4] *Ibid.*, pp. 37–38.

be expressed as a cost, provided there existed the requisite organization for consolidating a sufficient number of cases. But the term
uncertainty was restricted to cases of the non-quantitative type.
This unmeasurable risk, or uncertainty, is associated with economic
change; and 'The connection of profit with change is simply the
fact that decisions of a managerial sort either produce changes or
involve adaptations to change or both'.[1]

Knight drew a distinction between *a priori* probability where the
chances could be computed from general principles, and statistical
probability where the chance could only be determined empirically.
But 'Business decisions . . . deal with situations which are far too
unique, generally speaking, for any sort of statistical tabulation
to have any value for guidance. The conception of an objectively
measurable probability or choice is simply inapplicable. The
confusion arises from the fact that we do estimate the value or validity
or dependability of our opinions and estimates, and such an estimate
has the same *form* as a probability judgement; it is a ratio, expressed
by a proper fraction. But in fact it appears to be meaningless and
fatally misleading to speak of the probability, in an objective sense,
that a judgement is correct.'[2] For this reason Knight wished to
distinguish a third type of probability or uncertainty '. . . not
susceptible to measurement and hence to elimination. It is this *true
uncertainty* which by preventing the theoretically perfect outworking
of the tendencies of competition gives the characteristic form of
"enterprise" to economic organization as a whole and accounts for
the peculiar income of the entrepreneur.'[3]

Knight considered that he had been able to combine 'the conceptions of risk, of economic change and the role of business ability'.[4]
Given this view of profit, what part does the entrepreneur play?
With the perfect knowledge of ideal competition there is no call
for organization and management, and, by definition, no question
of uncertainty-bearing. 'With uncertainty present, doing things,
the actual execution of activity, becomes in a real sense a secondary
part of life; the primary problem or function is deciding what to do
and how to do it.'[5] Goods have to be produced for a predicted

---

[1] F. H. Knight, 'Profit', *Encyclopaedia of the Social Sciences*, XII (New York: The Macmillan Co., 1934) pp. 480–486, reprinted in American Economic Association, *Readings in
the Theory of Income Distribution* (Philadelphia: The Blakiston Company, 1946), p. 541.
[2] *Risk, Uncertainty and Profit*, p. 231.
[3] *Ibid.*, p. 232.   [4] 'Profit', p. 540.   [5] *Risk, Uncertainty and Profit*, p. 268.

market and the problem of forecasting is combined with the direction and control of production. These duties are 'concentrated upon a very narrow class of the producers and we meet with a new economic functionary, the entrepreneur'.[1] Enterprise and the wage system appear as a direct result of the fact of uncertainty. Under this system '... a special social class, the business men, direct economic activity; they are in the strict sense the producers, while the great mass of the population merely furnish them with productive services, placing their persons and their property at the disposal of this class; the entrepreneurs *also* guarantee to those who furnish productive services a fixed remuneration'.[2]

This system of organization implies two types of individual income: contractual income or rent and residual income or profit. For Knight the causal distinction between them is 'sharp and clear' although neither variety will ever be met in pure form. For example, the entrepreneur's income 'contains an element which is ordinary contractual income, received on the ground of routine services performed by the entrepreneur personally for the business (wages) or earned by property which belongs to him (rent or capital return)'.[3] These components were regarded by Knight as determined by competitive pricing, even though it may not be possible in practice to say what the remuneration is.[4] Further consideration of the profit component necessitates inquiry into entrepreneurial ability and its demand and supply conditions. First, it might appear that the possession of property (capital) is a necessary condition for assuming the entrepreneurial role. But Knight assumes away this restriction on the ground that 'demonstrated ability can always get funds for business operations'.[5] The prospective entrepreneur may, if he possesses sufficient capital, assume the entrepreneurial functions 'without convincing anyone outside himself of any special fitness to exercise them'.[6] Ability is a question of capacity to exercise responsible control and to guarantee the owners of productive services against uncertainty and fluctuations in their incomes.

On the demand side 'there is evidently a law of diminishing returns governing the combination of productive services with entrepreneurs. . . . The demand for entrepreneurs . . . depends directly upon the supply of the other agencies.'[7] On the supply side the important considerations are ability, willingness, and the

[1] *Ibid.*   [2] *Ibid.*, p. 271.   [3] *Ibid.*, p. 277.   [4] *Ibid.*, p. 278.
[5] *Ibid.*, p. 274, n. 1.   [6] *Ibid.*, p. 279.   [7] *Ibid.*, p. 282.

power to give satisfactory guarantees. The position is summarized in the following statement:

We have assumed in this first approximation that each man in society knows his own powers as entrepreneur, but that men know nothing about each other in this capacity. The division of social income between profits and contractual income then depends on the supply of entrepreneur ability in the society and the rapidity of diminishing returns from (other factors applied to) it, the size of the profit share increasing as the supply of ability is small and as the returns diminish more rapidly. If men are poor judges of their own powers as well as ignorant of those of other men, the size of the profit share depends on whether they tend on the whole to overestimate or underestimate the prospects of business operations, being larger if they underestimate.

These statements abstract from the question of possession of means to guarantee the fixed incomes which they contract to pay; limitations in this respect act as limitations on the supply of entrepreneur ability. If entrepreneur ability is of such high quality that it practically is not subject to diminishing returns, the competition among even a very few such men will raise the rate of contractual returns and lower the residual share, if they know their own powers. If they do not, the size of their profits will again depend on their 'optimism', varying inversely with the latter.[1]

The entrepreneurial function emerges as a dual one of risk-taking and control. The entrepreneur hires the other factors of production, undertaking to remunerate them at contractual rates.

If from the net receipts of the entrepreneur the imputed wages and interest and rent for the labour and capital contributed by the entrepreneur himself are deducted, the residual profit, which may be positive or negative, is ascertained. Is this residual the reward of any factor of production? It is ' . . . the remainder out of the value realized from the sale of the product after deduction of the values of all the factors in production which can be valued, or after all the product has been imputed to productive elements which can be imputed by the competitive mechanism. Profit is unimputable income, as distinguished from the total income of the business.'[2] In so far as some portion of the total income can be associated in advance with the ability of management, it ceases to be part of profit and becomes a wage. 'The true uncertainty in organized life is the uncertainty in an estimate of human capacity, which is always a capacity to meet uncertainty.'[3]

The entrepreneurial function can be discharged in several ways. 'The simplest division of entrepreneurship which we can think of is the separation of the two elements of control and guarantee and

---

[1] *Ibid.*, pp. 284–285.   [2] *Ibid.*, p. 308.   [3] *Ibid.*, p. 309.

their performance by different individuals.'[1] But in the real world, responsibilities can be shared or transferred. 'The natural result is a complicated division or diffusion of entrepreneurship, distributed in the typical modern business organization by a hierarchy of security issues carrying every conceivable gradation and combination of rights to control and freedom from uncertainty as to income and vested capital.'[2] Gordon has suggested that Knight's 'final concept of control becomes so attenuated as to be of little significance in any analysis of active business leadership'.[3]

The link between entrepreneurship and property has been touched upon and it is desirable to examine further Knight's views on this point. He considered that the entrepreneur must almost of necessity own some property and so could hardly be freed from all risk and responsibility. 'The importance of property-ownership in connection with profit will be even greater and more apparent if "goodwill", business connection, and established reputation, etc., be regarded as property.'[4] They should be classified as property if they are salable. Knight expressed the view that too much emphasis had been given to the relationship of profit and wages of management. 'The connection with property income is enormously more common, direct, and close. The residual share of income falls of necessity to the person in *responsible* control of a business; hence, in most cases to a person who also receives a property income.'[5]

Knight sums up in the following statement:

> The only 'risk' which leads to a profit is a unique uncertainty resulting from an exercise of ultimate responsibility which in its very nature cannot be insured nor capitalized nor salaried. Profit arises out of the inherent, absolute unpredictability of things, out of the sheer brute fact that the results of human activity cannot be anticipated and then only in so far as even a probability calculation in regard to them is impossible and meaningless. . . . And it is uncertainty in this sense which explains profit in the proper use of the term, the sense towards which economic usage has been groping, that of a pure residual income, unimputable by the mechanism of competition to any agent concerned in its creation.[6]

Profit is presented as a residual, non-factor income because, and only in so far as, the entrepreneurial agency, vital though it may be

---

[1] *Ibid.*, p. 289.   [2] *Ibid.*, p. 300.

[3] R. A. Gordon, 'Enterprise, Profits and the Modern Corporation', *Explorations in Economics* New York: McGraw-Hill Book Co., 1936), pp. 306–316, reprinted in American Economic Association, *Readings in the Theory of Income Distribution*, p. 563. Fritz Redlich comments: 'Knight's theory does not distinguish clearly between ownership, control, decision-making, and management—specifically between ownership and control on the one hand and decision-making and management on the other' ('Towards a Better Theory of Risk', *Explorations in Entrepreneurial History*, X (October 1957), p. 33).

[4] *Risk, Uncertainty and Profit*, p. 307.   [5] *Ibid.*, p. 306.   [6] *Ibid.*, pp. 310–312.

in economic activity, cannot be imputed a value through the competitive pricing process. Knight refers adversely to the conventional classification of productive agencies as land, labour, and capital. The classes are not homogeneous; substitution may take place and this is essential for the possibility of a competitive organization of society. 'The existence of a problem of distribution depends upon the coöperation of different kinds of agencies performing physically different operations in the creation of product, and the possibility of solving the problem depends on the equivalence of determinate amounts of the several services in contributing to the value result.'[1]

Although the proportion of decisions that involve true uncertainty has been whittled down by consolidation, specialization, diffusion, control of the future, and increased power of prediction, the society's power of applying such techniques must be taken as given. The category is too all-embracing, including as it does institutional arrangements, market structure, and even research of all types. Monopoly considerations were noted by Knight as the most important underlying difference between the theoretical model and the conditions of the real world; they could influence the rates of remuneration established for the services of factors of production. 'Free competition, of course, involves the complete separate ownership of every productive agent or natural unit, and the exploitation of every one in a way to secure its maximum yield value. Any sort of violent interference with competition manifestly contradicts this assumption and may be roughly designated monopoly.'[2] However, as pointed out in the previous chapter, the monopoly elements are part and parcel of the means of reducing or eliminating uncertainty.

It would appear worthwhile to trace the development of Knight's theory of profit through the subsequent years which witnessed the growth of the theory of monopolistic or imperfect competition, the advent of Keynesian theory of income and employment, and the considerable progress which is generally believed to have been made with interest theory. Weston has argued[3] that Knight did not attempt any major revisions in his subsequent writings, but he was challenged on this by Stockfisch[4] who drew attention to Knight's remark in 1935 that the theory as developed in *Risk, Uncertainty and Profit*

---

[1] *Ibid.*, p. 124.   [2] *Ibid.*, p. 185.
[3] J. Fred Weston, 'A Generalized Uncertainty Theory of Profit', *American Economic Review*, XL (March 1950), p. 41.
[4] J. A. Stockfisch, 'Comment', *American Economic Review*, XLI (March 1951), p. 170.

'needs to be entirely re-worked'.[1] This remark should be taken in context. Knight was criticizing Hayek's view of the relationship between investment and output according to which an increase in investment was identified with a lengthening of the production process or period of production. He pointed out that the theory of profit embodied in *Risk, Uncertainty and Profit* rested upon the general view of the firm buying productive services now, and selling the products in the future. He felt that the basis of computation of profit had been neglected: that basis could be a dated interval of time, a particular item of product, or a project or venture somehow defined, the first of these being the one usually adopted.

Knight argued that 'The *crucial* element in the profit problem in a society in which capital is employed has to do with asset values. It is a question of (expenditures and receipts and of) the relative values of assets at the beginning and end of the accounting period.'[2] He then declared that 'The main point for emphasis is that the outlays and returns compared to determine profit are not separated by any time interval, but belong to the same accounting period, however short it may be. For any outlay in business or production the corresponding return is not in the future, but contemporary. Time and uncertainty enter into profit in a different way altogether— namely, through the capital account, or specifically, through inventories and depreciation. But capital itself is always a matter of anticipation to the infinite future.'[3] However, this type of re-working of the theory was not carried through by Knight although it was advocated again in the note to the 1940 reprint of *Risk, Uncertainty and Profit*.

The adverse remarks about the traditional classification of factors of production were soon enlarged upon. The whole notion of factors of production was rejected;[4] along with 'wages, interest, and rent as distributive shares' it was classified as 'antiquated lumber'.[5]

---

[1] F. H. Knight, 'Professor Hayek and the Theory of Investment', *Economic Journal*, XLV (March 1935), p. 79, n. 1. See also *Risk, Uncertainty and Profit*, Additional note for the reprint of the 1940 issue (London School of Economics Reprints of Scarce Works, No. 16, 1946), pp. xxxvii–xxxix.

[2] 'Professor Hayek and the Theory of Investment', p. 80.   [3] *Ibid.*

[4] F. H. Knight, 'A Suggestion for Simplifying the Statement of the General Theory of Price', *Journal of Political Economy*, XXXVI (June 1928), pp. 367–370. Cf. the criticism of the marginal productivity theory from the general equilibrium point of view by William L. Valk, *The Principles of Wages* (London: P. S. King & Son, Ltd., 1928).

[5] *Risk, Uncertainty and Profit*, Preface to 1933 reissue, p. xxv. This view was again presented in the well-known article on 'The Ricardian Theory of Production and Distribution' (*The Canadian Journal of Economics and Political Science*, I (February and May 1935), Part I, pp. 3–25; Part II, pp. 171–196).

The land, labour, and capital classification was regarded as a carry-over from post-feudal Europe; for distribution theory is only 'a corollary or footnote to an exposition of the mechanism by which resources are apportioned among different uses, and organized in each use, under the forces of price competition'.[1]

The 1942 paper on 'Profit and Entrepreneurial Functions' adds little.[2] Pure profit is the residual after deducting wages and/or interest at the 'going rates' for the entrepreneur's labour and capital services. The entrepreneur's functions are innovation and adaptation. These functions are necessitated by the imperfection of competition, itself the consequence of error of human judgement. Knight pointed out that the tendency of the competitive process is to impute the whole product, leaving nothing, except for monopoly gain, for entrepreneurship. This tendency implies that pure profit will be temporary. 'While it exists, in a positive form, it may obviously be regarded as a phenomenon of monopoly, and some distinction, which can never be clear, must be made between temporary profit and permanent monopoly revenue.'[3] This type of temporary gain was treated in Schumpeterian fashion as the incentive to innovation.

Further opportunities exist to observe Knight's opinions. In 1953 he suggested that 'It is surely a significant fact that although the entrepreneur is dynamically the central figure in our free enterprise economy, his function in its purity and on the whole does not seem to share in the fruits of production, or even shares negatively. For both theory and statistics indicate that on the average the entre-preneur pays the productive agents he hires—labour and property— more than they actually yield and takes a lower remuneration for those which he furnishes himself.'[4] Profits are never secure and are usually not long continued. For this reason firms must, to avoid long-run losses, try to maximize profits when they are to be had.[5]

The difficulties of defining entrepreneurship and specifying its conditions of supply were revived when Knight argued the impor-tance of the non-economic interest, of 'the game aspect, the desire to achieve, to surpass, to win the race—and no doubt the gambling

[1] 'The Ricardian Theory of Production and Distribution', p. 171. This view was repeated in later works. See 'On the Theory of Capital: In Reply to Mr. Kaldor', *Econometrica*, 6 (January 1938), p. 81; 'Diminishing Returns from Investment', *Journal of Political Economy*, LII (March 1944), pp. 26–47.

[2] *Journal of Economic History*, Supplement, II (December 1942), pp. 126–132.

[3] *Ibid.*, p. 128.

[4] 'Discussion', *American Economic Review*, XLIV (May 1954), Proceedings, p. 63.

[5] Knight's comments suggest the Hicksian distinction between 'stickers' and 'snatchers'.

E

motive itself, as well'.[1] 'In so far as either winning or gambling is a motive, there is no mystery about the activity as a whole receiving no "pay", or less than none. The losses in these pursuits must at least equal the gains, and prizes may well add up to less than they cost by an indefinite amount.'[2] Profit 'is simply the difference between a value-output and a value-input in an enterprise, and the value-input is the worth of resources for the next best, or next better, alternative use'.[3] 'There is no difference in principle and no clear-cut distinction in practice between profit and monopoly gain. Profit is legitimate or justified monopoly revenues, and monopoly gain is that which is "too" large or lasts too long (or which rests on some "unfair" competitive practice).'[4] Temporary monopoly revenues are needed as an incentive to innovate, but as the aggregate need not be positive it is not a question of a reward for risk-taking. Knight repeated his view about probability: 'I find much nonsense—sheer irrelevance—in writings applying probability theory to profit or to economic events or human choices in general'.[5]

In Knight's more recent comments the entrepreneur's role is 'to improve knowledge, especially foresight, and bear the incidence of its limitations'.[6] Uncertainty accordingly explains profit and loss, but profit, when it occurs, is not a reward for risk-taking. Entrepreneurship is not a factor of production on a par with others 'since it is not in at all the same sense measurable or subject to varying proportions and marginal imputation. Profit (when positive) is not the price of the service of the recipient, but a residual, the one true residual in distribution.'[7] More recently still he has stated: 'It is "uncertainty" distinguished from insurable risk that effectively gives rise to the entrepreneurial form of organization and to the much-condemned "profit" as an income form. Most criticism misrepresents the nature of profit, and ignores the fact that it is often negative and may be so on the average of all enterprises.'[8]

These remarks included a hypothetical case where two workers are carrying out a project together without using any other factors.

They would have a choice: either to negotiate agreement in advance on all details of what is to be done by each and the sharing of the result, or, a much simpler arrangement would be for one of them to take charge and assure the other a more

---

[1] *Ibid.*, p. 63. [2] *Ibid.* [3] *Ibid.* [4] *Ibid.*, p. 65. [5] *Ibid.*

[6] *Risk, Uncertainty and Profit.* Preface to the 1957 Reprint, p. lix.

[7] *Ibid.* Knight now stresses that there is no connection between profit and the use of property.

[8] 'Social Economic Policy', *Canadian Journal of Economics and Political Science*, 26 (February 1960), p. 31.

or less definite return, his own 'share' (positive or negative) to depend on the outcome. In a social ethos of free contract, the latter seems to be the more natural recourse, unless there is a 'familial' relation between the parties. This hypothetical case exemplifies all the theoretical essentials of entrepreneurship and profit.[1]

Such an exceedingly simple model surely omits too much that is relevant to profit-seeking behaviour. It omits the initial distribution of property, the existence of business organizations, relationships between the various types of productive agencies, and above all the expectations of the parties concerned. Even within this simple model it would still be necessary to explain which of the two workers would become the entrepreneur; there would need to be some difference in capacity, say, in experience and hence in expectations and judgement.

SOME CRITICAL COMMENTS

The distinction drawn by Knight between risk and uncertainty is, to say the least, imprecise. In essence it represents an attack upon the application of the probability calculus to *some* decisions; and it leaves the impression that these decisions are not only crucial but, embracing both innovation and adaptation, also widespread. Before any conclusions on this aspect can be reached it is necessary to examine the nature of some attempts to proceed along the subjective, psychological road indicated by Knight.

Mention has already been made of Weston's contribution, the nature of which should be apparent from his definition of profit as the difference between *ex ante* and *ex post* incomes. This profit is clearly not a functional return; it is a measure of an error in forecasting. How did Weston proceed to generalize Knight's theory? First, he suggested that risk is a subset of uncertainty and that Knight's measurability criterion is an inadequate basis for distinguishing the types of uncertainty that give rise to profit. His criticism here stems from the fact that uncertainty that cannot be measured can nevertheless be reduced through customs, traditions, and conventions:

The relevant distinction for profit theory is not between risk and uncertainty, but between transformable risks and non-transformable risks. The term, *transformable*, is preferred to the term, *transferable*, because the latter conveys the impression that risks are transferred to insurance producers or other institutions. The significant point is, however, that through the insurance process, through utilization of the services of specialists, and through the use of other institutions and devices,

---

[1] *Risk, Uncertainty and Profit*, Preface to the 1957 Reprint, p. lxi.

risks are reduced, eliminated or substantially eliminated, not simply transferred. The economic basis of these institutions rests upon their risk-reduction accomplishments.

If a risk is transformed or converted into a definite cost through some risk-administering device or institution, it has been eliminated and expectations with regard to the item may be represented by a probability distribution with a narrow range of dispersion. If a risk is not so converted, future events may deviate from planned events and thereby give rise to profit. Non-transformable or non-transformed uncertainty causes profit.[1]

As a second step Weston wished to dispose of the distinction between contractual returns and non-contractual returns, the recipient of the latter being identified as the entrepreneur, and to adopt instead the distinction between *hired* and *unhired* factors. The unhired factors are paid remuneration which is not determined in absolute amount before the results of the productive activity are known, but they may be paid according to predetermined formulae; for example, a percentage of turnover or an amount related to accounting net profit. The return to the unhired factors can then be analysed in terms of supply and demand conditions in much the same way as was done by Knight. 'The returns to unhired factors depends on the value of their functional contributions and upon the influence of uncertainty.'[2] The firm may attempt to predict the unpredictable changes that will occur in demand and supply functions during the contract period or production period. 'The objective of decision-makers of the firm is to achieve *situations* where the revenue-cost relationships for the firm are such that maximum net revenue returns may be achieved.'[3] Here Weston is obviously dealing with *ex ante* values; so the firm may visualize a divergence between the anticipated total cost and the anticipated total revenue. This can be called the anticipated net revenue. 'It is an anticipated factor return which motivates the decision-makers of the firm to carry on productive operations in the industry of which the firm is a member. It *illustrates* Marshall's concept of quasi-rent.'[4] Profit will be the difference between this quasi-rent as it was anticipated and as it has proved to be.

Weston's article stimulated an interesting discussion.[5] It is possible to draw out and add to the threads of criticism. Firstly, the analysis

---

[1] *Op. cit.*, p. 44. See also 'The Profit Concept and Theory: a Restatement', *Journal of Political Economy*, LXII (April 1954), pp. 156–157.
[2] *Ibid.*, pp. 47–48.   [3] *Ibid.*, p. 54.   [4] *Ibid.*, p. 53.
[5] Including Anatol Murad, 'Comment', *American Economic Review*, XLI (March 1951), pp. 164–169; J. A. Stockfisch, *op. cit.*; J. Fred Weston, 'Rejoinder', *American Economic Review*, XLI (March 1951), pp. 175–181; G. L. S. Shackle, 'The Nature and Role of Profits', *Metroeconomica*, III (December 1951), pp. 101–107.

is confined to the short period. This limitation is of importance if the theory of profit is to be integrated with discussion of the pricing and marketing policies of firms under oligopolistic conditions. As Weston says, this short period analysis proceeds on the assumption that there is a structure of competitive prices.

If the horizon of the time period is extended, however, so that expectations could be revised and resources could be shifted between firms and industries as a consequence of changed expectations, the competitively established prices would be changed. Economic profit would then be defined in terms of potential shifts of these types. Under these assumptions, economic profit is the difference between factor payments actually received and the payments that would have been received if there had been complete knowledge of all events as they worked themselves out. In this framework it is likely that every type of factor return would contain an element of profit.[1]

This is a view that had been suggested by Knight: he had contrasted the British empirical approach with the United States usage which had sought 'for rigorous differentiation of a theoretically distinct form of income'.[2] 'If this . . . procedure is followed through to its logical end, the result is a definition of profit as the difference between any income as it actually is and what it would be in the theoretical position of general equilibrium of the economic system as a whole. . . . It is evident that in this highly theoretical sense every income, with accidental exceptions, contains an element of profit.'[3] Weston dismissed this aspect of the problem: 'Since change is itself a breeder of uncertainty, it would be extremely difficult to utilize this . . . concept of profit. The subsequent analysis will in consequence refer to profit as the difference between *ex ante* and *ex post* returns in "the short period".'[4] In so far as this possibility is admitted, it becomes difficult to speak of profit as a distinct share in distribution.

The same conclusion follows if profit is treated as the change in capital values; and here the problem has short-run implications as well because the revision of capital values can be a continual process.[5] If, as Knight pointed out, 'profit in the theoretical sense (including loss) is largely a matter of changes in the value of assets, not a difference between current income and outgo . . .',[6] the important point is whether institutional conditions permit capitalization of the expected income streams. Clearly this is not the case with labour. When discussing this view of the determination of profit, Stockfisch's

---

[1] Weston, 'A Generalized Uncertainty Theory of Profit', p. 51.
[2] 'Profit', p. 537. [3] *Ibid.* [4] 'A Generalized Uncertainty Theory of Profit', p. 51.
[5] Cf. Stockfisch, *op. cit.*, p. 173.
[6] F. H. Knight, 'The Quantity of Capital and the Rate of Interest', *Journal of Political Economy*, XLIV (August 1936), Part 1, p. 463.

remarks imply a definition of profit as the difference between successive *ex ante* long-run returns.[1] Weston pointed out that this was consistent with his definition, 'if in successive couplets of *ex ante* returns, one of the two returns is considered an *ex post* return'.[2] Weston went on to indicate some advantages and disadvantages of this approach. It views every owner of sources of services as an economic unit seeking to maximize the present worth of an income stream and it emphasizes generality of the profit component in incomes through the omnipresence of capital (training, experience, etc.). All agents clearly bear uncertainty. It might be argued that it shows the errors in other presentations because, with continual revision of asset values, all assets would be reflected in the cost curves and price would equal average cost under pure competition. But measurement and identification problems become even more baffling. For example, what is the appropriate revision time period?

In its essentials Weston's generalization of the uncertainty theory of profit seems to boil down to the substitution of the difference between *ex ante* and *ex post* net revenue for unimputed net income. 'Now the distinction between imputed and unimputed net income does not necessarily correspond to the distinction between net returns *ex ante* and *ex post*. . . . The former distinction may, for instance, represent in part the difference between the entrepreneur's anticipations and those reflected in the market.'[3] The distinction between transformable and non-transformable risks does not advance the argument any further than Knight's distinction between risk and uncertainty, for there is a great deal of difference between transformable and transformed.

A further important issue raised by Stockfisch is the nature of expectations.[4] Quite early in the discussion of Knight's work Hicks had challenged the importance of 'true uncertainty'. For Hicks it was not enough to know 'in what economic phenomena we are likely to find an explanation of profit'; it was necessary to know 'exactly what profit is, and what are the causes that determine its magnitude'; and it could be assumed that 'in any economic operation whose result cannot be certainly foreseen, there are objective chances of various results'.[5] From this he went on to argue that 'Those "unmeasurable risks" or "true uncertainties" which escape

[1] *Op. cit.*, pp. 173–175.   [2] 'Rejoinder', p. 180.
[3] R. M. Davis, 'The Current State of Profit Theory', *American Economic Review*, XLII (June 1952), p. 247.
[4] *Op. cit.*, pp. 173–175.   [5] 'The Theory of Uncertainty and Profit', pp. 170–171.

any such classification, and which bulk so large in Professor Knight's theory, must justify their claim to a large measure of our attention by showing that a satisfactory theory of profit cannot be constructed without paying special attention to them'.[1] Despite an extensive literature, agreement has not yet been reached on this issue. Briefly, a frequency ratio probability approach has to be contrasted with attempts, notably that of Shackle, to develop the psychological or subjectivist approach of Knight.

As a preliminary step, the main problems that arise in Knight's treatment can be reviewed. Firstly, there is the unsuccessful attempt which appears to lead to the adoption of control as the single criterion to define entrepreneurship; control being the power to appoint the chief executive. Such an approach seems inadequate for dealing with the location of power within the firm, and the diffusion, both within and without the firm, of influence upon the firm's decisions. The identification of the entrepreneur and the firm and the view of the firm as an organization as set out in the previous chapter seem essential to the solution of this problem. Secondly, there is Knight's assertion that aggregate profits may be negative. The functional approach to risk bearing, as taken in most versions of the theory that treats profit as the reward for risk bearing, clearly does not have this in mind. Consider, for example, those theoretical contributions which made the share of profits in aggregate income depend upon the degree of monopoly. To argue that the distributive share of profit depends upon aspects of market structure is to link profit with actual conditions. Nevertheless, the degree of monopoly hypothesis can be tested only if it can be shown how those market relationships determine the price-cost ratio.[2] Full cost theory failed on this score because it left the 'normal' level of profits undetermined. One possible answer to this last criticism is provided by recent analysis of oligopoly pricing: overhead costs are spread at capacity operation with allowance for seasonal and cyclical variations while the profit margin is the greatest that can be charged without inducing new entry.[3] An alternative approach in terms of 'satisfactory' profit will be indicated in the next chapter.

[1] *Ibid.*, p. 171.

[2] Cf. N. Kaldor, 'Alternative Theories of Distribution', *Review of Economic Studies*, XXIII (1955–56), pp. 92–93; Davis, *op. cit.*, pp. 248–252.

[3] See, for example, P. W. S. Andrews, *Manufacturing Business* (London: Macmillan & Co., Ltd., 1949), Chapter V; Joe S. Bain, *Barriers to New Competition* (Cambridge: Harvard University Press, 1956); Franco Modigliani, 'New Developments on the Oligopoly Front', *Journal of Political Economy*, LXVI (June 1958), pp. 215–232. R. B. Heflebower, 'Stability in Oligopoly', *Manchester School*, XXIX (January 1961), pp. 79–93.

It is clear that the degree of monopoly contributions, and for that matter most theorizing about the profit share, are based upon the zero profit concept and do not consider the possibility of negative aggregate profits; such a possibility is logically inadmissible. There is a need to examine the conditions necessary for the emergence of a positive total profit, the more so because the search for profit underlies capital accumulation, so it is said, and because market structure may influence the total profit share or determine the sharing of a total profit between firms. In any case there is a lack of evidence on the magnitude of pure profits.

Thirdly, there is Knight's distinction between risk and uncertainty. There are many lines of criticism.[1] The division is not clearly defined. The dividing line has been drawn in the wrong place. The classification compounds risk, ignorance and economic indeterminacy. There is really no dividing line. Or, finally, there is no necessity to draw such a distinction. A very important point is 'the concealed assumption that a statistical series will project itself unchanged into the future, permitting the operation of the law of large numbers'.[2] These criticisms are all relevant to the uncertainty theory of profit for which a satisfactory definition of uncertainty is surely a prerequisite.

The Certainty Equivalent Approach

Now consider the simple probability description which Hicks first developed with reference to schemes of investment.[3] The chances of return could be represented by a probability distribution, which need not be known but might be merely an estimate, yielding a generalized ordering of the probability distributions for a variety of investment schemes. In the same way, funds available for investment were grouped, each group having attached to it some index of caution. As part of the equilibrating process, there could be redistribution of funds between these groups. But the intermediary role of the entrepreneur or the business organization was ignored.

---

[1] See K. J. Arrow, 'Alternative Approaches to the Theory of Choice in Risk-Taking Situations', *Econometrica*, 19 (October 1951) pp. 416–417; E. R. Rolph, *The Theory of Fiscal Economics* (Berkeley: University of California Press, 1954), pp. 292–293, n. 6; Martin Shubik, *Strategy and Market Structure* (New York: John Wiley & Sons, Inc., 1959), pp. 172–174; Hardy, *op. cit.*, pp. 46, 53–55; R. S. Weckstein, 'On the Use of the Theory of Probability in Economics', *Review of Economic Studies*, XX (1952–53), pp. 191–199; Lucien Foldes, 'Uncertainty, Probability and Potential Surprise', *Economica*, N.S., XXV (August 1958), pp. 246–254.

[2] R. S. Weckstein, 'Probable Knowledge and Singular Acts', *Metroeconomica*, XI (Aprile-Agosto 1959), p. 116.   [3] *Op. cit.*

Hicks in 1934 used the mean and the standard deviation as the measures of the desirability of a probability distribution;[1] but he adopted the mean in 1935,[2] and in *Value and Capital*[3] changed to the mode, or most probable value, plus or minus an allowance for uncertainty. Hicks did not regard this certainty equivalent approach as entirely satisfactory for he suggested that there ought to be an economics of risk which lay beyond his own economic dynamics. Lange recommended the mode as 'a more realistic descriptive device because an idea of it can be formed without any computations by mere ranking. It does not require that probabilities be measured.'[4] But in application cardinal probabilities reappear.[5] By postulating a preference for more definite expectations rather than for less definite expectations, it is possible to translate any value expected with some degree of uncertainty into a certainty-equivalent value. Uncertainty could be measured by the standard deviation, coefficient of variation, or practical range. Even a comparatively recent treatment of this subject which endeavoured to take account of the work of Marschak, Makower, Tintner and others, does not achieve any significant advance. Outcomes are assigned likelihoods which are not probabilities but only subjective feelings based in a vague way on 'a combination of experience, analysis, and hunch'.[6] These are, however, treated as probabilities in order to permit the derivation of certainty-equivalents.

Several difficulties arise with this certainty-equivalent approach. For example, there is the difficulty associated with the meaning of profit maximization.

Under uncertainty there corresponds to each decision of the firm not a unique profit outcome, but a plurality of mutually exclusive outcomes which can at best be described by a subjective probability distribution. The profit outcome, in short, has become a random variable and as such its maximization no longer has an operational meaning. Nor can this difficulty generally be disposed of by using the mathematical expectation of profits as the variable to be maximized. For decisions which affect the expected value will also tend to affect the dispersion and other

---

[1] J. R. Hicks, 'Applications of Mathematical Methods to the Theory of Risk', Abstract, *Econometrica*, 2 (April 1934), pp. 194–195. In the case of a normal distribution, which Hicks appears to have had in mind in his 1931 *Economica* article, this is equivalent to knowing the entire distribution. Cf. Arrow, *op. cit.*, p. 422.

[2] 'A Suggestion for Simplifying the Theory of Money', *Economica*, N.S., II (February 1935), pp. 1–19.

[3] *Value and Capital* (Oxford at the Clarendon Press, 1939), pp. 125–126.

[4] Oscar Lange, *Price Flexibility and Full Employment* (Bloomington: The Principia Press, Inc., 1944), p. 29, n. 2.   [5] As pointed out by Arrow: *op. cit.*, p. 411.

[6] See W. J. Baumol, *Economic Dynamics*, 2nd ed. (New York: The Macmillan Company, 1959), p. 89.

characteristics of the distribution of outcomes. In particular, the use of debt rather than equity funds to finance a given venture may well increase the expected return to the owners, but only at the cost of increased dispersion of the outcomes.

Under these conditions the profit outcomes of alternative investment and financing decisions can be compared and ranked only in terms of a *subjective* 'utility function' of the owners which weighs the expected yield against other characteristics of the distribution. Accordingly, the extrapolation of the profit maximization criterion of the certainty model has tended to evolve into utility maximization, sometimes explicitly, more frequently in a qualitative and heuristic form.[1]

The certainty model also omits a major consideration in business decisions about fixed investment, working capital, and organization; namely, flexibility. Emphasis of this aspect has been the important contribution by Hart.[2] The following illustration shows that reduction to certainty-equivalents eliminates some essential aspects of business decision-making. Facing an uncertain future, a firm which is now planning output for a year ahead will seek to be able to modify the rate of output without too great variation in cost per unit of output. If it faces the choice between two different cost curves having the same minimum level but one being much shallower than the other, then ignoring the possible use of stocks as a buffer, the greater the uncertainty about the future rate of output, the more attractive the shallower cost curve becomes in terms of minimizing the average cost of goods produced over a period of time. Similarly the significance of liquidity is largely omitted from the certainty model because liquidity is a necessary condition for flexibility in response to changing knowledge.[3] It makes possible the adaptation of policy to unfolding events whether they be favourable or unfavourable.

SHACKLE'S THEORY OF DECISION

Shackle's theory of decision,[4] which has been developed primarily with regard to the decision to invest, shares with Knight's approach the view that traditional ideas of probability are inapplicable to

[1] Franco Modigliani and M. H. Miller, 'The Cost of Capital, Corporation Finance and the Theory of Investment', *American Economic Review*, XLVIII (June 1958), p. 263.

[2] A. G. Hart, *Anticipations, Uncertainty, and Dynamic Planning* (Chicago: University of Chicago Press, 1940).

[3] Cf. A. G. Hart, 'Shackle's System and the Theory of Liquidity Preference and of Money', *Metroeconomica*, XI (Aprile-Agosto 1959), p. 42. See also, A. G. Hart, 'Assets, Liquidity and Investment', *American Economic Review*, XXXIX (May 1949) Proceedings, pp. 171–181.

[4] The development of Shackle's ideas may be traced in *Expectations, Investment and Income* (Oxford University Press, 1938); *Expectation in Economics* (Cambridge University Press, 1949); *Uncertainty in Economics and Other Reflections* (Cambridge University Press, 1955); *Time in Economics* (Amsterdam: North-Holland Publishing Company, 1958); *Decision, Order and Time*

economic activities. What is the general nature of this theory? If all relevant consequences of all possible action-schemes are known and can be ranked in order of preference, there would be no need of decision' in any non-empty sense. Uncertainty is the necessary condition for decision-making, but it must be bounded uncertainty; it must be possible to set limits to the possible consequences of any action. If the consequences are actuarially certain, then there is no uncertainty; but if the event is unique and non-repeatable, the frequency idea must be abandoned.

When the outcome of a given action is envisaged as a number of rival hypotheses all equally possible, the notion of positive confidence in any one such hypothesis also loses its meaning, and must be replaced by the idea of *disbelief*. For any one action-scheme, those hypotheses of its outcome will be selected, as the basis of imaginative anticipation, for which 'marginal disbelief' is just balanced in its effect on the power of the hypothesis to arrest attention by marginal desirability or undesirability of pure *content* or 'face-value'.

Our discussions of how 'non-empty' decisions are made would be meaningless if, in fact, the apparent freedom to decide were illusory. If the process of history is merely the working-out of a design complete from the 'beginning of time' and human 'decisions' are mere mechanical links in a chain of predestinate situations, then again the word 'decision' has lost the meaning that it has in our ordinary consciousness and attitude to life. *Freedom* to decide implies that decisions are *creative*, capable of injecting something essentially new into the stream of events, something which was not already implicit in past history. Freedom of decisions implies that decisions can be creative, perhaps we may say *inspired*, and therefore essentially unpredictable.[1]

While there may be some doubts as to the desirability of Shackle's emphasis upon free will, he has made an important contribution by emphasizing, and stimulating discussion of the proposition, that most economic decisions are, or are regarded by the decision-maker as, unique or virtually unique. This uniqueness derives in the main from the quality of crucialness; that is, the decision creates a

in Human Affairs (Cambridge at the University Press, 1961). As important items in a growing literature see J. de V. Graaf and W. J. Baumol, 'Three Notes on "Expectation in Economics"', II', *Economica*, N.S., XVI (November 1949), pp. 338–342; J. Mars, 'A Study in Expectations: Reflections on Shackle's "Expectation in Economics"', Part I', *Yorkshire Bulletin of Economic and Social Research*, 2 (July 1950), pp. 63–98 and 'Part II', 3 (February 1951), pp. 1–36; K. J. Arrow, *op. cit.*; B. S. Keirstead, *An Essay in the Theory of Profits and Income Distribution* (Oxford: Basil Blackwell, 1953); C. F. Carter, G. P. Meredith and G. L. S. Shackle, eds., *Uncertainty and Business Decisions* (Liverpool: Liverpool University Press, 1954. Second edition revised and enlarged, 1957); M. J. Bowman, ed., *Expectations, Uncertainty, and Business Behavior* (New York: Social Science Research Council, 1958); *A Symposium on Shackle's Theory of Decision*, *Metroeconomica*, XI (Aprile-Agosto 1959); J. W. Angell, 'Uncertainty, Likelihoods, and Investment Decisions', *Quarterly Journal of Economics*, LXXIV (February 1960), pp. 1–28; R. A. D. Egerton, *Investment Decisions Under Uncertainty* (Liverpool: Liverpool University Press, 1960).
[1] *Time in Economics*, pp. 107–108.

new set of circumstances so making repetition of the experiment impossible. The frequency ratio approach is applicable only when the expectation can be based upon a large number of trials under comparable conditions. Having rejected this probability approach on the ground that the law of large numbers has no relevance to unique ventures, Shackle proceeded to substitute the concept of potential surprise.

The degree of such *potential surprise* can lie . . . anywhere in the closed interval from zero up to that degree that represents absolute disbelief in a suggested answer to some question, absolute exclusion of some hypothesis. Zero potential surprise attached to a hypothesis means that this hypothesis is looked on as 'perfectly possible', as perfectly consistent with all the individual's existing knowledge. The number of distinct answers to some one question, to which a person can simultaneously assign zero potential surprise, is unlimited. Because certainty of the truth of some hypothesis implies that all rival hypotheses are completely excluded, it implies that these rivals are assigned the *absolute maximum* of potential surprise while the hypothesis itself is uniquely assigned zero potential surprise. Thus potential surprise, though representing disbelief, is something quite other than the mere inverse of the degree of positive belief or confidence; for if it were such an inverse, subjective perfect certainty of the truth of a hypothesis could be represented by merely assigning to it zero potential surprise.[1]

Contemplation of any action-scheme will yield a range of hypotheses varying from considerable loss to substantial gain. Outside this range will lie the outcomes which are rejected as impossible. 'But if . . . there will ordinarily be in [the decision-maker's] mind a widely diverse range of entertained hypotheses, will there not be within this range an "inner" range of hypotheses to each of which the degree of potential surprise attached is not merely less than the absolute maximum, but is actually zero?'[2]

The next step is to develop the idea of a stimulation function. The decision-maker is interested in things that can happen, so his consideration is clearly limited to hypotheses having some degree of potential surprise less than the absolute maximum. Outside the range of zero potential surprise will lie possibilities which are doubted in varying degrees increasing to the limit of absolute disbelief. The degree of potential surprise is a continuous function $y = y(x)$ where x is the consequence of the action-scheme. The stimulation function 'associates, with each pair of values of face value and potential surprise, a measure of the degree of interest or power to arrest attention that this element has for the individual

[1] Shackle, 'Expectation and Liquidity', Bowman, *op. cit.*, p. 30.   [2] *Ibid.*, p. 31.

enterpriser'.[1] This yields Shackle's ϕ surface, ϕ being an increasing function of x and a decreasing function of y and being zero for impossible outcomes. Shackle points out that ϕ may be zero for some perfectly possible outcomes if x is small.

This introduces the concept of the 'neutral outcome'. Some outcomes will not improve the position of the decision-maker nor will they cause any deterioration. Shackle then makes two simplifying assumptions. 'The difference between the largest and the smallest of these "neutral" values of x will be only a small proportion of any such value of x, and thus we can . . . telescope all these values into a single "neutral outcome". Moreover, we can reasonably take this to be a zero gain or loss. Thus we have $\phi = 0$ everywhere on the line $x = 0$.'[2] More recently Shackle has mentioned the need for more careful definition of this neutral outcome.[3] This is one of the most difficult features of his theory of decision as it raises questions of perceptions and thresholds, and is, as Shackle himself suggests,[4] linked to a level of aspiration and so, as will be argued later in this chapter and when discussing alternative profit criteria in Chapter IV, to such economic concepts as normal and satisfactory profit.

When all outcomes are judged perfectly possible or perfectly impossible, Shackle argues that the decision-maker will come to a decision by considering the best and worst outcomes having zero potential surprise; that is, the best and worst outcomes would be the upper and lower limits of the inner range. When this condition is not fulfilled it is necessary to ascertain the points where ϕ is a maximum value both in the positive and negative ranges. These

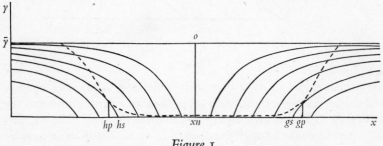

Figure 1

$\bar{y}$ maximum degree of potential surprise	*gs*	standardized focus gain
xn neutral outcome	*hp*	primary focus loss
gp primary focus gain	*hs*	standardized focus loss

[1] *Ibid.*, p. 32. [2] *Ibid.*, see Figure 1. [3] *Time in Economics*, pp. 48–49. [4] *Ibid.*

points—the primary focus outcomes—are found at the points of tangency between the potential surprise curve $y = y(x)$ and some member of the family of contours $\phi =$ constant. This is depicted in Figure 1. For purposes of comparison y can be disposed of by standardizing the primary focus value. This is done by tracing down the contour curve to the x axis. The comparison is then made in terms of two x values, the procedure having the effect of extending the inner range.

The final step to compare action-schemes, given such a pair of standardized focus outcomes, can be shown by means of a gambler indifference map such as appears in Figure 2. The indifference curves slope upwards to the right because gain and loss are not

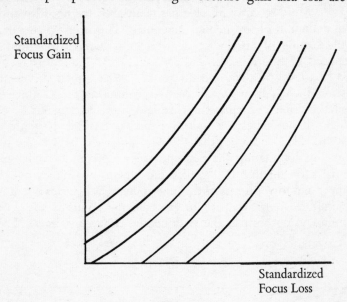

Standardized
Focus Gain

Standardized
Focus Loss

Figure 2

substitutable, the upward curvature reflecting degrees of caution and the curves to the right being asymptotic to a vertical representing according to Shackle, the enterpriser's whole fortune.[1] The indifference curve passing through the origin ' ... stands for all those possible combinations of focus gain and focus loss that are neither more nor less attractive to the enterpriser than the certainty of making, in terms of money, zero gain and loss, which is the prospect represented by the origin itself'.[2]

[1] 'Expectation and Liquidity', p. 35.   [2] *Ibid.*

Shackle's theory does not represent an entirely new departure. It shares with other theories of choice under conditions of uncertainty, the principle of weighting of different possible outcomes. However, mention should be made of the concept of seriability originally presented by Shackle in *Uncertainty in Economics and Other Reflections*.[1] It has been suggested already that the frequency ratio approach is applicable only when the event can be repeated many times under the same conditions. Bowman has argued that the concept of degrees of seriability might be used because sequential repetition has obvious empirical counterparts. 'Degree of seriability may be considered as a function of several factors: (1) the proportion (or weight) of those factors influencing the outcome that are repeated from one event in a series to the next; (2) the length of the time intervals between events in the sequence; (3) the ability of the firm to survive an initial series of unfavourable outcomes long enough to realize on a high average outcome.'[2]

SHACKLE'S TREATMENT OF PROFIT

Shackle's application of his theory of decision to the profit problem begins with several earlier articles but finds its fullest expression in 'Expectation, Income and Profit' which appeared in 1955 and, in revised form, became Chapter XXVIII of *Decision, Order and Time in Human Affairs*.[3] This treatment of profit is an application of the focus gain focus loss approach based upon Lindahl's concept of income.[4] Lindahl's presentation was limited to certain and unique expectations and sought to measure income as a change in capitalized value of future receipts between two points in time. Following Shackle, this may be summarized. Let

s = the distance of a variable point of time from some fixed earlier point

t = the distance of the person's viewpoint from the fixed date $s = 0$

$f(s)$ = the value in money units of stable purchasing power of the services expected by the person to be yielded per unit of time at date s by all the concrete property he owns at the viewpoint and by his own powers

---

[1] Chapter 2.   [2] Bowman, *op. cit.*, p. 4.

[3] 'The Nature and Role of Profit', *Metroeconomica*, III (December 1951), pp. 101–107; 'The Economist's View of Profit', *Company Accountant*, N.S., 26 (1953), pp. 8–13; 'Professor Keirstead's Theory of Profit', *Economic Journal*, LXIV (March 1954), pp. 116–123; 'Expectation, Income and Profit', *Ekonomisk Tidskrift*, LVII (December 1955), pp. 215–232; *Decision, Order and Time in Human Affairs*, Chapter XXVIII.

[4] Erik Lindahl, 'The Concept of Income', *Economic Essays in Honour of Gustav Cassel* (London: George Allen & Unwin, Ltd., 1933), pp. 399–407. See also 'The Concept of Gains and Losses', *Festskrift Til Frederik Zeuthen* (København: Nationalo$konø$misk Forening, 1958), pp. 208–219.

r = the rate of interest ruling at the viewpoint on loans of all terms

ρ = $\log_e (1 + r)$

v = capital value, at the viewpoint, of the expected services.

Then
$$v = \int_t^\infty f(s)\, e^{-\rho(s-t)}\, ds$$

and
$$\frac{dv}{dt} = \rho \int_t^\infty f(s)\, e^{-\rho(s-t)}\, ds - f(t)$$
$$= \rho v - f(t)$$

ρv—Lindhal's measure of income—is the appreciation of services, other than the next one to be realized, by virtue of the passage of time, while $-f(t)$ is the service deleted from capitalized value and called realized receipts by Shackle. Income will depend upon the policy adopted, in the sense of committing the resources to a certain course of action. Each policy will appear to lead on to a variety of courses of events to each of which corresponds a particular value of capital if expectations are fulfilled. To those imaginable capital values Shackle

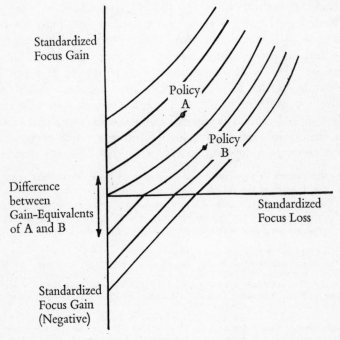

Standardized
Focus Gain

Policy
A

Policy
B

Difference
between
Gain-Equivalents
of A and B

Standardized
Focus Loss

Standardized
Focus Gain
(Negative)

Figure 3

applies his general theory of decision: the potential surprise function, the ϕ surface, and the gambler indifference map.

The possible concepts of profit that emerge may be indicated by reference to the gambler indifference map shown in Figure 3. If A and B represent the outcomes of two different policies, there are several ways of comparing their profitability. They could be ranked by vertical height on the indifference map, that is, by their standardized focus gain, but as this would neglect the danger of loss there would be no room for liquidity considerations.

The differential measure of standardized focus gain is open to the same objection. Alternatively, absolute profit may be measured by the intercept on the vertical axis, that is, the gain-equivalent of the policy, with a corresponding differential concept. From this model Shackle derives interesting results. Profit in these four senses will be small, but not zero, for contractual incomes and tend to be large for ' . . . those who command large funds which they commit to the construction of particular kinds of factories and plants and concrete production systems, who both make the decisions about the specific form that these investments shall take, and who stake their reputations and even their personal capital, or as we can say in a broad sense their "fortunes", on the success of the productive units which they create'.[1] Shackle considers that the functions of decision-making and uncertainty-bearing cannot be usefully separated, even conceptually, because pure decision-making would involve neither 'tension' nor coherence in the making of the choice.[2]

The next stage in Shackle's analysis is to compare two locations of the viewpoint. As the state of knowledge changes so the potential surprise curves will be modified. Likewise the gambler indifference map may alter. In particular, the right hand side limit to which the curves are asymptotic could shift. The comparisons that can meaningfully be made will depend upon the flexibilities of policies. But assuming that choice is possible, the gain-equivalents of the preferred policies may differ. As this involves a move to a higher indifference curve it implies an improvement in outlook and a profit concept which Shackle labels dynamic increment of gain-equivalent. As the analysis is being conducted at the subjective level an almost infinite variety of elements can enter into the determination of this dynamic increment.

---

[1] *Decision, Order and Time in Human Affairs*, p. 263.   [2] *Ibid.*

F

Or the *ex post* value can be compared with those *ex ante* values which carry zero potential surprise. Within the inner range Shackle sees the possibility of a narrower range of non-revision of expectations. If so, it is possible to consider the difference between the *ex post* value and the upper and lower limits both of the inner range and of the range of non-revision. In the first case there is a measure that Shackle calls windfall realized receipts by analogy to the Keynesian windfall profit. Provided less than the maximum degree of potential surprise had attached to the outcome, the windfall realized receipt would not be attributable to luck but to decision-making and uncertainty-bearing.

In the second case the difference between the *ex post* value and the upper and lower limits of the range of non-revision would be considered. This is the variable upon which the dynamic increment of gain-equivalent will depend. The longer the period between the viewpoints, the greater the range of outcomes carrying zero potential surprise. The improvement of knowledge as the future viewpoint is advanced in time will tend to eliminate possibilities. For a short period remote in the future, the inner range will be great but the range of non-revision may shrink and disappear. These considerations lead Shackle to argue that 'as we shift our attention from a short interval remote in the future to ones which are successively nearer the viewpoint, the two ranges will tend more and more closely to coincide'.[1] The usefulness of this procedure depends upon the planning horizon, and many studies suggest that firms' planning horizons are not far distant. In these circumstances windfall realized receipts is the variable on which the dynamic increment of gain-equivalent depends. Shackle concludes by suggesting that elasticity of gain-equivalent can be defined as the proportionate change in gain-equivalent associated with a given proportionate difference in windfall receipts.[2]

Shackle's scheme certainly goes far towards unifying the treatment of profit. His work has stimulated much valuable discussion of decision-making processes. There are, however, several points that must be raised. These are concerned with the neutral outcome, business organization, the nature of policy, information, and sequentiality.

---

[1] *Ibid.*, p. 270.   [2] *Ibid.*

The Neutral Outcome

The neutral outcome was defined by Shackle as 'a hypothetical outcome whose realization would leave the decision-maker feeling neither better nor worse off than he does at present'.[1] Arrow remarked that 'The exposition is greatly complicated by... [Shackle's] insistence on differentiating between gains and losses. It is completely unclear ... what the meaning of the zero-point would be in a general theory; after all, costs are usually defined on an opportunity basis only.'[2] Reconsideration has led Shackle to feel that the concept needs elaboration. Because the sense of well-offness depends upon expectations, 'We cannot in general define a neutral outcome for one action-scheme alone. The neutral outcome of one action-scheme will be higher or lower according to the possible outcomes which he discerns for the other action-schemes which seem open to him.'[3] Shackle adds that there may be some connection between neutral outcome and level of aspiration.[4]

It might be possible to avoid 'such psychological complications if it were only a matter of choosing between actions, but it might be unavoidable in the attempt to provide an explanation of the choice between action and inaction'.[5] Inaction can be treated as a policy but it need not furnish the subjective stability that seems to be basic for Shackle's theory of decision-making. There might be a range of outcomes associated with a policy of inaction and so the neutral outcome may not be a single value. This seems the more likely if, instead of the single enterpriser considering the disposal of given resources, the decision-maker is a business organization which has to make prior decisions about the amount of funds to be raised in the capital market to supplement the internal flow of undistributed profits and depreciation allowances. Subject to intricate problems of capital structure, there will be no easily defined boundary on the right hand side of a firm's gambler indifference map.

Suppose that the neutral outcome is not a single value but a range of satisfactory outcomes. This range of neutral outcomes lies within Shackle's inner range which carries zero potential surprise. What is the relationship between this neutral range and the range of non-revision? When an actual value fell outside the range of non-revision it caused revision of expectations about the future. Now it is

---

[1] *Time in Economics*, p. 48.
[2] K. J. Arrow, 'Alternative Approaches to the Theory of Choice in Risk-Taking Situations', p. 432.   [3] *Time in Economics*, p. 48.   [4] *Ibid.*, p. 49.
[5] Weckstein, 'Probable Knowledge and Singular Acts', p. 112.

doubtful if this question can be answered, because Shackle's theory seems to assume that the change in the state of knowledge with the passage of time occurs without any search activity on the part of the decision-maker. However, the firm is not passive. The distinction between policies is not merely one of being cautious or audacious. One policy may be concerned with gathering information; and information-gathering activity should, perhaps, be elevated to the same level as production.

As in the discussion of the firm's production function, so in the theory of decision-making there has been a tendency to take as given, the decision-making unit. In earlier chapters it was suggested that this procedure is unwarranted. In the present context it might be suggested that one policy that may be adopted is modification of the decision-making unit itself. In a sense, a policy of information-gathering does this. Furthermore, the existence of learning processes and likely variation in policy criteria in a business organization imply that the decision-making unit is undergoing continual change. This situation is far removed from the assumption that the decision-maker is of unchanging temperament.[1]

It may well be that Shackle and the followers of Knight have overemphasized uncertainty and paid too little attention to the 'judgement' which can be exercised by a business organization. Knight, and more recently, Shackle, wished to link the decision-making and uncertainty-bearing activities. This led Knight to treat the ordinary shareholder as the entrepreneur, choosing the men to make the decisions and also bearing the uncertainty. Eastham suggested that 'It seems more realistic to select the professional director, who may or may not have a shareholding interest beyond the minimum to qualify him as a director. Such an individual endeavours to expand the firm for the sake of his own prestige and professional pride as well as for the sake of his pocket, and is much more likely to regard his shareholders as rapacious creditors to be paid as little as possible than to think of them as the makers of the policy he pursues.'[2] Even this procedure seems to stop short of the desirable solution; namely, treatment of organization and information as inputs in the production function and of decision-making as the equivalent of a production process.

[1] See Shackle, *Time in Economics*, p. 53.
[2] J. K. Eastham, 'A Redefinition of the Boundary between Interest and Profit Theories', *Dundee Economic Essays* (Dundee School of Economics, 1955), p. 49.

But because of the nature of the firm, its ability to initiate change, including change in its own internal structure and policy criteria, and its capacity to gather information, it seems worthwhile to consider the possibility that there is an intermediate category between complete fulfilment of the conditions of the frequency ratio approach and the truly uncertain or unique events emphasized so much by Knight and Shackle. Keirstead's objective uncertainty—subjective certainty case approximates such an intermediate category. Is it possible, as Keirstead has attempted to do,[1] to classify the things about which expectations will be held and so simplify the situation? He classified expectations and suggested relevant time periods for which they would be held. Particular expectations referred to values particular to the firm like its costs, prices and sales. General expectations referred to quantities general to the economy as a whole such as national income, savings and exports. Keirstead suggested that the nature and pattern of response differed as between these two categories. Within this context Keirstead wished to distinguish a third situation between risk and uncertainty, namely, objective uncertainty—subjective certainty. Although an objective risk calculation is impossible, 'Nevertheless, empirically the entrepreneur or his expert technical advisers, possess present data which they can, with some confidence, extrapolate into the future. These data . . . are single-valued projections and are sufficient to determine the entrepreneur's decision. In these situations the entrepreneur regards the single-valued projections as given quantities and behaves as though no uncertainty were present. He is subjectively certain—or behaves as though he were subjectively certain—even though the situation is formally one of objective uncertainty.'[2]

THE ORGANIZATION AS DECISION-MAKER

But in all this activity it is the organization that is important. The emphasis should be shifted from the elusive entrepreneur to the firm, and to the study of the firm's perceptive capacity, communication system, and response mechanisms. For the time being it seems wise to seek only a theory of decision-making for one type of decision-maker. It may, of course, be found that decision-makers of various types, for example, firms, governmental bodies and individuals, adopt similar processes. This shift of attention to the organization gives greater scope for emphasis upon sequentiality. Hart, for

---

[1] Keirstead, *op. cit.*   [2] *Ibid.*, p. 21.

example, refers to decisions 'taken in the consciousness that they are part of a developing chain'.[1] Decisions are not only interdependent one with another at the time when they are made, but also through time. An investment decision today may determine not only the result of a production decision next year but also the content of a further investment decision a year after that.[2] Sequential decision-making is the essence of the dynamics of business activities and a theory of decision needs to be adequate for its study. Perhaps the most valuable comment made in this connection is Hart's suggestion that the potential surprise concept can be used in the study of learning processes, for 'to learn is to be surprised'.[3] But even when it is known that surprise leads to revised expectations, it is still necessary to ascertain the consequent revision of policy. Here policy is used in the sense indicated in the previous chapters; that is, rules of action rather than direct arranging of action.

Recognition that the decision-maker is a firm, a business organization, and that conditions of capital structure and supply are involved, as against the simple allocation of a predetermined sum of finance, may well reduce the subjective uniqueness of action-schemes. The firm is stressed here as the decision-maker because the firm may survive unfavourable outcomes by replacing the 'entrepreneurs' responsible for them, and because the state of knowledge is not a constant given independently of the actions of the decision-maker. Furthermore, there is an aspect of sequentiality that may counterbalance differences in events; or alternatively, it might be said that insufficient attention has been given to the nature of the event. A management team, even though its composition has been changing, may develop confidence in its ability to deal with an unspecified problem within the context of its own 'industry'; or where a process of routine diversification takes place, a similar confidence may be built up over a period of time. This would contribute to Keirstead's objective uncertainty-subjective certainty situation, and may also affect the speed of decision-making quite markedly.[4] Perhaps the level and rate of change of past profits, as related to the various activities, would be correlated with this degree of confidence,

---

[1] Comments reported by Bowman, *op. cit.*, p. 6.

[2] It is true that even when uncertainty is involved this can formally be reduced to the problem of a single decision. However, this seems a little like reducing the multi-product firm to a single-product firm.   [3] *Ibid.*

[4] Discussion of price and product policy of the firm has tended to avoid the issue of the speed of response. This certainly reinforces any tendency towards non-price competition that might otherwise exist in oligopoly situations.

small fluctuations in profits having only minor influence. The stability of the internal management structure and an absence of tension would no doubt also be indicators.

EMPIRICAL TESTING OF UNCERTAINTY THEORIES

What possibility is there of subjecting any of these uncertainty theories to empirical test? There are serious limitations upon measurements of realized profits but they are slight compared with those involved in the measurement of expectations as required for the testing of uncertainty theories of profit. To illustrate the nature of the problems involved here, accounting profits are much more closely related to realized receipts than to accretion of wealth—in the Lindahl-Shackle terminology, with $-f(t)$ rather than with ρv. The uncertainty theories shift attention to ρv. What is required are measures of expected or *ex ante* profits, of standardized focus gains and losses, limits of inner ranges, ranges of non-revision, and neutral outcomes. Consequently there is little to be derived in this respect from studies of accounting profits.

An alternative approach would be to study planning records. If budgeted profits are the expected outcome, it is possible to compare *ex ante* and *ex post* values. But such figures are not usually available on a product basis and it is doubtful whether they represent an expected profit in the sense of a standardized focus gain. It seems more probable that they are formed either as residuals in an incomplete estimation procedure, or simply as a minimum target. Some modern developments of budgeting techniques allow for various outcomes but where responsibility and outcome are linked, and, especially where a number of people or departments are successively concerned in their preparation, it seems inevitable that both operating and capital budget figures involve understatement. Another possible approach is through dividend decisions but these decisions may be as much a reflection of liquidity as of current estimates of profit.

Nor does there seem to be much empirical evidence available as yet to support the Shackle theory of decision. Gambling games may give decisions inconsistent with the theory, but it is business behaviour that must be studied because the attempt to establish pairs of focus values ought to show in the ways in which firms go about the gathering and presentation of the information on which their decisions are based. The single representative values of revenues and cost recorded in business decision-making may result largely from the delegation of financial work and authority; consequently, a good deal of importance attaches to the supplementary information. Although there may not be supporting evidence for Shackle's specific concept of which computations are made, it does seem that a process of simplification takes place and only a limited number of criteria are employed. Some empirical studies of investment decisions to which reference will be made in Chapter V, suggest that maximization is of limited applicability and that feasibility may be more important on some occasions.

Concluding Remarks

In a single chapter it has been quite impossible to do justice to the richness and complexity of the discussion of 'the inevitable connection between profit and uncertainty'. Nevertheless, it is hoped that this selective treatment has succeeded in indicating the main lines of that discussion. From the point of view expressed in the earlier chapters this critical review draws attention to several important deficiencies of the uncertainty theory of profit.

Does profit maximization have any precise meaning under conditions of uncertainty? If this question is answered in the negative, consideration must be given to the formulation of alternative hypotheses with respect to profit-seeking behaviour. In the next chapter it will be shown that while some such attempts have been made and have progressed as far as recognition of the importance of the firm's perception and responsiveness as an organization, no alternative analytically useful statement of the profit objective has been achieved as yet. In Chapter VII an attempt at such a formulation will be undertaken, by way of defining the concept of 'satisfactory' profit. The nature of this task may be illustrated by reference to Shackle's theory of decision. The telescoping of the range of satisfactory outcomes to give a single-valued neutral outcome may have excluded significant aspects of the behaviour of the firm. For example, it is desirable to inquire into the consequences of the various possible relationships between the actual outcome and the *ranges* of non-revision and neutral outcome for changes in expectations and changes in the firm's policy. Shackle has praised Boulding's application to the firm of the biologist's notion of homeostasis, or the desire to maintain an existing state of affairs. An existing state of affairs might be defined in terms of a policy which yields a 'satisfactory' profit, such a policy concept bearing some relationship to Boulding's *image*, Hansen's *end index* and the social psychologist's concept of *primary task*.

Is probability analysis applicable to the firm's decision-making? The discussion of this question reveals a sharp division of opinion. Those who favour the certainty equivalent approach do not explore the means by which single-valued estimates are reached by the firm. Such means include the following of policy rules, search activity, adaptation of production activities, and changes in asset and liability structure, organization and policy criteria; and these changes may have significant influence upon the decisions made by the firm. Those who argue against the probability approach have failed, through over-abstraction, to appreciate some of the ways in which the uniqueness and crucialness of decisions are reduced. Firstly, despite incomplete information decisions may be reached by the use of policy rules even though those rules do not provide an optimum solution; secondly, the firm may add to its stock of information or, alternatively, change its policy criteria; thirdly, the uniqueness of a decision should be judged by taking account both of circumstances external to the firm and previous decision-making experience within the firm; fourthly, the crucialness of events has been emphasized unduly if the analysis is to be applied to the large self-financed, multi-product firm which has access to the capital market. A generalization of the gambler indifference map treatment of the investment decision to be presented in Chapter VII will draw these threads together and link the analysis with the concept of 'satisfactory' profit.

There has been a tendency to view consolidation or transformation of uncertainty as achieved by transactions between the firm and other firms, some of which may be newly created for a specific transaction. However, the large firm can seek the same result through internal change—a procedure involving a choice comparable in some respects to the decision to make or buy materials or equipment. This aspect of the firm's activities, as with the theoretical issues of the meaning of profit maximization and the applicability of the probability approach, requires explicit treatment of the firm itself—of its organization and information—in order that its decisions can be understood and, perhaps, predicted. Change internal to the firm is relevant to 'the inevitable connection between profit and uncertainty' and recognition of its importance may prove a helpful guide in empirical work.

CHAPTER IV

ALTERNATIVE PROFIT CRITERIA

THE view that the firm seeks to attain a satisfactory level of profit rather than a maximum level has received a good deal of attention in recent writings.[1] However, the affinity of the concept to the normal, ordinary and fair profit discussed by Marshall, Chamberlin and Andrews should not be ignored. When dealing with the large, multi-product, oligopolistic firm whose particular (and general) expectations are held with uncertainty, the hypothesis is clearly a plausible one. Business management will frequently be thinking in terms of simultaneous, discontinuous changes in the large number of variables with which it is concerned and will have recourse to conventional procedures, one of which may be the adoption of a profit target. Study of such profit budgeting procedures has been inadequate. The target may be indicated according to a variety of methods, for example, a percentage on turnover or capital employed, and pursued by a single policy under stable conditions. But changes in such things as the degree of integration, factor proportions, capital structure, and the value of money may all lead to divergences depending upon the method adopted.

The use of such targets has interesting implications for the definition of profit. As noted earlier, profit might be regarded, in the Knightian tradition, as the divergence, positive or negative, between the realized net revenue and the expected net revenue. But can the target be substituted for the expected value? In a given period the firm might expect net revenue to exceed the target. Or could realized net revenue be regarded as exceeding the expected net revenue if the firm is a sales revenue maximizer and has decided already to absorb any such surplus by additional selling costs in

[1] For example, R. A. Gordon, 'Short-Period Price Determination', *American Economic Review*, XXXVIII (June 1948), pp. 265–288; R. M. Cyert and J. G. March, 'Organizational Factors in the Theory of Oligopoly', *Quarterly Journal of Economics*, LXX (February 1956), pp. 44–64; H. A. Simon, 'The Role of Expectations in an Adaptive or Behavioristic Model', M. J. Bowman, ed., *Expectations, Uncertainty, and Business Behavior* (New York: Social Science Research Council, 1958) pp. 49–58; W. J. Baumol, *Business Behavior, Value and Growth* (New York: The Macmillan Company, 1959), Chapters 6–7; Don Markwalder, 'Satisfactory Profits as a Guide to Firm Behavior: Comment', pp. 682–684 and R. M. Cyert and J. G. March, 'Profits as a Guide to Firm Behavior: reply', pp. 684–685, *Quarterly Journal of Economics*, LXXIII (November 1959); D. M. Lamberton, 'Alternative Profit Criteria', *Quarterly Journal of Economics*, LXXIV (November 1960), pp. 635–640.

subsequent periods? Before these questions could be settled it would be necessary to define the profit target in precise terms. If the profit target is a budget forecast with which realized net revenue does not coincide and the divergence is small, it may lead to minor revisions of plans within an existing policy framework; for example, the seeking of alternative sources of finance. But if the target is to be regarded as a minimum level, then even a downward movement towards that minimum level might occasion such minor revision. A fall in profit below the minimum level could lead to a general review of policy, for example, product abandonment or diversification.

This brings up one of the major problems of profit maximization under conditions of uncertainty. Decision-making becomes a sequential process and there is a premium on additional information;[1] the consequences of actions in one period contribute to the basis for future decisions. The satisfactory profit of the present period is, as a source of finance and an influence upon borrowing capacity, a precondition for other decisions relating to future periods. In these circumstances a model of the firm in which all decisions are made in equilibrium terms, and in which there is no uncertainty, is an inadequate one for the analysis of actual behaviour of firms. Of course, the additional information must bear appropriately upon the decisions to be made and must be in a form in which it can be utilized by the firm's personnel. Otherwise it could tend to introduce confusion to the decision-making processes.

To a major extent the formulation of the firm's objectives in terms of satisfactory profit is a response to the economist's difficulties in giving a precise meaning to the customary profit maximization criterion which dictates equation of marginal cost and marginal revenue; some of these difficulties arise even under conditions of certainty. Some meanings of profit maximization will now be distinguished, emphasis being given primarily to decisions other than those of an investment nature because the decision to invest will be discussed in Chapter V. Such an arbitrary division is, of course, unwarranted, as questions of long-run pricing and entry cannot be separated from investment decisions. This chapter will consider

[1] Cf. K. J. Arrow: 'The uncertainty, in turn, puts a premium on information. Traditional economic theory stresses the sufficiency of the price system as a source of information for guiding economic behavior, and this lis correct enough at equilibrium' ('Toward a Theory of Price Adjustment', M. Abramovitz et al., The Allocation of Economic Resources (Stanford: Stanford University Press, 1959), p. 47).

some of the criticisms of the profit maximization hypothesis, the responses to those criticisms, alternative profit criteria, and, finally, some empirical evidence.

The equilibrium price and output of the firm under conditions of imperfect or monopolistic competition are determined by the intersection of the marginal cost and marginal revenue functions and excess profit is the product of output and the difference between average revenue and average cost. Profit, defined as the difference between *ex ante* amd *ex post* net revenue may correspond to this excess but need not do so. This is because the cost and revenue functions depict conditions which are expected by the firm to hold in the future but may not be fulfilled. These functions are of little use in dealing with conditions that are constantly changing in unpredictable ways. The equilibrium approach is one which abstracts from questions of time and uncertainty; it has meaning in the sense that expectations held in the past have been fulfilled and will be fulfilled again in the future. And it cannot be argued that somehow the cost and revenue functions take account of all possible future developments. Nor can the fact that cost and revenue estimates will probably not be single-valued be ignored.

Given certainty of expectations, the maximization of profit is 'a problem in boundary maxima'.[1] The firm would seek to increase its holdings of goods to an infinite amount whenever it knew that price was to rise; and reduce them to zero whenever it knew that price was to fall. This pattern bears so little similarity to the actual behaviour of firms that it is necessary to ask what limits profit? The conditions of exchange may not be independent of the volume of transactions; alternatively, uncertainty may have the same limiting effect. Once time and uncertainty are introduced the problem is much more complicated. If it is assumed that current costs and revenue conditions will hold for the next period but may change in subsequent periods, then to say that the firm seeks to maximize profits is not to say anything precise about the behaviour of the firm. To do that it is necessary to introduce a time dimension and assign weights to future profits,[2] not neglecting the fact that the future profits are themselves uncertain.

[1] K. E. Boulding, *The Skills of the Economist* (London: Hamish Hamilton, 1958), p. 57.
[2] Cf. M. J. Farrell, 'Deductive Systems and Empirical Generalizations in the Theory of the Firm', *Oxford Economic Papers*, N.S., 4 (February 1952), pp. 45–49; 'An Application of Activity Analysis to the Theory of the Firm', *Econometrica*, 22 (July 1954), pp. 291–302.

Clearly maximization in each successive short period need not lead to maximization over a long period because the policy pursued in each short period may bring about changes in cost and revenue conditions in subsequent periods. The distinction drawn by Hicks between 'stickers' and 'snatchers' has some value;[1] but is a firm likely to remain in, say, the 'snatcher' category? New firms, especially small ones, faced with problems of capital supply may be 'snatchers' especially in a growing industry. But if as time passes there is a greater degree of stability in inter-firm relationships and in other external relationships, for example, with suppliers of factor inputs and with government, firms may not only have less need to pursue such policies but also less scope for pursuing them, because they would conflict with established practice. Many, perhaps most, firms are multi-product firms and in new development departments 'snatcher' behaviour might occur even though the firm as a whole might be characterized as a 'sticker'. Of course, the stability of behaviour patterns will be dependent not only upon external relationships; the internal organization and recruitment of personnel will need to be adapted to the firm's pricing policy. Even so, it is possible that a 'sticker' could be obliged, for reasons of capital supply, to adopt a 'snatcher' policy, albeit a temporary measure. Such a need could be imposed through the rate of growth, perhaps of a particular department, to which the firm aspired, given its rate of profit, or alternatively through the impact of controls over capital and credit supply. Granted such differences, an important question remains: what is it, under conditions of uncertainty, that the business organization might seek to maximize over a period of time? Clearly it can be expressed as a rate of return on some measure of capital, for example, the entrepreneur's capital or total assets. An alternative expression would be the present value of all future net revenues capitalized at market rates of interest. Market value of the firm's securities has been used as a measure of size, and so can serve as an alternative maximand. Under conditions of certainty, profit maximization and maximization of market value of shares yield the same results, because the cost of capital is equal to the rate of interest. But under conditions of uncertainty neither of these formulations suffices to determine the behaviour of the firm.

[1] J. R. Hicks, 'The Process of Imperfect Competition', *Oxford Economic Papers*, N.S., 6 (February 1954), pp. 41–54.

QUALIFICATIONS TO PROFIT MAXIMIZATION

A report by The Committee on Business Enterprise Research ended by indicating some general research areas. It suggested that the purpose of studying business behaviour was to test the validity of the profit maximization hypothesis and called for a careful re-appraisal of this assumption in the light of accumulating evidence.[1] Some tentative steps towards such a reappraisal may begin by looking at some of the qualifications to the profit maximization hypothesis that have been suggested.[2] A complete catalogue of such qualifications would be very lengthy but it would include such items as: social status; interest in craftsmanship and technical progressiveness; empire-building; moral and ethical considerations; poor intelligence; sheer inertia; desire for loyal and contented workers; reluctance to experiment; the role of the firm as consumer; business costing practices, including such matters as historical accounting and naïve use of full costing; a desire for more secure profits which might lead firms to limit current profits to discourage potential competition, to restrain those responsible for anti-monopoly action and wage claims, and to maintain and extend customer goodwill; and conflicts of interest such as those arising from the separation of ownership and control. The responses to mention of these qualifications have been varied. Some are dismissed entirely. It is said, perhaps with welfare aspects in mind, that most of the qualifications relate to revenue rather than to costs. Or again that there are important limits to the divergence from profit maximiza-tion set by the degree of competition, the need for profit, and the maintenance of liquidity.

It is said that there is a functional relationship between profits and the degree of attainment of these other objectives. Take as an example the 'ever-growing discord' in industry which Marshall saw arising from the transference of authority and responsibility from the owners of business to salaried managers and officials.[3] Keirstead considers that profit can be regarded as the measure or

---

[1] See H. R. Bowen, *The Business Enterprise as a Subject for Research* (New York: Social Science Research Council, 1955), p. 73.

[2] See, for example, P. H. Douglas, 'The Reality of Non-Commercial Incentives in Economic Life', R. G. Tugwell, ed., *The Trend of Economics* (New York: Alfred A. Knopf, 1924), pp. 153–188; P. J. D. Wiles, *Price, Cost and Output* (Oxford: Basil Blackwell, 1956), Chapter 11.

[3] See Alfred Marshall, *Industry and Trade* (London: Macmillan & Co., Ltd., 1919), p. 307; B. S. Keirstead, *An Essay in the Theory of Profits and Income Distribution* (Oxford: Basil Blackwell, 1953), p. 43; W. J. Baumol, *Business Behavior, Value and Growth*, Chapter 6. Jack Downie, *The Competitive Process* (London: Gerald Duckworth & Co., Ltd., 1958), p. 64.

criterion of the executive's success, but Baumol thinks that sales revenue is better for this purpose. Downie argues that business standing depends upon the volume of assets controlled and the amount by which they have grown under the executive's stewardship. Of course, these criteria, especially growth, are closely related to profit. Because of interdependence it can be expected that there be a reasonable correlation between these and other criteria, such as the number of employees. But it is doubtful if the problem can be disposed of as simply as some of these writers apparently have believed. It seems an open question, for example, whether status and business power are best measured by gross or net capital (or profits). While it might seem obvious that managers do not wish to be in control of worn-out equipment, depreciation allowances might not be applied to replacement but to the acquisition of new and different assets. It might seem that all these problems are avoided by those who take the view that the firm maximizes long-run profit. However, this brings in once again the difficulties that follow from uncertainty and it is some time now since Rothschild remarked that 'Any theory . . . which tries to explain price behaviour in terms of marginal curves derived from *long-term* demand and cost curves really by-passes the problem of uncertainty, and thus the very factor which gives rise to that desire for security which the theory tries to explain'.[1]

THE SUBJECTIVE TREATMENT OF PROFIT MAXIMIZATION

Another response has been to develop a subjective treatment of profit maximization according to which profit is only one item in computing satisfactions.[2] Figure 4 shows a net income curve for conditions of imperfect or monopolistic competition. An increase of output, that is, a decrease of entrepreneurial inactivity, lowers price per unit and so leads eventually to a reduction of income. The net income curve cuts the zero income level where entrepreneurial inactivity is at a maximum and output is nil, and where output is so high and price so low that the firm starts to work at a

---

[1] K. W. Rothschild, 'Price Theory and Oligopoly', *Economic Journal*, LVII (September 1947), pp. 299–320 reprinted in American Economic Association, *Readings in Price Theory* (London: George Allen & Unwin Ltd., 1953), p. 451.

[2] See, for example, B. Higgins, 'Elements of Indeterminacy in the Theory of Non-Perfect Competition', *American Economic Review*, XXIX (September 1939), pp. 468–479; T. Scitovsky, 'A Note on Profit Maximization and its Implications', *Review of Economic Studies*, XI (1943), pp. 57–60; J. de V. Graaf, 'Income Effects and the Theory of the Firm', *Review of Economic Studies*, XVIII (1950–51), pp. 79–86; J. P. Nettl, 'A Note on Entrepreneurial Behaviour' *Review of Economic Studies*, XXIV (February 1957), pp. 87–94.

loss. The higher indifference curve is tangential to the net income curve at the point of maximum satisfaction. Net income can be divided into wages of management and a profit residual. By invoking a concept of the minimum profit that will induce the entrepreneur to carry out entrepreneurial functions, the position of the lower indifference curve in Figure 4 can be fixed. This

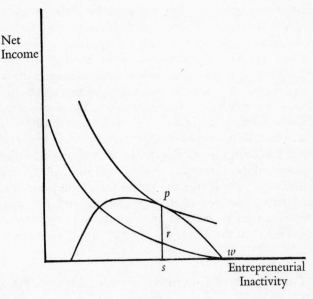

Figure 4

curve will reach the zero income level at the point *w*. Then *rs* will be the wages of management, and *pr* will be the profit residual. For maximum profit, that is, net income less wages of management, to coincide with maximum satisfaction, each indifference curve must be a vertical displacement of the next so that the tangents to the indifference curves are, for a given level of inactivity, parallel.

The further the making and consumption of profit can be removed from each other, the more likely an objective policy of profit maximization becomes. The more the entrepreneur is motivated by his spending habits, the further he will depart from a policy of profit maximization. From this point of view some of the qualifications appear as necessary conditions for profit maximization. As Tobin remarked, 'The firm's utility function may differ from a simple linear function of profits, implying constant marginal utility, in so far as it reflects a fear of going out of business, an idea of normal profits, a tradition of sharing an oligopolistic market, or a fear of an unfavourable public reaction to high profits'.[1]

Dunning developed this approach further, and sought to show ways in which the non-pecuniary elements might be evaluated when output-profit preference schedules are introduced. The usual equilibrium solution assumes a constant and zero marginal rate of substitution between output and profit so that the point of tangency between the indifference curve and the curve of total profit will be at the maximum profit output. But when the rate of substitution is not zero a different result is achieved. Dunning sought to distinguish three measures of non-pecuniary elements:[2] compensating money profit variation, or the amount of additional money profits with which an entrepreneur would require to be compensated if he were forced to produce at other than the equilibrium level of output, where satisfaction is maximized, and yet still retain the same measure of well-being as enjoyed at that output; equivalent money profit, or the amount of money profits equivalent to the loss of satisfaction experienced through being forced to produce at an output other than that consistent with maximum satisfaction; and appropriate money profit variation, or the monetary evaluation of the satisfaction gained or lost at any one point on the total net profits curve as the result of the introduction of non-pecuniary elements as depicted in the businessman's output-profit preference pattern.

Although the shape of the indifference curves is not known—it is difficult to visualize them at all for a business organization rather than an individual in control of a firm—and it would be extremely difficult to assign any values to these measures proposed by Dunning, this sort of analysis does help to clarify the possible influences of non-pecuniary elements. Departures from profit maximization may occur through failure to minimize costs, failure to charge the price consistent with profit maximization, and failure to produce and sell at the profit maximizing output.[3] The impact of the non-pecuniary elements on cost, price, and output policies need to be distinguished. This analysis is limited, however, to the effects of failure to produce the profit maximizing output which is implied by the existence of an output-profit preference pattern. Such indifference curve analysis

[1] James Tobin, 'Discussion', *American Economic Review*, XXXIX (May 1949), Proceedings, p. 208.
[2] J. H. Dunning, 'Non-Pecuniary Elements and Business Behaviour', *Oxford Economic Papers*, N.S., 11 (October, 1959), pp. 232, 234, 236.   [3] *Ibid.*, pp. 239–240.

G

does not cope with non-fulfilment of the other conditions which would affect the position and shape of the profit curve itself.[1] Dunning concluded by suggesting that a completely determinate theory would involve the study of the relationships between all these variables. And then the analysis would need to be extended beyond its static framework.

The last-ditch defence seems to be that realism is irrelevant, that the traditional model of the firm is best since it is sufficient to predict the behaviour of the firm. This view has been discussed in Chapter I. Prediction of an equilibrium position is of little value if it is never reached. Both in the study of the individual firm and for purposes of economic policy, it is desirable to know the process that goes on, the path to the equilibrium position, and this involves knowledge of the detailed rules of behaviour of the firm. And it can legitimately be asked whether there is a record of successful prediction based on the profit maximization hypothesis alone.

These are the responses to the qualifications suggested to the profit maximization hypothesis. The orthodox view might be that taken by Joan Robinson: ' . . . the most valid simple generalization, is that the aim of the entrepreneur is for the firm first to survive, and secondly to grow. To this end he must pursue profit. . . .'[2] But is it necessary to maximize profit in order to survive and grow? Or is there some margin within which profits can be sacrificed for other objectives? Can such a margin be a permanent one? If so, what determines its magnitude? Having attained a satisfactory level of profit can the firm then give priority to maximization of sales, or to achieving technical leadership in its field? Might the firm experience a loss of drive to sustain and improve its position, with the result that organizational inefficiency makes its appearance? Can meaning be given to this idea of satisfactory profit? Or does it cover all the motives that might influence business decisions? If so, the statement that the firm seeks satisfactory profit would seem to have no empirical content.

[1] Cf. Dunning: 'Just as the equilibrium point along the profits curve is fundamentally determined by the character of the output/profit indifference schedule, so likewise are the nature and shape of the "equilibrium" cost and revenue curves (i.e. those curves chosen out of all possible cost and revenue curves as most conducive to satisfaction), a reflection of the business man's preference for profits in relationship to a particular non-maximizing price or cost policy' (*Ibid.*, p. 241).

[2] 'Imperfect Competition Revisited', *Economic Journal*, LXIII (September 1953), p. 582.

SATISFACTORY PROFIT

As pointed out already, some critics of the profit maximization hypothesis have put forward the goal of satisfactory profit. These critics, who should not be identified with anti-marginalists, are not developing an entirely new approach. In his *Principles* Marshall discussed a 'fair' or normal rate of profit; in *Industry and Trade* he moved close to modern views when he spoke of conditional monopoly and the policy of far-sighted trusts:[1] '... a conditional monopoly must take account of the cost of production which its competitors must meet'. The far-sighted trust was concerned with the 'potentialities of independent output in the future'. A well-managed trust '... adjusts its price rather closely to the cost of production *including profits* on which a newcomer in an ordinary competitive market would base his calculations. But it adds to this something for the insurance against extra risk which a newcomer into this market would expect to face.' Marshall's rate of profit offered stability in the industry; it was influenced by both existing and potential competition; and it was the rate that would be allowed by a Court.

Chamberlin originally introduced the objective of 'ordinary rather than maximum profits' to demonstrate one set of conditions that could lead to an equilibrium with excess capacity.[2] He stated subsequently that 'conceptions of "good" and "reasonable" profits rather than maximum profits, perhaps because of a genuine desire not to "profiteer", or perhaps through a fear of adverse publicity or inviting public regulation' are 'real forces', though by no means as strong as 'a fear of attracting competitors'.[3] Despite the emphasis Chamberlin has wished to place upon the brief passage in *The Theory of Monopolistic Competition*, it does seem that the departure from profit maximization indicated there was of minor importance and certainly not a central feature of his analysis.[4]

Normal cost theory is reminiscent of Marshallian analysis and would seem to be a formulation, perhaps the most fully elaborated,

---

[1] See *Industry and Trade*, pp. 523–524.

[2] *The Theory of Monopolistic Competition*, 4th ed. (Cambridge: Harvard University Press, 1942), pp. 105–106.

[3] *Towards a More General Theory of Value* (London: Oxford University Press, 1957), p. 58.

[4] Chamberlin's writings do not accord recognition to the remarks on the interlacing and interpermeation of competition and monopoly that are to be found in Marshall's *Industry and Trade*. No reference to *Industry and Trade* is to be found in *The Theory of Monopolistic Competition* or *Towards a More General Theory of Value*.

of the satisfactory profit hypothesis. For example, Andrews refers to the businessman quoting a price which 'would enable [the firm] to cover its estimated average costs of production plus a fair profit'.[1] The allowance for net profit made by an established business 'will be a matter of experience' and must be 'a fair return'.[2] The addition made to average direct costs is the amount the businessman thinks 'he can take from the market without giving possible competitors an opportunity to cut into it (or into his share of it) in the long-run'.[3] A new business might accept a negative profit provided it saw the possibility of satisfactory profits after it had passed through an establishment phase.[4] Gordon explicity recommended the substitution of satisfactory for maximum profits: ' . . . vague as that criterion is, [it] is frequently a more accurate description of the primary objective. . . . Given the fog of uncertainty with which he must operate, the limited number of variables his mind can juggle at one time, and his desire to play safe, it would not be at all surprising if [the businessman] adopted a set of yardsticks that promised reasonably satisfactory profits in the long run and a maximum of stability in his relations with customers, suppliers and competitors.'[5]

The concept of satisfactory profit has been clarified by some recent writings. An attempt has been made to provide a plausible psychological basis for it, by emphasizing that opportunity cost refers to expectations and that, in turn, aspiration level is closely related to opportunity cost. Simon considers that 'The doctrine that a firm seeks reasonable rather than maximum profits does not mean that the firm prefers less to more profit or even that it is indifferent as between less and more profit. Among the courses of action it perceives as available to it, it may be expected to choose the most profitable. But the point is that failure to earn a reasonable profit will lead to a search for new alternatives, will stimulate the innovative processes.'[6] How would Simon define the reasonable level of profit? Recently attained levels will be important; comparison with other firms will play a part; and a level of profit might be judged to have been unsatisfactory if it directly stimulated efforts towards improvement. Baumol saw the minimum profit constraint as 'some vaguely defined minimum level' of profits which is 'just acceptable'.

[1] P. W. S. Andrews, 'Industrial Analysis in Economics', T. Wilson and P. W. S. Andrews, eds., *Oxford Studies in the Price Mechanism* (Oxford at the Clarendon Press, 1951), p. 163.
[2] P. W. S. Andrews, *Manufacturing Business* (London: Macmillan & Co., Ltd., 1949), pp. 165–166.
[3] *Ibid.*. p. 174.   [4] See Andrews, 'Industrial Analysis in Economics', p. 146.
[5] *Op. cit.*, p. 271.   [6] Simon, *op. cit.*, p. 55.

He viewed its determination as 'a major analytical problem', and suggested that it rests upon long-run considerations: it must yield enough dividends to make future share issues attractive to potential shareholders and enough retained profits to finance current expansion plans.[1]

Boulding took the view that the profit rate is a homeo-static variable. 'If actual profits fall below the homeostatic rate management becomes agitated, holds conferences, schemes schemes, and devises devices to cut costs or to increase revenues and so raise profits again. If it rises above the reasonable rate managerial activity slackens off, more golf is played, labor and customers are given concessions more easily and less pressure is placed on engineers to cut costs.'[2] The homeostatic rate of profit can be reconciled with marginal analysis if it is viewed as yielding the profit that gives the greatest amount of satisfaction.

All these attempts at definition place the emphasis upon long-run considerations. But the satisfactory or reasonable level so determined would seem to be open to a wide variety of influences and might also be subject to sudden changes. Changing relations with customers, suppliers, labour, and competitors could call for revision; aspiration levels should adjust to past performance; economic policy decisions on such matters as taxes and tariffs could have their impact; the general climate of opinion can change; certainly finance requirements for expansion plans and the satisfaction of existing and potential shareholders will vary. In view of all these considerations, it would be almost surprising if the satisfactory level displayed stability. But there is evidence of long-run stability of gross margins, at both industry and firm levels, and some firms have employed the same profit rate criterion for investment outlays during quite long periods of changing economic conditions. But not very much is known about the extent of divergence between the expected and realized profits.

SALES MAXIMIZATION

Baumol's suggestion that managerial success might be more closely related to total revenue than to profits has been noted already. His sales maximization hypothesis is closely linked to this proposition and, advanced in the oligopoly context, appears to rest basically on the separation of ownership and control. Before examining

---

[1] 'On the Theory of Oligopoly', pp. 187–188. [2] *Op. cit.*, p. 76.

Baumol's theoretical contribution[1] and exploring some of its implications, it should be noted that the hypothesis had been suggested elsewhere. The possibility that the firm might sacrifice profit in order to increase output had already been suggested, for example, by J. M. Clark. In his well-known article on workable competition he stated that 'There is a tendency to strive to maintain and increase output, as if this were an end in itself, aside from the resulting net earnings and perhaps at a short-run sacrifice of net earnings which a more grasping policy might secure'.[2] In a later article, Clark stressed the fact that in a dynamic context zero profit had been given a misleading precision. If cost, or the minimum return necessary to attract capital and enterprise, includes the large elements of unpredictable obsolescence which arise in the dynamic conditions of the real world, zero profit may be 'an indefinite, but substantial quantity. This makes it rational to prefer larger to smaller volume, at zero profit; and this seems clearly to accord with the characteristic American business emphasis on the importance of growth.'[3] This idea received further elaboration:

This inexactness of elements of cost impairs the validity of what appears superficially to be a self-evident proposition; namely, that a firm will prefer a profit on a smaller volume to no profit on a larger volume; and if it faces a sloping individual-demand function, it will raise prices until the resulting elimination of physical volume cancels the gain by raising unit costs. Yet actual firms attach much importance to growth in volume and would be surprised to be told that they deliberately limit their volume to less than the most efficient scale. The paradox is resolved when one realizes that 'no profit' includes a substantial, but highly indefinite, amount of income accruing to ownership, management and enterprise; with the result that it is quite rational to prefer 'no profit' on a larger volume to 'no profit' on a smaller volume, or even to a precarious and temporary 'profit' on the smaller volume. The importance which firms attach to growth may contain some irrational elements, but it rests on a rational basis.[4]

Similarly, the sales maximization hypothesis is related to the subjective treatment of profit maximization, although it is a significant improvement. On the one hand, there is added realism because the output-profit relationship has been linked with organizational

---

[1] Op. cit.; see also 'Marginalism and the Demand for Cash in Light of Operations Research Experience', Review of Economics and Statistics, XL (August 1958), pp. 209–214.

[2] 'Toward a Concept of Workable Competition', American Economic Review, XXX (June 1940), pp. 241–256 reprinted in American Economic Association, Readings in the Social Control of Industry (Philadelphia: Blakiston Company, 1949), p. 461.

[3] 'Competition: Static Models and Dynamic Aspects', American Economic Review, XLV (May 1955), Proceedings, p. 458.

[4] 'The Uses of Diversity: Competitive Bearings of Diversities in Cost and Demand Functions', American Economic Review, XLVIII (May 1958), Proceedings, p. 477.

conditions and no longer rests upon the concept of an entrepreneur as an individual having preference for leisure as against increased income. On the other hand, it indicates possible extension of the model because it suggests ways in which the profit curve might be modified as a result of the introduction of an output-profit preference pattern.

If the minimum level of profit that the firm regards as satisfactory is taken as single-valued and given, then unless that level equals the maximum profit, it is clearly necessary to introduce some other criterion (or criteria) to determine the equilibrium position. This can be seen from Figure 5. Given these cost and revenue conditions the profit maximizing output is OP. If the satisfactory level of

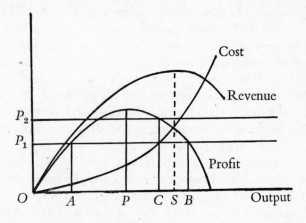

Figure 5

profit is OP1, then it can be achieved by any output equal to, or greater than OA, but not greater than OB. Because of the curvature of the profit function, the range of such outputs narrows as the satisfactory level rises. While the satisfactory level lies below the maximum, and the firm is assumed to take only the satisfactory amount, profit is only a constraint and not a determinant of an equilibrium position. These comments apply provided the satisfactory level is below the maximum level. This proviso is usually implicit in statements of the satisfactory profits hypothesis although it removes part of the usefulness of the aspiration level concept.

Baumol proposed that the needed criterion is sales revenue maximization. The sales maximizing output would be OS where the marginal revenue becomes zero, that is, the point of unit elasticity in the firm's demand curve. Sales equal to *OB* could be reached with the profit constraint at *OP*1. But to achieve profit of *OP*2, sales would have to be contracted to *OC*. From the output *OP* where profit is maximized, the firm would be able to lower price and expand sales, sacrificing some part or the whole of the difference between the maximum and satisfactory levels of profit. It also follows that if the profit constraint is not satisfied at the sales maximizing output, and if the constraint is less than the maximum level of profit, the firm will contract sales and raise price. The multi-product firm will choose the combination of outputs that yields the greatest sales revenue. Baumol considers that the constraint is ordinarily effective so that sales maximization does not leave a surplus profit. In these circumstances there is a fund of surplus or sacrificeable profit which can be applied to increase sales revenue. As some part of this fund must be sacrificed to increase sales of an individual product, the equilibrium product-mix of the sales maximizing firm is indicated by equality of the ratios of marginal revenue product and marginal profit yield for all products.[1]

The sales maximizing firm will usually spend more on advertising than the profit maximizing firm, provided it believes that advertising will increase physical sales, the surplus profit being applied to increased selling costs. This provides a partial explanation of oligopolistic preference for non-price competition; whereas the effects of price changes are uncertain, increased selling costs are assumed to yield increased sales. There are, of course, other explanations: the timing of responses may tip the scales in favour of non-price competition in an oligopoly situation. This alternative explanation would not require abandonment of the profit maximization hypothesis but it would involve the introduction of dynamic considerations. At this point a general criticism of the Baumol approach can be illustrated: price rigidity might also result from the existence of a *range* of satisfactory profit levels rather than of a single-valued constraint. This seems the more likely in the case of a business organization operating under conditions of uncertainty.

Marginal analysis suggests that changes in overhead costs will not affect the firm's equilibrium price and output. But firms do argue that rising overheads call for consideration of higher prices. This response is plausible in the light of the sales maximization

---

[1] See Baumol, *Business Behavior, Value and Growth*, p. 59.

hypothesis.[1] A rise in overhead will lower the profit curve shown in Figure 5 and, incidentally, reduce the range of satisfactory profit outputs. If the firm is producing the profit maximization output, as marginal analysis assumes, then no change takes place. But if output had been the sales revenue maximizing output because the firm was seeking only a satisfactory level of profit, then output would be contracted with a rise in price. Changes in rates of taxation can be treated in similar fashion. The sales maximizing firm will regard an increase in taxation as lowering the profit curve. In normal cost terminology, the firm could regard the rise in overhead or taxation charges as the justification for a higher price. Such justification will be sought in oligopolistic conditions, especially if adverse official and public reaction to price increases is considered probable. Such a model helps also to deal with the question whether the firm seeks to maximize profits before or after tax. Different formulations of the satisfactory level concept, while not altering any of the general propositions put forward above, would need to be taken into account. If the satisfactory level is defined as a percentage of turnover, the contraction of turnover and the associated rise in price following a rise in overhead would be less than if the satisfactory level had been defined as a given money amount of profit. If it is defined as a percentage of equity, problems would arise with issues of new shares. If defined as a percentage of capital employed, the result would depend upon the measurement of capital adopted and would need to take account of additional capital introduced during a period.

The key point of Baumol's explanation of the determination of the profit constraint is the dependence of the firm upon the capital market and the cost of borrowing. 'This means that, in obtaining capital by the issue of stocks, [the firm] must be prepared to meet competitive pricing conditions—the yield on its stocks will be determined by the forces of competition.'[2] As the return to the shareholder can be either in dividend payments or capital gains, an explanation of the distribution ratio must be provided: 'We may then surmise that the minimum acceptable rate of profits is that which just satisfies stockholders when it is divided between dividends and re-investment in the manner which most closely accords with stock-holder preference'.[3] The same balancing of current and future

---

[1] Normal cost theory also provides an explanation of such a response to changes in overhead costs.　[2] *Ibid.*, p. 50.　[3] *Ibid.*, pp. 51-52.

capital requirements and shareholder preferences takes place in the long-run.

A formal analysis would make use of stock-holder demand functions (which include past dividend payments as variables) and a dynamic model which describes sales over time as a function of the firm's investment history. That plan (a stream of dated dividend payments, investments, etc.) would be chosen which maximizes the capitalized present value of the stream of expected sales or some other measure of long-run sales. . . .

In practice, the determination of a minimum acceptable profit level probably comes down to no more than a rough attempt, again partly by rule of thumb, to provide competitively acceptable earnings to stock-holders while leaving enough over for investment in future output expansion at the maximum rate which management considers to be reasonably safely marketable.[1]

This analysis places great emphasis upon the separation of ownership and control and has prompted the comment that it must be interpreted as tending to eliminate excess profits above a competitive level, established by the need to attract funds; and that the original feature is that this result comes about not because of error in predicting the reactions of other firms, but from the nature of managerial objectives.[2] But this is to carry the emphasis too far. Growth and the consequent capital supply problems in themselves make for and reinforce the tendency for separation of ownership and control. Even if the owners of the firm exercised effective control over management, they may still adopt a satisfactory profit policy. And the rationale for this is to be found in the business organization's decision-making processes under uncertainty which create a need for complex internal organization and policy rules.

Furthermore, the argument in favour of the elimination of excess profits appears to consider the problem simply as a divergence from profit maximizing output. While it may be reasonable to assume that price will be maximized in the entry-forestalling sense, the treatment of costs is by no means so straightforward. If the existing producers permit their cost levels to rise with the emergence of organizational inefficiency and conspicuous consumption, they may find subsequently that there is a lack of downward flexibility. Excess profit will be eliminated but not necessarily by competition, unless this concept is taken to include imitative behaviour on the cost side. The excess profit interpretation would make satisfactory profit, in the long-run equilibrium sense, equivalent to normal

---

[1] *Ibid.*, p. 53.
[2] William Fellner, 'Professor Baumol's New Approach to the Theory of the Firm', *Kyklos*, XIII (1960, Fasc. 1), p. 111.

profit. But for a firm in a continuing state of disequilibrium, the meaning is an entirely different one. It is a target to be achieved by product differentiation, diversification, investment—including the gathering of information—and modification of the decision-making unit itself. When profits are less than normal the firm leaves the industry; when they fall, or are expected to fall, below the satisfactory level, the firm can change product-mix, seek cost reductions, and generally revise its policy. When an entry-fore-stalling policy results in unsatisfactory profit, such a policy would be intended to hold a position only temporarily.

Although Baumol described the satisfactory level of profit as 'vaguely defined' and discussed the ways in which the complexities of internal organization lead to the adoption of rules of thumb, his analysis shows inadequate recognition that a range of profit, however it be measured, is involved. Questions of perception and thresholds are important. How is the satisfactory level implemented? Perhaps by some sort of break-even chart approach which indicates when the satisfactory profit has been achieved and accordingly when the other objectives can be pursued? Budgeting and accounting techniques are obviously important if this is the case. Can the firm know the results of its activities soon enough, or does the firm plan for the entire period and sacrifice expected profits for expected extra sales? It would seem necessary to know a great deal more than is known at present about the budgeting methods of firms. What circumstances induce firms to depart from budget plans, to introduce supplementary budgets? How do the results of one period enter into the budget plans for the next and subsequent periods?

Another difficult feature is that the model is determinate only when the rate of expansion is given. Baumol surmises that this is why oligopolistic firms undertake market research investigations.[1] But the expected demand may be beyond the growth capacity of the firm. Managerial organization may not be able to develop rapidly enough. Even growth by merger will be subject to constraints. A number of surveys of investment behaviour have stressed sales or the level of demand as the most important single factor in the determination of the current level of capital expenditures. So the sales maximization hypothesis affords a possible means of co-ordinating price and investment theory. The possibility that the

[1] *Ibid.*, p. 53.

growth constraint be operative cannot be ignored. Presumably, the firm's reaction to such a constraint will depend on whether the realizable rate of growth permits it to maintain its share of the market, although the desired growth may be achieved through diversification.

The real weakness of the sales revenue maximization hypothesis is revealed when an attempt is made to clarify its meaning with regard to the long-run. It has minimized the importance of oligopolistic interdependence in routine matters like pricing and advertising expenditures, although it is largely this interdependence that warrants the adoption of the routine procedures. But in the long-run more radical changes take place and they may involve substantial investment decisions. Here competitive reactions may be important; and long-run cost and revenue functions cannot be treated as given under conditions of uncertainty.

EMPIRICAL EVIDENCE

What empirical evidence has been offered in support of the satisfactory profit hypothesis? The nature of the business organization and its decision-making processes, excessive costs, sales maximizing behaviour, restrained price policies, profit rate statistics, distribution ratios, and the stimulus to innovate all seem to provide some evidence consistent with the hypothesis, even if they do not provide conclusive evidence. Here again it is difficult to exclude consideration of investment decisions from the discussion, but such decisions will be taken up once more in the next chapter.

Nature of the Business Organization and Its Decision-Making Processes

Some of the complexities of the internal structure of the modern large business organizations have been discussed in Chapter II. The facts about the separation of ownership and control have been known and accepted for some considerable time.[1] The legal rights of shareholders to select directors have very little importance in the majority of companies because the large number of small shareholders is not organized and seems to lack sufficient interest to exercise any effective control over management. A minority group could perhaps exercise control with as little as 15, or even 10, per cent of voting rights. The most frequent situation is one in which

[1] See A. A. Berle and G. C. Means, *The Modern Corporation and Private Property* (New York: Macmillan, 1932); P. Sargant Florence, *The Logic of British and American Industry* (London: Routledge & Kegan Paul, 1953).

capital has been collectivized and control vested in a small group which selects its own successors. The pattern of ownership and control is similar in Britain, the United States, and Australia. The problem with such studies of control is that they have employed the concept of *ultimate* control, or the power to select or change the management of the firm. This is a serious deficiency, for to show where power is located is insufficient because that power may not be exercised. No simple generalization seems possible. Where ownership is associated with control, according to the 51 per cent criterion, it may not be effective because of conflicts within the ownership group. Ultimate control measured in such a way does not imply power of decision-making. Proxy battles provide ample evidence of this. And individual shareholders, especially institutional investors, may have an influence quite out of proportion to their shareholding; an influence sometimes strengthened by financial press comment. Actual control could be determined only by a case study approach and it is doubtful if the information could be obtained by an outside observer. Because of these problems it would be difficult to test this aspect of the sales revenue maximization hypothesis. Separation of ownership and control would occur in varying degrees and it would not be possible to assign precise values.

Top management is not easily demarcated from lower levels because, in a sense, everyone employed by the firm participates in the making of policy. But within the firm the delegation procedure may mean that performance is geared to satisfactory levels. Modern business organization seems to necessitate that minimum standards be set by management and it has been suggested that once this has been done, actual performance will tend to approximate to the standard.[1] Several observations might be made about this tendency. Internal competition, as in promotion, will be a strong counteracting force. The attitude of lower management will depend to a considerable extent upon employees' knowledge of the firm's activities. Variability and bias in answers by employees to questions about the firms in which they are employed are great.[2] Such conditions may be interpreted in a direct manner as consistent with satisfactory profit behaviour; or it might be argued that the firm is tolerating excessive levels of cost. At the level where decisions

---

[1] Cf. Cyert and March, *op. cit.*, p. 48.
[2] See D. R. Fagg, Carl Kaysen and R. N. McKean, 'What the Factory Worker Knows about his Factory', *Journal of Business of the University of Chicago*, XXXI (July 1958), pp. 213–234.

are made formally, it is essentially a matter of a group activity. Setting aside the contributions made to policy formation at lower levels, decisions must be seen as matters of compromise. The participants have different backgrounds. Sales personnel will emphasize turnover; production people, cost savings; research and development departments, technical performance. The highest levels will attach heavy weights to consequences in the capital market and in political spheres. And these participants may differ in their time preference and their interpretations of policy criteria. Given the composition of the management personnel, policy will always be a compromise. Perhaps, almost unconsciously, a managerial group will tend to preserve a balance between the various elements.

The budgeting methods adopted by firms, at first glance, appear to confirm the importance of the acceptable or satisfactory level of profits as a day-to-day working principle. Texts on budgeting point out that when unexpected changes take place in cost and revenue conditions, budgets are used by management to determine the consequential changes in plans which must be made to achieve the profit target. Against this it might be pointed out that recent developments in accounting of the cost-volume-profit type could be bringing the firm's decisions into line with marginal analysis. The new flexible cost accounting, which aims at providing control and evaluation of specific operations and policies, is directed to the increase of profit. Similarly, Baumol points out that many business-men 'are delighted to learn the techniques and adopt many of the results of a marginal analysis'.[1]

Excessive Costs

Two types of excessive costs can be distinguished. High and rising levels of profit will encourage expenditure on such things as cars for executives, subscriptions to journals, improved amenities, research departments, information services, and greater advertising. Here the firm is a consumer and these items go to make up its standard of living. It might be argued that such items are really appropriations of profits already earned. But they are paying-out costs[2] and many of them will be reduced only under very adverse

---

[1] 'Marginalism and the Demand for Cash in Light of Operations Research Experience', pp. 212–213. Baumol believes that this is the important contribution of operations research.

[2] Costs which have to be met in cash payments. Some such costs may be really investment expenditures.

circumstances. The longer these items of expenditure exist, the truer it is to speak of them as costs rather than appropriations. They may seem to have little bearing upon productivity, but employee reactions to severe cuts in this part of the firm's budget may be unfavourable even when the existence of the firm is threatened. Such items of expenditure also have a competitive aspect in so far as they bear upon the conditions of supply of labour and managerial personnel and the determination of goodwill. Cost reduction of a more general kind may result in a more efficient management achieving lower costs with the same production technique; or it might lead to lower costs through new managerial or technological techniques. Firms will possess, in varying degrees, the quality of progressiveness.[1] Improvement in this quality may yield rapid reductions in costs; alternatively, loss of drive may push costs up. Such changes are not only long-run consequences of changing managerial resources; they seem to be bound up with business fluctuations and rates of growth. Andrews speaks of the effects of 'an enervating period of inflation'[2] and implies that competitive forces will be sufficiently strong to ensure that the firm will be obliged to bring its costs into line with those of other firms. There is some evidence that cost conditions can and do deteriorate and that cost reduction can be effected when adverse circumstances oblige the firm to look to these opportunities.

Sales Maximizing Behaviour

This hypothesis has been outlined already. What is the empirical evidence? The separation of ownership and control is well advanced. But it is not known for certain whether the remuneration of management is more closely related to size—measured by sales revenue—than it is to profits.[3] However, the hypothesis is really based upon Baumol's experience in the course of work done for a management consulting firm. He reported that firms frequently made a conscious

---

[1] Cf. C. F. Carter and B. R. Williams, *Industry and Technical Progress* (London: Oxford University Press, 1957), Chapter 16; P. W. S. Andrews, 'Competition in the Modern Economy', *Competitive Aspects of Oil Operations* (London: The Institute of Petroleum, 1958).

[2] *Op. cit.*, p. 29.

[3] Cf. Baumol, *Business Behavior, Value and Growth*, p. 46, n. 2. An American study of companies reporting to the Securities and Exchange Commission over the period 1945–50, concluded that executive compensation (salary and bonus and company contributions to deferred compensation but not including stock options) is related significantly to size of company (net sales) but not to profits (net income before taxes, long-term interest and executive compensation). See D. R. Roberts, 'A General Theory of Executive Compensation based on Statistically Tested Propositions', *Quarterly Journal of Economics*, LXX (May 1956), pp. 270–294; *Executive Compensation* (Glencoe, Illinois: The Free Press, 1959).

decision to take less than maximum profits, both in the short- and long-run, in order to maximize sales revenue.[1] Baumol is confident in his interpretation of the evidence but that evidence has not yet been presented. Like evidence of restrained price policies, it is open to interpretation as long-run profit maximization.

Profit Rates

Statistics of profit rates also have been employed in an attempt to show that satisfactory profit rates exist. A pilot survey of small manufacturing business reported some evidence that a profit rate— that is, the percentage of gross profit to total assets—of 10–15 per cent was 'a comfortable one, that firms earning this kind of rate think they are doing well enough and bend their efforts to preserving their position without thinking much of expansion—apart, perhaps, from the risks it would entail'.[2] Above the 15 per cent level, the firms thought predominantly of expansion. Below 10 per cent, the wish to expand was strong but not as strong as above 15 per cent. There appeared to be some pattern between the desire to expand, the profit rate, and the method of financing.

Broadly speaking, internally financed firms are either firms with a very high rate of profit which have recently expanded and wish to expand further, presumably because of this very high level, or they are firms with a fairly high rate of profit which have not expanded in the past and do not wish to do so in the future, presumably because their profits are high enough to be 'comfortable' but not high enough to push them into taking the risks of expansion. In other words, if one is to depend solely on one's profits, they must be at a comfortable level; and it would seem that if they are just high enough for that (10 per cent–15 per cent?) then, one's horizon adapts itself to that level.[3]

Horizon is used here not in the usual planning sense but to indicate the level to which the firm both wishes to expand, and believes it within its power, given sufficient time, to reach. There was a preference for financing expansion out of profits. But this could only be done, and provide a reasonable income at the same time, if profits were at a comparatively high level. The sample covered a wide range of small manufacturing business and the possible influence of such factors as size, age of business, ownership structure, and market position was obscured. As the figures related to the averages

---

[1] See 'Marginalism and the Demand for Cash in Light of Operations Research Experience', pp. 211–213.

[2] Colin Bruce, F. A. Burchardt and E. B. Gibb, 'Small Manufacturing Businesses: A Preliminary Report on a Pilot Survey', *Bulletin of the Oxford University Institute of Statistics*, 17 (August 1955), p. 278.   [3] *Ibid.*, p. 279.

for 1952 and 1953, the analysis left open the question of how the standard of 'comfort' was revised in the light of past attainments. Furthermore, the survey was concerned with small business and the results cannot be applied to large firms with their complex managerial structures.[1]

Profit rates of large and small firms have been compared.[2] It has been argued that because of the separation of ownership and control the large firm is less interested in profits than the small one, irrespective of relative monopoly strength. The large firm minimizes costs and avoids losses, but lacks interest in increasing profits. Such argument is based on the work done by Crum and McConnell who used aggregations of income tax returns and Securities and Exchange Commission registration statements. Crum related net profit to the book value of equity; that is, share capital plus reserves plus accumulated profits. McConnell revised these figures to allow for excessive salary payments in the small companies, and extended the analysis to 1942, as Crum's figures related only to the period 1931–36. The largest firms appeared to be less profitable than all but the smallest in prosperity, whereas the largest firms were the most profitable in the 'thirties.[3]

Such computations involve many problems. They relate to the average rate of profit according to size of company. If the entire distribution of the profit rates is examined, rather than of the averages alone, the picture is not so clear. There is greater variability of profit rates amongst small firms; and when full allowance has been made for excessive salary payments, it no longer seems to be clearly established that the small firms earned at lower rates in the 'thirties.[4]

There is a further point to be taken into account. The profit figures used were net profits after depreciation. This could be

[1] The taxation system may operate to depress after-tax earnings of small companies. For example, English tax law limited the amount of directors' remuneration that could rank as expense for profits tax in the case of director-controlled companies whereas the remuneration of a whole-time service director, whose shareholding did not exceed 5 per cent, was allowable without limit. Cf. *Royal Commission on the Taxation of Profits and Income, Final Report* (London: H.M.S.O., 1955), para. 1031.

[2] W. L. Crum, *Corporate Size and Earning Power* (Cambridge: Harvard University Press, 1939); J. L. McConnell, 'Corporate Earnings by Size of Firm', *Survey of Current Business*, 25 (May 1945), pp. 6–12 and '1942 Corporate Profits by Size of Firm', *Survey of Current Business*, 26 (January 1946), pp. 10–16, 20; R. C. Osborn, 'Efficiency and Profitability in Relation to Size', *Harvard Business Review*, 29 (March 1951), pp. 82–94.

[3] See '1942 Corporate Profits by Size of Firm', p. 10. These figures are ratios of net profits before taxes to equity for all corporate industry.

[4] See S. S. Alexander, 'The Effect of Size of Manufacturing Corporation on the Distribution of the Rate of Return', *Review of Economics and Statistics*, XXXI (August 1949), pp. 229–235.

H

important. If a straight-line method of depreciation is used when depreciation is increasing from one period to the next, reported profit figures will be understated for new assets and overstated for old assets.[1] Changes in the reported profit rates will then depend upon the age distribution of the firm's assets. A new firm would report a lower profit rate than an old firm; a growing firm would report a lower profit rate than a stationary or declining firm. If the rate of growth is a determinant of the reported profit rate, and if the very largest firms are growing faster than other firms, the slight downturn in profit rates in the largest size classes shown in the more recent American figures might be accounted for.[2] Even if this point is not wholly justified and if there is no uniform practice with regard to depreciation methods, the influence of growth upon profit rates makes for difficulties of interpretation. Furthermore, large and small business concerns are not really comparable; the large firms may, for example, undertake research and development activities that are ignored by smaller firms which subsequently benefit from the findings.

Aggregate figures have also been put forward as supporting evidence. Phelps Brown's estimate of the rate of profit on the aggregate current replacement value of industrial capital in the United Kingdom is approximately as follows: 17 per cent in the earlier 1870's; 15 per cent from 1878 to 1900; 14 per cent from 1901 to 1913; a pronounced fall with the First World War is followed by fluctuations around 11 per cent up to 1940.[3] The series showed inertia and displacement which were explained by means of a conventional rate of profit which might obtain in highly competitive as well as oligopolistic markets.[4]

Distribution Ratios

The market value of shares seems to be more closely related to dividend rates than to undistributed profits, so that distribution policies would seem to leave shareholder preferences unsatisfied. Nevertheless, shareholder attendance at company meetings is

[1] Cf. E. O. Edwards, 'The Effect of Depreciation on the Output-Capital Coefficient of a Firm', *Economic Journal*, LXV (December 1955), pp. 654–666.

[2] S. J. Prais has endeavoured to show that in recent years the largest English companies have been growing more rapidly than smaller companies ('The Financial Experience of Giant Companies', *Economic Journal*, LXVII (June 1957), pp. 249–264).

[3] E. H. Phelps Brown, 'The Long-Term Movement of Real Wages', J. T. Dunlop, ed., *The Theory of Wage Determination* (London: Macmillan & Co., Ltd., 1957), Chapter 4.

[4] *Ibid.*, p. 349. Phelps Brown relied upon uncertainty considerations without giving explicit recognition to forms of business organization.

generally poor and difficulty is often experienced in obtaining a quorum. The lag of dividends behind current profit could be interpreted in terms of a satisfactory profit standard. The firm might have dividend rates applicable to high, satisfactory, and low levels of profit and this standard might change in the light of profit results. If profit rose continuously such a standard would yield results similar to those given by dependence of current dividends upon current profit and last year's dividend.

Innovation

In line with the suggestion that adverse changes in the position of the firm will lead to attempts at cost reduction, it might be argued that the firm will innovate when performance falls short, or is expected to fall short, of some previously established satisfactory level. Can the empirical relevance of this proposition be tested? One method is to examine the reasons that firms give for acts of innovation. But there is room for differences of interpretation and a single cause would not usually tell the whole story. 'For example, some of the innovation ascribed to research and development and to successful trials in other countries or industries were in fact sought out and developed or adopted because of the desire to strengthen the competitive position of the firm.'[1]

A second method would be to predict the expansion of sales of the individual firm in an industry group according to the satisfactory or unsatisfactory nature of its cost and revenue conditions at some base date. Firms with satisfactory profit and cost conditions, as compared with their competitors, would not be as likely to seek to increase sales as would those with unsatisfactory profit and cost conditions. Unsatisfactory profit could be measured by the initial ratio of sales to break-even point, an arbitrary standard being selected.[2] Unsatisfactory costs could be indicated by a more than proportionate increase in costs, the median being the standard. The general proposition would be that firms having unsatisfactory profit and/or costs, would be more likely to expand sales than those having satisfactory profit and/or costs, the divergence from the standard being treated as the motivating influence. On these

---

[1] Carter and Williams, *op. cit.*, p. 57.
[2] Let F be fixed costs and V the ratio of variable costs to sales. If S equals sales at the break-even point then $S-V(S)-F=0$; $S(1-V) = F$; and $-S = F/1-V$. But see J. L. Meij, 'Some Critical Remarks on the Significance and Use of the Break-even Point', *Journal of Industrial Economics*, I (April 1953), pp. 132–139.

assumptions firms can be ranked according to their sales expansion expected by some future date.

This second method was followed by Cyert and March.[1] Data on seven firms engaged in the manufacture of farm implements were used and comparisons made of 1946 with the average for 1935–39. The rank correlation co-efficient between the predicted and observed rankings was found to be significant. Overhead costs were mentioned as of equal importance with variable costs but were not taken into account because of lack of information. Unless there was reason to believe that such costs had no influence, there seems little point in making the test. In practice, the significant figure from the point of view of the firm wishing to expand may be accounting net profit plus depreciation allowances. Discussion in earlier chapters of the nature of the decision-making unit is relevant here. During a period of nine years, and the experience of a war economy, the given decision-making units may have changed a good deal. The unsatisfactory profit, through its influence on capital supply, may have been an effective barrier to growth even though the firms wished to expand. Business fluctuations could provide the incentive to look for improvements but at the same time could deter firms from undertaking the actual investment outlays. Or if the stimulus was provided by the cost reductions achieved by competitors, copying of these new techniques might be explained in terms of lesser costs borne by a firm that copies rather than originates the change, without introducing the satisfactory profit concept. Why attribute motivating influence to the firm's position in an industry ranking? Might not the firm be more interested in the cost levels that might be achieved by potential competitors? As these remarks suggest, the satisfactory levels themselves may be changing.[2] For example, a firm may wish to step up its rate of profit from year to year, or to secure an additional x per cent of the market each year. Empirical testing of the satisfactory profit hypothesis becomes a very difficult task in such circumstances.

Furthermore, innovation may become self-generating. Modern business organizations frequently have executive staff, and sometimes special units within the organization, devoting their efforts to change, rather than to routine administration. 'The levels of aspiration of executives are, then, generally attached to rates of change, and hence the executive hierarchy may be expected to be a frequent source

---

[1] *Op. cit.*, pp. 55–58.   [2] Cf. Simon, *op. cit.*, p. 56.

of demands for innovation.'[1] Carter and Williams are taking the same point of view when they suggest that the divergence from profit maximization is less likely 'the greater the importance in the company of a specialist function of creating and evaluating technical and market possibilities'.[2]

The empirical evidence is on the whole consistent with the satisfactory profit hypothesis, even though it has to be hedged in with qualifications. The ability of the firm to cut costs may indicate nothing more than that it is an inefficient firm, rather than that the firm has consciously permitted a divergence from minimum cost levels. In those cases where the cost reductions involve new technical or managerial arrangements, these developments may require time. The proposition that innovation is a response to a failure to achieve a satisfactory profit is difficult to test, not only because of measurement problems, but also because innovation tends to become institutionalized, or self-generating, within the firm. When allowance is made for excess payments to executives and the influence of growth upon profit rates, there may not be a great deal of difference between rates beyond the smallest size classes. The *Small Business Survey* was, after all, limited to small business and the 10–15 per cent comfortable rate reported appears to be bound up with methods of financing and retention of control. Budgeting methods and all the various forecasting procedures employed by the firm are perhaps the strongest justification for the assumption of a satisfactory profit target and the stability of that target. This type of *ex ante* data might tell more than could examination of realized profits.

UNSETTLED QUESTIONS

Although there is some supporting evidence from empirical studies, these attempts to formulate a profit criterion alternative to maximum profit have not yet achieved analytical usefulness in that they lack a definition of 'satisfactory' profit and have failed to furnish an explanation of the determination of profit. This has been so largely because they have attempted to explain profit in terms of conditions external to the firm.

The full and normal cost approach[3] encounters the problems of fixing a normal rate of output and of determining a profit margin.

---

[1] *Ibid.* [2] *Op. cit.*, p. 46.
[3] See P. W. S. Andrews, *Manufacturing Business* (London: Macmillan & Co., Ltd., 1949); N. D. Ruggles, 'Recent Developments in the Theory of Marginal Cost Pricing', *Review of Economic Studies*, 17 (1950), pp. 107–126; Elizabeth Brunner, 'Competition and the Theory of

The first of these problems is resolved if constant costs can be assumed;[1] and solution of the second problem appeared to have been furthered by the development of ideas concerning barriers to new competition and entry-forestalling price levels. However, such an extension of modified full cost theory has been only partially successful for two reasons. Firstly, barriers to new competition are not as impregnable as the Bain long-run comparative static analysis suggested because firms may gain a foothold in a sub-market, cross industry boundaries, or take advantage of conditions arising in the course of business fluctuations and from growth of the industry.[2] While these considerations reduce the importance of barriers to new competition, they do not require adoption of the view that long-run competitive forces are so strong that the competitive price level for the industry's product cannot long be exceeded and that only fair or normal profits will be earned. The opportunity to earn some excess profits may well remain over a lengthy period. Of course, this discussion is meaningful only if the concept of a competitive price level can be applied in non-competitive situations and this may well be unwarranted because different industry structures may generate different cost conditions. Secondly, the existence of barriers to new competition could do no more than set an upper limit to price and a lower limit to output. Given the structure of the industry, the level and stability of price would depend upon inter-firm differences, the qualities of the individual firms, the prospects for collusion, the number of potential entrants, and the resulting process of competition.

The sales revenue maximization hypothesis fails to the extent that it has been presented in terms of known cost and revenue functions in a traditional marginalist manner. In the conditions under which firms make their decisions, optimum solutions to technological, production, and marketing problems are not defined objectively. They depend upon the firm's perceptions and responses

the Firm', *Economia Internazionale*. Part I: V (Agosto 1952), pp. 509–526; Part II: V (Novembre 1952), pp. 727–747; H. R. Edwards, 'Price Formation in Manufacturing Industry and Excess Capacity', *Oxford Economic Papers*, N.S., 7 (February 1955), pp. 94–118; C. L. Schultze, 'Recent Inflation in the United States', Joint Economic Committee, Study Paper No. 1, (Washington: Government Printing Office, 1959), pp. 55–59.

[1] For an assessment of empirical findings, see J. Johnston, *Statistical Cost Analysis* (New York: McGraw Hill Book Company, 1960), Chapters 5–6.

[2] Cf. H. H. Hines, 'Effectiveness of "Entry" by Already Established Firms', *Quarterly Journal of Economics*, LXXI (February 1957) pp. 132–150; R. B. Heflebower, 'Stability in Oligopoly', *Manchester School*, XXIX (January 1961), pp. 79–93.

which follow from its experience, present capacities and expectations. The task of defining 'satisfactory' profit by references to conditions internal to the firm will be taken up in Chapter VII; and it will be helpful to use the principle of average cost pricing—as justified by uncertainty, multi-product production, and decision-making procedures within business organizations—and managerial preference for growth. However, in a context of disequilibrium where long-run processes of adjustment have yet to work themselves out, maximizing sales revenue and maximizing profit may not be in conflict if price is stable but in excess of marginal cost.

CHAPTER V

THE INVESTMENT DECISION

THE purpose of this chapter is not to present a theory of the investment decision but rather to examine some theoretical and empirical work done in this field and to seek out its major implications for a theory of profit. This leads, for example, to emphasis upon the significance of profit as a source and determinant of capital supply; and, in turn, this has implications for the concept of profit that is relevant to business decision-making, for it suggests that accounting measures of profit may be more important than 'pure' profit however interpreted. Or if the profitability of investment is viewed as the inducement to undertake capital outlays, interdependence between such outlays complicates profit measurement. In earlier chapters it was suggested that profit residuals might be attributable to the business organization. This is linked with the important question of capital-output ratios and the role played by organization in technological change and economic growth.

Attention may be focused on capital investment in an individual business because there is a distinct gap between the pure theory of investment and managerial decisions to acquire assets, despite a number of empirical studies of investment decisions in individual firms, groups of firms, and the economy as a whole, by means of interview and other survey techniques and by time series analysis.[1] Some of these findings are difficult to reconcile with any simple theory of profit maximization, or for that matter with the belief that profit plays a significant part in the determination of the nature

[1] For a useful survey of such studies see Robert Eisner, 'Interview and Other Survey Techniques and the Study of Investment', Franco Modigliani, ed., *The Problems of Capital Formation: Concepts, Measurements, and Controlling Factors* (Studies in Income and Wealth, Vol. XIX, Princeton: Princeton University Press for the National Bureau of Economic Research, 1957), pp. 513–584. Some more recent contributions are M. D. Brockie and A. L. Grey, Jr., 'The Marginal Efficiency of Capital and Investment Programming', *Economic Journal*, LXVI (December 1956), pp. 662–675; John R. Meyer and Edwin Kuh, *The Investment Decision* (Cambridge: Harvard University Press, 1957); W. H. White, 'The Rate of Interest, the Marginal Efficiency of Capital and Investment Programming', *Economic Journal*, LXVIII (March 1958), pp. 51–59; Robert Eisner, 'Expectations, Plans, and Capital Expenditures: A Synthesis of Ex Post and Ex Ante Data', M. J. Bowman, ed., *Expectations, Uncertainty, and Business Behavior* (New York: Social Science Research Council, 1958), pp. 165–188; Robert Eisner, 'A Distributed Lag investment Function', *Econometrica*, 28 (January 1960), pp. 1–29; B. G. Hickman, 'Diffusion, Acceleration, and Business Cycles', *American Economic Review*, XLIX (September 1959), pp. 535–565.

and rate of economic growth. For example, there is the failure of statistical analysis to reveal any consistent relations between accounting profits and investment expenditure.[1]

MARSHALL'S IDEA OF THE DECISION PROCESS

It is helpful to begin by noting the emphasis that has been placed upon the principle of substitution. In the writings of Marshall the entrepreneur combines the factors of production, at each volume of output, in such a way as to get their least expensive arrangement, and pushes ' . . . investment of capital in his business in each several direction until what appears in his judgement to be the outer limit, or margin, of profitableness is reached; that is, until there seems to him no good reason for thinking that the gains resulting from any further investment in any particular direction would compensate him for his outlay'.[2] Allowance had to be made for the time distribution of costs and revenues: 'Looking backwards we should sum up the net outlays and add in accumulated compound interest on each element of outlay. Looking forwards we should sum all the net incomings, and from the value of each subtract compound interest for the period during which it would be deferred.'[3] Uncertainty was acknowledged; the successful manufacturer had always to look forwards: 'he needed to study the past indeed; but his main concern with it was that he might consider how far the future would differ from the present, as the present differed from the past'.[4] Marshall stated also that ' . . . the margin of profitableness is . . . a boundary line cutting one after another every possible line of investment, and moving irregularly outwards in all directions whenever there is a fall in the rate of interest at which extra capital can be obtained'.[5]

A number of interesting questions emerge. At what rates of interest are the sums accumulated and discounted? Does the entrepreneur consider investment outside his own business? Is the nature of the business, its organization and its range of products, to be taken as fixed or can it diversify and cross industry boundaries? What are the conditions of supply of finance? How would the cost of internal funds be reckoned? Gaps such as these prompted

---

[1] For a summary of empirical findings see Meyer and Kuh, *op. cit.*, pp. 23–35.

[2] Alfred Marshall, *Principles of Economics*, 8th ed. (London: Macmillan & Co., Ltd., 1920), p. 356. See also pp. 404–406, 435, 514–515.   [3] *Ibid.*, p. 354.

[4] Alfred Marshall, *Money, Credit and Commerce* (London: Macmillan & Co., Ltd., 1923), p. 71.   [5] *Principles*, pp. 520–521.

the criticism that Marshall's theory of investment decisions failed to allow for uncertainty about the yield from investment.[1] However, elsewhere Marshall says of business undertakers that 'each one tries every opening, forecasting probable future events, reducing them to their true relative proportions, and considering what surplus is likely to be afforded by the receipts of any undertaking over the outlay required for it'.[2] It is true that many economists have been content to assume that investment opportunities are created through happenings external to the economic system, or through the functioning of a system of competition.[3] But from the wider sources of *Industry and Trade* and Marshall's other works, it is possible to challenge the view that he assumed an unwarranted certainty of yield, and to show that he did take account of many of the factors increasing technical opportunities to invest and the conditions affecting the willingness of firms to accept those opportunities.

The Marginal Efficiency of Capital

More recently, the marginal efficiency of capital concept has been developed to indicate the profitableness of investment outlays by comparison of the future returns yielded from capital expenditures with the cost of capital. The definition of the marginal efficiency of capital, r, is given by the following equation:

$$C = \frac{R_1}{(1 + r)} + \frac{R_2}{(1 + r)^2} + \cdots\cdots + \frac{R_n}{(1 + r)^n}$$

where C is the capital expenditure and $R_1 \ldots R_n$ the expected annual returns. Then r can be compared with the rate of interest, i, or a demand price equation can be written in the form

$$V = \frac{R_1}{(1 + i)} + \frac{R_2}{(1 + i)^2} + \cdots\cdots + \frac{R_n}{(1 + i)^n}$$

and V compared with C.

[1] For example, C. F. Carter and B. R. Williams, *Investment in Innovation* (London: Oxford University Press, 1958), Appendix on 'Traditional Ideas of the Decision Process', p. 155.

[2] Alfred Marshall, *Economics of Industry*, 3rd ed. (London: Macmillan & Co., Ltd., 1899), pp. 300–301.

[3] See *Investment in Innovation*, p. 149. To Carter and Williams, Marshall is apparently no exception. Unfortunately, they have continued in the tradition of emphasizing the content of the *Principles*, and ignoring that of *Industry and Trade*. Cf. H. H. Liebhafsky, 'A Curious Case of Neglect: Marshall's *Industry and Trade*', *Canadian Journal of Economics and Political Science*, XXI (August 1955), pp. 339–353. Some exceptions are A. J. Youngson, 'Marshall on Economic Growth', *Scottish Journal of Political Economy*, III (February 1956), pp. 1–18; D. C. Hague, 'Alfred Marshall and the Competitive Firm', *Economic Journal*, LXVIII (December 1958), pp. 673–690.

The approach to the computing problem in the investment decision, implied by the marginal efficiency of capital concept, is very close to that of Marshall. But in a wider sense there is an important difference which is bound up with the determination of the rate of interest. In the one case, the rate of interest is determined by the demand for and supply of money; in the other case, the rate of interest is determined by the marginal productivity of capital and the real supply cost. The solution to this problem of two theories of the rate of interest must be solved by reconsidering distribution and the theory of capital. 'It may be that the relations between the anticipated earnings of borrowed funds, the realized productivity of real capital, and the rate of return paid the capital-supplying stockholder are less direct and more complicated than has been thought.'[1]

The Keynesian concept leads to difficulties in regard to both the earnings and the cost of capital. Confusion has stemmed from the use of *cost of capital* for both the rate at which funds can be borrowed or new equity obtained, and the rate at which a stream of future cash flows should be discounted to measure its present value; that is the borrowing and lending rates. The first is what the firm must pay for funds. The second is the rate that can be obtained outside the firm, either in the capital market or more directly by investment in some other enterprise. The distinction between these two rates is acknowledged frequently but seldom maintained. Although the cost of capital can be regarded as showing the return on funds diverted from internal use to market investments, 'This opportunity-cost principle has a tone of unreality, . . . since it implies that the stockholder is king and that financial policy is aimed solely at maximizing the value of his capital'.[2] The view implied here is that the firm should discount its future income at an outside lending rate which differs from the borrowing rate. At the margin, the firm should not make a capital expenditure within the business if it can do better elsewhere, subject to legal and taxation considerations.

Because of the difficulties of estimating the lending rate, the borrowing rate has been made to serve both purposes. The firm's alternative to investment within the business may be the purchase of government bonds, as these involve no credit risk, with the result

[1] B. S. Keirstead, 'The Structure and Accumulation of Capital', *Canadian Journal of Economics and Political Science*, XXIII (November 1957), p. 446.

[2] Joel Dean, *Capital Budgeting* (New York: Columbia University Press, 1951), p. 44. See also Friedrich and Vera Lutz, *The Theory of Investment of The Firm* (Princeton: Princeton University Press, 1951), pp. 22–24, 35–37, 38, 39, 60, 131, 195–197.

that the lending rate is lower than the borrowing rate. But there is the possibility that investment in other lines of business may occur. This suggests that the lending rate could be measured in terms of the rate which the firm believes it could obtain by taking equity interests in other firms that appear to involve an element of risk about the same as that involved by further investment within the firm.[1] But this leaves unsolved the problem of how to incorporate uncertainty into the analysis. Alternatively, the real situation may be that firms are indifferent to the opportunity costs of capital. It may be, for example, that a large firm pursuing a policy of expansion has no marked time preference. Precise calculations of earnings may not be carried out; other considerations may predominate. There has been a tendency to assume that future profits might be estimated on the basis of past business results, given the rate at which future costs and revenues will be discounted to arrive at their present value. Such a procedure suits the purposes of model building and econometric investigation, but it is doubtful if it can be reconciled with the observed behaviour of firms. In particular, it would be necessary to decide what measure of profit it is that is extrapolated into the future.

THE INTERDEPENDENCE PROBLEM

An investment decision usually involves more than a simple comparison of the return from a single new investment outlay with a rate of interest. Multiple outlays and uncertainty are normal. To postulate dependence of investment decisions upon current and/or recent profits would seem to enable such problems to be avoided but this procedure is unwarranted for several reasons. Firstly, it leads to the conclusion that the economy should be much more unstable than it is observed to be; interdependence between investment projects means that firms have only limited choice and this contributes to the stability of capital expenditures. Secondly, it is inconsistent with the observed behaviour of the individual firm.

Contributions discussed in Chapter III have clarified the uncertainty problem. In this connection attention must be drawn to several aspects of the investment decision which have tended to be neglected in the literature. Firstly, the element of contingent plan has been neglected. The firm's investment decisions have some

---

[1] Cf. H. V. Roberts, 'Current Problems in the Economics of Capital Budgeting', *Journal of Business of the University of Chicago*, XXX (January 1957), p. 14.

flexibility and should not be regarded as once-and-for-all matters. Accordingly, they should be amenable to a type of sequence or period analysis. Secondly, the firm is seldom concerned with an isolated investment outlay but rather with an investment programme ranging over a number of products and extending into future planning periods. This is important in the assessment of the marginal return from a given new investment outlay. Such an outlay may add to the returns from existing activities; alternatively, it may cause them to diminish, as in the obvious case of a new, self-competing product. But a more important, and less easily detected, case is where managerial, and perhaps technical, resources have to be diverted. This will be an important case if it is assumed that managerial capacity is more or less fixed, or if the rate of growth of the firm exceeds that of managerial resources. The need for periods of consolidation is well known.

The structure of assets can provide a convenient starting point for a consideration of this interdependence problem. This initial stock of capital is not homogeneous; its component parts complement each other; and time lags in use may be involved. If thought of as the fixed assets of the firm, this initial stock must be used in conjunction with working capital or the investment in current assets, that is, cash, debtors, and materials stocks. Working capital is changing in structure continually, the maintenance of an optimum structure being an important aspect of financial management because it adds flexibility to business operations. Additional capital projects normally create create a need for additional working capital. A further part of this initial stock is managerial capacity or organization, which provides the entrepreneurial services. An aspect of this capacity is the planning that is undertaken. As the planning and implementation of an investment decision, or rather an investment programme, take time, the speed of response to a given stimulus, say, a change in demand, will depend upon the quality of preparedness or the extent to which planning is a continuing function in the organization. And this quality is unlikely to be one that can be acquired quickly. At a given point in time, the firm looks to the future but its decisions are subject to the constraints that have come down from the past and are embodied in the initial stock of capital. Of course, the past is relevant in another sense. As Marshall pointed out, the differences between the past and the present should create an awareness that the present should not be projected into the future.

Penrose has stressed this dependence of investment opportunities upon internal conditions. 'The "productive opportunity" which invites expansion is not exclusively an external one. It is largely determined by the internal resources of the firm; the products the firm can successfully produce, the new areas in which it can successfully set up plants, the innovations it can successfully launch, the very ideas of its executives and the opportunities they see, depend as much on the kind of experience, managerial ability and technological know-how already existing within the firm as they do upon external opportunities open to all.'[1] As a matter of history the firm, at a given point in time, may have a surplus of these various types of resources. The managerial organization may have been expanded in preparation for the new activities; funds may have been built up in order to finance new projects and to ensure adequate working capital when those projects reach fulfilment; equipment may have been purchased and stored in preparation for planned developments.

The fact that investment activity is a continuous process deserves emphasis, not least because much of the theory of investment has been confined to a single investment outlay and has excluded problems of flexibility and interdependence. In contrast, actual investment decisions are observed at some point in the process, not as taken from some initial equilibrium point. Many considerations will enter into decisions on individual investment projects and these can vary in relative importance with fluctuations in the general level of business activity and with changes in technology, information and organization. As circumstances alter, different weights may be attached to present and future profits. It may be that different theories are needed for different phases of the trade cycle and for different economic and social environments, for example, for oligopoly situations as opposed to competitive situations.

To concentrate attention on the single investment project which involves simply an extension, in a balanced form, of an optimal asset structure seems to leave out a major part of the investment process. An investment project may complement the existing assets; it may replace existing assets; or it may aim at expansion without altering the structure. In each case it will probably be a continuation of an earlier growth process; in each case some technological improvement will no doubt be embodied in the

---

[1] E. T. Penrose, 'Foreign Investment and the Growth of the Firm', *Economic Journal*, LXVI (June 1956), p. 225.

project. In a list of investment opportunities open to a firm, projects *a*, *b*, and *c* may be alternatives, at least for the present; project *d* may be a diversification venture that is loosely linked to existing activities through common managerial, technical, financial, and marketing resources; project *e* might be improvements in equipment which will reduce the cost of project *f* at some later date. A similar argument might be presented about research investment. Instead of seeing it in isolation, it should be regarded as part of a larger investment programme, as a measure which reduces risks by keeping up a supply of investment opportunities.

Consequently, in calculating the profitabilities of individual investment projects account must be taken of the repercussions on existing revenues and costs; the interdependence with other investment projects that might be undertaken concurrently; and the interdependence with other investment projects that might be undertaken in the future. A type of sequence analysis is called for. Classification in capital expenditure budgets has sometimes distinguished between essential, desirable, and contingent items. This classification seems to bear some relationship to the situation envisaged in such sequence analysis. Some immediate actions must be taken; some others may be taken; and yet others are contingent upon the choices that have yet to be made. The foregoing remarks simply stress the contingent nature of most investment plans. From a given starting point it is necessary to make different estimates of earnings for a given project, for each path that might be followed. Horizons will differ as between firms and in the same firm as between projects and over time. Such conditions as age of firm, capital structure, managerial structure, rate of growth, and general economic conditions would have to be taken into account.

Briefly, it must be recognized that investment decisions are being made in a growth context and that there may be flexibility in investment programmes. Sequence analysis is applicable. The additional knowledge generated as a consequence of events in one period provides a basis for decisions in the next and subsequent periods. The firm moves from the decisions and outcomes of one period, revising its plans, correcting for errors of judgement, improving upon the flow of information, and extending its horizon, to the decisions of the next period. However, the flow of information need not be a smooth and continuous one. It may be more realistic to see the firm as lacking adequate information in the sense that no one course of action stands out as being the most appropriate in the circumstances and so deciding to postpone the decision until more information becomes available. Changes compel decisions; to take no action in a changing environment is in itself a decision.

CLASSIFICATION OF INVESTMENT DECISIONS

This process view of investment activity underlies at least some of the simple classifications of investment decisions that have been presented in recent discussions. The following are illustrations:

Voluntary and Forced Decisions.[1] Voluntary decisions are those taken by the firm when it is not compelled to do so, for fear of what will happen if it does not. They are decisions taken when there is an adequate supply of investible funds, when the firm is inclined to be venturesome, and when there has been adequate time to investigate the alternative uses of funds. Forced decisions are those taken to avoid or minimize a threatened setback or loss; decisions taken because the firm considers that if things are left as they are the position will deteriorate further, and intended to restore the firm to its former situation.

Habitual and Genuine Decisions.[2] Habitual investment decisions are those in which the firm feels that it has no choice and in which expectations about the future play practically no part. The firm considers that it is compelled to expand, say, by an increase in demand. But some decisions are of a genuine nature. Some investments are made to improve the position of the firm, to raise sales or increase profits, to keep up with competitors, or reduce costs. Decisions in this second category are influenced by definite expectations.

External and Internal Factors.[3] Much capital expenditure might be classified as unavoidable in the sense that it is influenced by factors outside, or at least only partially within, the direct control of the firm: safety regulations, conventional working conditions and amenities for staff, the activities of competitors, the importance of maintaining the earning power of existing assets, government

---

[1] See H. R. Parker, 'Voluntary and Forced Decisions', *Metroeconomica*, IX (April 1957), pp. 116–124.

[2] See George Katona, *Psychological Analysis of Economic Behavior* (New York: McGraw-Hill Book Company, 1951), pp. 240–263.

[3] See L. G. Norton and J. E. Wall, 'Control and Oversight of Capital Expenditures within Unilever', *Journal of Industrial Economics*, I (July 1953), pp. 241–253.

policies, the pace of technical development, and errors in commercial planning. These items belong in the external category.

Earnings-justified and Policy Expenditures.[1] Here a contrast is drawn between decisions reached on the basis of estimated earnings likely to arise from the expenditures, and those dictated by policy considerations. However, policy expenditures are often intended to keep the firm's producing machine going and might be regarded as measures to maintain the earning power of existing assets. Such expenditures may have a very high rate of return whatever method of computation is employed.

These classifications provide insight into the investment decision-making process. They recognize that the decision must be implemented at some point in time and that the position of the firm at that time—its stock of fixed equipment, liquid assets, organizational resources, market situation, etc.—delimit the possible courses of action that might be followed. Certain actions will be performed of necessity to carry on the current activities; that is, to implement existing policy. But other actions will stem from revisions of policy, prompted by changes in the environment or from changes internal to the firm. Of course, the policy change may involve extension of existing activities or change in the pattern of existing activities. It is this policy continuity very largely that constitutes a business organization and distinguishes a firm from a mere collection of factor services.

SIZE OF INVESTMENT AND RATE OF RETURN

The structural or process view of investment activity is relevant to the relationship between size of investment outlay and rate of return. *A priori* no systematic relationship between the size of investment project and the estimated rate of return seems likely. The size may be measured as a percentage of, say, the firm's average total investment outlay over a period of time. Consider the proposition that while there is considerable variability in expected earnings from projects under consideration, the smallest projects generally show substantially higher rates of earnings than do the larger projects.[2] In an oligopoly situation, it would be necessary to consider the effects of increased output resulting from the expanded capacity. Small increases might not lead to any significant changes.

[1] See P. W. S. Andrews and Elizabeth Brunner, *Capital Development in Steel* (Oxford: Basil Blackwell, 1951), pp. 353–360.   [2] *Ibid.*, p. 354.

I

But such analysis would encounter difficulties of classification in the case of the multi-product firm. Similarly, qualifications apply to the cost side. Small projects may be absorbed by the existing managerial capacity; they may have the benefit of existing over-heads. And allowance must be made for changes in working capital requirements. Are these omitted or deemed to be unnecessary for small projects but brought to account for large ones? In so far as small projects tend to be replacements, it is likely that they will bring about reductions in working capital requirements.

Can it be said that the small investment opportunities are, because of capital rationing, accessible to a much larger number of firms? This might mean that the small project would have a lower rate of return, on an argument parallel to that employed to explain the alleged tendency for the rate of profit on capital employed to increase with the size of firm. However, it seems unnecessary to evaluate this argument. Suffice it to point out that rather special assumptions about the nature of investment opportunities are involved.

The method of calculation of rates of return may favour either the short- or long-lived asset. Firms may adopt a pay-off period which is shorter than the period during which the asset will con-tribute some reasonable return. This introduces a bias against the long-lived asset, because if depreciation is included in the returns estimated for paying off the investment outlay, short-lived assets can better meet any set pay-off requirement than can long-lived assets that have relatively lower rates of depreciation. On the other hand, a method may discriminate in favour of long-term projects, or introduce 'a rather complex bias for assets of various durabilities'.[1] Thus the method of calculation may favour the short-lived assets; but if the very short-lived assets are also small, they may not even be treated as capital expenditures. Along with these considerations it is possible that fewer people will be concerned with individual small projects. The costs of decision may be lower; there may be less weighing of intangibles and so less risk allowance built into the estimates. There may be less careful costing and less careful con-sideration of the interdependencies. These remarks have been concerned with investment plans. No strong case for any systematic relationship between size of outlay and rate of return seems to emerge. But this proposition about *ex ante* values is not tested by looking at realized results even if it can be shown that for investment

[1] Eisner, 'Interview and Other Survey Techniques and the Study of Investment', pp. 544–545.

projects actually carried out, expectations have been proved accurate; for the rate of return on projects abandoned or postponed has been neglected. If it is a policy rule that small projects should have higher rates of return than large ones, it is not possible to learn about the small projects never brought forward.

Several arguments have been advanced to account for the observed relationship; that is, higher realized returns on small than on large projects. It has been suggested that the element of technological change is more important for small than for large investment projects.[1] This seems to rest upon a judgement as to the way in which technology changes. Would all industries have the same experience? Although technical change of a substantial kind will not be a continuous process, there may be more continuity in some industries than in others. Would it not be necessary also to take account of the point in time? A second reason that has been advanced is the relative frequency with which minor improvements become possible.[2] This argument seems to depend upon the type of investment project. It can apply to small replacements but can it apply with equal force to small additions to capacity—ignoring the fact that even the small replacements will normally involve some additional capacity? The answer to this question depends upon the relationship between the new investment activity and existing productive operations. The weaker the link the less force this argument has. Clearly nuisance value is important. But it should be brought into account when assessing the rate of return. In terms of the process nature of investment activity, it could perhaps be argued that the more small projects being carried out in a given period of time, the higher their costs and the lower their rates of return. Much the same applies to the large projects; the overall rate of growth may be limited by the availability of managerial resources and, perhaps, also

[1] Cf. Andrews and Brunner: 'Small schemes are generally more of the kind affected by technological change than larger ones; it is more likely that a piece of ancillary equipment in the steel industry will be substantially superior to older equipment or methods than will be the case with larger schemes which will be more concerned with steel making and working processes proper, and, there, technical change of a substantial kind occurs more rarely' (op. cit., p. 271).

[2] Cf. Andrews and Brunner: 'The more frequent they are, the more likely it would be that a low earnings standard would result in recently installed plant being replaced on the average before it had paid for itself. Another factor telling in the same direction is the relative nuisance value of alterations to plant. Unless, on the average, small replacements can be fitted into normal programmes of maintenance, etc. they would tend to interfere with productive operations. The restrictions on upsets to production, which management will normally impose, will be factors tending to cause such projects as are adopted to show relatively high earnings' (Ibid.).

by shortages of money capital and physical assets. The time distribution of investment activity might be more significant than the size distribution.

EMPIRICAL STUDIES

The varied nature of the findings of empirical studies of investment behaviour calls into question any simple conceptualization of the investment process. And this is understandable because the organizational and environmental conditions of the decision-making units differ; because the studies have related to different points in time and have employed different methods; and because the investment process implies disequilibrium.[1]

A theory of investment decisions is required to be more than a forecasting device; that would not necessarily give any explanation of behaviour. If attention is focused on, say, a change in demand, it is desired to know the conditions, internal and external to the firm, under which the firm will be most responsive. The nearness to capacity output might be the most significant; or the availability of funds; or some level of planning activity. Because investment is a process through time, it is possible that the expansion of capacity might be carried out before the increase in demand materializes; funds may be raised now because capital market conditions are not expected to be as favourable later on; planning may be carried out in advance; and research activity might be treated as part of planning activity.

What common elements are there in the empirical findings? Broadly speaking, two types of theoretical approach can be distinguished: the first is associated with the profit maximization hypothesis and the second with the acceleration principle. Studies based on the first approach encountered the difficulties arising from incomplete knowledge and the related question of organizational and institutional conditions. In its simplest form, for example, as shown in the quotations from the writings of Alfred Marshall given earlier in this chapter, the profit maximization approach stressed the

[1] Cf. E. Lundberg: 'My simple premise is that the investment process can be understood only when the reference basis is an economy perpetually out of static equilibrium. There is a more or less continuous flow of disturbances brought about by technical change as well as by other changes in demand and supply conditions. The resulting disequilibrium positions create investment opportunities, and then the investment process is continually creating new disequilibria. Only a minor part of the investment problem can *a priori* be regarded as a static substitution problem. If this view is accepted as plausible, then an effort to use the production function as an instrument to explain long-term growth must be considered as very inadequate ('The Profitability of Investment', *Economic Journal*, LXIX (December 1959), p. 662).

role of the rate of interest but empirical findings indicated that changes in cost of capital had little effect on investment expenditures. Planned and actual investment outlays do not tend to diverge with changes in the cost of capital. In fact, there is some evidence pointing to a belief on the part of firms that increased costs will be accompanied or followed by increased selling prices and increased, or at least maintained profits, provided the changes in costs are within reasonable limits.

The importance of expectations should not be underestimated. It has been reported that the plans of firms for investment outlays are normally most definite with regard to the near future, becoming more tentative as the horizon is extended. This can result from the planning procedures that are followed by the firm and suggests that certainty-equivalents cannot tell the whole story. Expectations are also relevant to the belief that rising costs will be taken care of without any direct action. While this presupposes certain oligo-polistic response patterns between the firms in the industry, it rests also upon an expected positive growth rate which will act as a corrective for any excess capacity produced through too rapid expansion. The significance of the market share criterion, under conditions of uncertainty and assuming constant or decreasing costs, may well be that it serves as an indication of a minimum target rate of growth.

The findings have also emphasized the complexity of managerial motives, and restraint by top management in approving investment projects. The latter point can be dealt with in terms of organization and planning procedures. The former point has led to a shift from profit maximization to utility maximization. The importance of internal liquidity considerations and preference for internal financing fit somewhat uneasily into the theoretical framework, until the dual function of profit as incentive and as the major determinant of the supply of finance to the firm is recognized.

The second approach in terms of the acceleration principle has been employed widely. The original application of this principle was to the behaviour of the firm but it has been extended into business cycle and growth theories. The findings in these areas have emphasized the level of sales or demand. This does not imply that profitability is being disregarded. Granted the expectation of demand, the estimated turnover is assumed to yield a flow of profit. What is the relevant rate of profit that is projected in this way? It could be a rate determined under oligopoly conditions with price set at the highest level that will keep out potential entrants and on the basis of existing cost levels. And this, of course, depends upon the growth of capacity in relation to the growth of the total market. Here again the market share criterion has a rationale. For there is little use a firm keeping down its price and foregoing current profits unless it can, at a later date, meet available demand. Alternatively, the rate of profit might be viewed as a matter of attaining or maintaining a normal or satisfactory level of profit, in which case it becomes necessary to explain the determination of that level. This approach places a desirable emphasis upon expectations because there has been a tendency to treat the acceleration principle as a purely technological matter deriving from a fixed capital–output ratio.

Investment studies have not given much attention to stocks although the assumption of a desired stock-sales ratio has an important place in discussions of business fluctuations.[1] Consider the following illustration. J. Lyons & Company, operating a chain of restaurants and caterers, carry substantial stocks. Their accounts for 1955 and 1956 showed stock-in-trade and consumable stores at £16·4 million and £10·8 million respectively, equal to 43 per cent and 31 per cent of the firm's total current and fixed assets. Price changes were of considerable importance at that time. In 1953 the Chairman had noted a 10 per cent rise in the balance sheet figures of stock-in-trade and had commented that 'This is no more than normal having regard to the recent freeing of certain commodities from control and rationing, and the continued upward trend of food prices. Our stocks are, of course, very carefully watched, and their volume is not excessive having regard to the total volume of business.'[2] But what is meant by 'normal' here? Is there a stable relationship between stocks and sales, apart from seasonal change? What part do stocks play in oligopoly strategy?

There are several reasons for holding stocks. There are economies of bulk purchase; production flows can be smoothed; purchases can be made in anticipation of price increases; buffer stocks make it possible to avoid turning customers away; and it may be essential to take up stocks in the case of a good that is not in continuous supply. But these reasons do not seem to dictate a constant stock-sales ratio. How can the frequent references to this ratio in business

[1] Norton and Wall (op. cit.) stress working capital requirements. See also Ruth P. Mack. 'Characteristics of Inventory Investment; the Aggregate and its Parts', Problems of Capital Formation, pp. 471–487; Franco Modigliani, 'Business Reasons for Holding Inventories and their Macro-economic Implications', Problems of Capital Formation, pp. 495–506.
[2] The Times, July 7, 1953.

practice be explained? It may help management to judge the efficiency of individual production and purchasing activities. And, of course, financial commentators attach a good deal of significance to this ratio. Consequently, company reports tend to explain stock movements lest they be wrongly interpreted as evidence of declining sales or inefficient management.

To these general comments on empirical findings will now be added a more detailed examination of some recent investigations.

A Cross-section Study

The Meyer and Kuh investigation employed the techniques of multivariate analysis. The sample included five years of observation, 1946–50, in twelve United States manufacturing industries whose securities were registered with the Securities and Exchange Commission. Some firms had to be excluded for reasons such as lack of crucial information or exceptional experience. Using fixed assets as a measure, a 40 per cent coverage was achieved in all industries, with at least an 80 per cent coverage in five of the twelve groups. The main explanatory variables used were: depreciation expenditure, sales, profits, capacity utilization, current change in sales, depreciation reserves, and liquidity stock. The variables were deflated by gross fixed assets in order to justify the assumption of normality. Cross-section multiple regression equations were then computed. Unlagged values were found superior to lagged values; the profit variable in the paper and pulp, petroleum, and fabricated metal products industries and depreciation expense were the only flow variables lagged, as were the two stock variables, net quick liquidity and depreciation reserves.

The relationship between depreciation expenditure and investment was found to be significant under conditions of stability or deceleration but not under converse situations. This was held to be due primarily to liquidity considerations and was not dependent upon differences in the durability of equipment.[1] Depreciation reserves measured the age of assets and negative regression coefficients predominated. This led to a theory of behaviour called the 'senility effect',[2] which stressed the continuity in the behaviour of the firms. Firms that possessed old equipment at present, reached that condition by investing at a low rate in the earlier periods. The investigation showed that during the period 1946–50 such firms continued to

---

[1] *The Investment Decision*, p. 115.   [2] *Ibid.*, Chapter VI.

invest at a low rate. Where firms were losing their status in the industry and earning falling profits and their capital equipment was old, typically they did not take action to reverse this trend. In contrast, the firms that had pursued a policy of change possessed new equipment and tended during the period investigated to maintain their higher rate of investment. It was also found that the firms with old assets also had larger stocks of net liquid assets.[1]

Relationships between investment and sales, profits, capacity, and liquidity[2] were not stable throughout the period; this was most noticeable with the business fluctuation of 1948–49. While markets were growing quickly and liquid funds were readily available, capacity considerations were dominant. But in recession the emphasis shifted to liquidity flows as shown by profits and depreciation expenditure. On an industry basis, the decreased importance of the accelerator and the increased importance of profits were accompanied by a fall in the average rate of profit in the industry. Liquidity emerged as the key explanatory variable because it was a necessary condition for the operation of the accelerator. In the long run capital-output relationships seemed more important than financial considerations. When the results from the annual and averaged data models were compared, the importance of sales and profits were almost reversed, sales being more important in the latter.

There was a strong reluctance to finance needs from external sources, but when this was overcome long-term debt was strongly preferred to equity. Competitive pressure and rapid growth were slightly related to the use of external finance. As regards the retention ratio, the conclusion was 'that firms in growing industries not only needed outside funds and consequently good relations with the money market more than did stagnant industries but also stood the best possibility of deriving appropriate benefits from a more generous dividend policy'.[3] Small firms showed greater sensitivity to the liquidity flow variables than did large firms, but, in the period studied, were able to more or less maintain their position.[4]

Interest rates did not exert an important influence. However, share prices could be influential. Meyer and Kuh point out that 'The observed outcome about stock prices is subject to two interpretations, the first holding that stock prices and investment are influenced in common by similar economic phenomena, while the

---

[1] *Ibid.*, p. 100.　　[2] *Ibid.*, pp. 134–135.　　[3] *Ibid.*, p. 158.　　[4] *Ibid.*, pp. 179–180.

second interpretation stresses the causal relation between stock market actions and investment expectations. The data were insufficient to permit a clear-cut choice between these alternative explanations of the observed relationship.'[1]

Meyer and Kuh have taken the firm as their unit of observation. While recognizing that it would be desirable to have smaller units such as machines, processes, and plants, they defend the selection on the grounds that capital budgeting is centralized.[2] The sampling procedure has led to the inclusion only of firms which are 'incorporated, well established, fairly large, and frequently selling in an oligopolistic market',[3] and these firms will tend to be multi-product firms. It would seem that an aggregation problem is involved here. The output of the large multi-product firm is typically composed of expanding and contracting lines with varying margins of profit. If expansion takes place in the most profitable lines, it seems reasonable to query whether there should be any positive correlation between the total new investment expenditure and the aggregate of profit for all products. This question seems to have been ignored. Although newly organized firms were excluded on the grounds that their behaviour was not governed by the same factors as established firms, the parallel with new and old products within the firm was not taken up.

This problem would not seem to have been solved by the industry grouping adopted. The study began with categories of the three established government classification manuals (Securities and Exchange Commission, Standard Industrial Classification, and the Bureau of Internal Revenue). Firms were allocated to large group classifications on the basis of that product whose value was the greatest share of total sales value in 1948.[4] Then it became apparent that the industry definitions employed in these classifications would be too gross for purposes of the investigation. There was too much variation, within the industry groups, in the capital intensity of physical production processes. If industries with widely different capital intensities were included in the sample, then the same value of a variable for firms with disparate capital intensities would imply different fixed investment decisions.[5] The solution adopted was to break the industry groups into their smaller component industries and then regroup until statistically insignificant differences in the

---

[1] Ibid., p. 189.   [2] Ibid., p. 53.   [3] Ibid., p. 46.   [4] Ibid., pp. 48–49.
[5] Ibid., p. 49.

central tendency of capital intensity were found for all classifications.[1] The small industries rejected were then regrouped 'wherever possible, with fellows of like intensity and products'.[2]

It seems likely that the effects of aggregation could have been accentuated by the measure of investment employed. This included all purchases of new and used investment goods. Disinvestment in capacity for some lines of production could be occurring simultaneously. That this might assume some importance is suggested by the findings on inter-firm differences. The older the existing equipment, the less investment undertaken. Firms with high sales also had a high rate of investment and new equipment. And the lines where this disinvestment was occurring might still be contributing to the measure of net profit; that is, 'that final or ultimate profit figure left after accounting for all possible costs, non-recurring additions and deductions, corporate income taxes, etc.'.[3] Consequently, while investment decisions may be made at the centre, the use of the firm as the unit of observation leads to an aggregation problem that partially conceals the relationship between investment expenditures and profitability.

While cross-section analysis imposes limitations, it also possesses certain advantages: '. . . micro data are much less likely to grossly violate the assumption of independence in successive observations, or to be damagingly collinear, or to require simultaneous equation techniques because of interdependencies between error terms and explanatory variables'.[4] It is true also that there is a greater chance of stability in the universe from which the sample values are derived when the investigation is limited to a few years. But the method does not permit measurement of variables that change only over time.

Briefly, the investment behaviour of the firm was studied by observing the extent to which it diverged from average behaviour; the movement of the average itself from one period to another was not revealed. There is the possibility that the expectations, capital supply conditions, and other factors bearing on investment decisions are common to all firms. If this is so then to employ the cross-section method of analysis might lead to failure to consider the more significant determinants of investment. Nor can it be assumed that the firm's deviation from the average behaviour is produced by

---

[1] *Ibid.*   [2] *Ibid.*, p. 52.   [3] *Ibid.*, p. 65.   [4] *Ibid.*, p. 53.

the same factors that cause the aggregate changes to take place.[1] It may be significant that the limited time series analysis carried out suggested that share prices could exert some influence on investment decisions. The movement of share prices might provide a composite measure of expectations that would tend to be a common factor to all firms.

What were the general findings of this study and what role were profits found to have? The principal existing theories of investment were found to contain a varying amount of empirical truth but none was justified in any claim to superiority. Meyer and Kuh were led to put forward an alternative theory of a highly eclectic nature.[2] They confined their attention to a modern industrial economy where oligopoly was the dominant market situation. Ownership and control of the large companies were assumed to be widely separated and the capital market was assumed to be highly imperfect. The theory makes investment expenditure on fixed and working capital, in the short-run, a residual, equal to the surplus funds realized from current operations, the dividend distribution being treated as established or conventional. Investment expenditure need not be exactly equal to this surplus. The discrepancies would be related to changes taking place in the markets for the firm's products because the maintenance of some sort of fixed relationship between capital stock and output is 'a desired long-run objective of most producers'.[3] The speed with which a firm responds to a change in demand by increasing or decreasing output was held to depend upon the character of the market structure and the extent of competition for market share.[4]

With regard to profits it was reported that 'On a year-by-year basis profits were observed to be generally superior to sales in their ability to explain investment'.[5] 'When the long-run or averaged data results were examined, however, the comparative importance

[1] Cf. Yehuda Grunfeld, Review of Meyer and Kuh, *The Investment Decision, Journal of Political Economy*, LXVI (October 1958), p. 451. See the following comments by Eisner: 'However, a substantial problem in both model formulation and estimation remains because of the intermingling of transitory or stochastic, and permanent changes in sales. We should not expect capital expenditures to be related to transitory changes in final output. Yet regressions such as these, which involve cross section deviations from the means of variables at given points of time, by eliminating the effects of movement of the mean (economy as a whole) over time may reduce the ratio of permanent to transitory variance of sales changes. This may occur because firms may be largely interested in movements of their industry and of the economy and may consider variations around that mean (i.e., variations in market share) as essentially stochastic' ('A Distributed Lag Investment Function', Abstract, *Econometrica*, 27 (April 1959), p. 308).   [2] *The Investment Decision*, pp. 204–205.
[3] *Ibid.*, p. 205.   [4] *Ibid.*   [5] *Ibid.*, pp. 131–132.

of sales and profits is reversed. Sales turns out to be the more powerful explanatory variable with its partial correlation with investment on the average exceeding that of profits with investment by 0·110.'[1] This result was confirmed by Eisner's study: 'Profit variables, while showing positive zero order relations with capital expenditures, do not generally reveal significant coefficients in multiple regressions including sales change variables; profit co-efficients are indeed frequently negative'.[2] This led Eisner to his view that the positive relationship sometimes observed between *ex post* profits and investment stems from the role of profits as a proxy variable for other factors, especially changes in sales which had brought pressure on capacity.

Elsewhere Meyer has referred to an emerging consensus of opinion that investment behaviour can be explained in terms of a capacity-type accelerator model provided the economy is expanding and expectations are buoyant.[3] If this is so, the model should have its best application to industries which are growing rapidly and have considerable growth potential. But this growth context requires that capital be freely available. Such a simple model is inadequate to deal with the full range of investment behaviour. Price expectations, technological change, market share strategy, and product development could have a substantial influence.

Acceleration and Diffusion

The interdependence problem has been implicit in much of the criticism of the investigation carried out by Meyer and Kuh. When the firm is the unit of observation the interdependence between individual investment projects within the firm is ignored. The cross-section analysis concealed the interdependence of invest-ment projects carried out by different firms. Hickman attempted to develop, through disaggregation, an explanation of the downturn in the trade cycle, alternative to the acceleration hypothesis and taking account of the correlation between retardation and diffusion. His analysis can be adapted to the investment behaviour of individual firms.

Hickman challenged the validity of invoking the accelerator to explain how downturns in aggregate investment may occur when total output is retarded; he stressed the importance of other determinants. He sought to show that fixed investment in most manufacturing industries is more nearly a function of the level of output than of its rate of change and that accelerator-induced investment may play a minor role in downturns. His ' . . . positive contribution is to emphasize the fact that a business expansion becomes less widely diffused over the economy as aggregate activity retards, and to show how the individual production *declines* which regularly accompany aggregative *retardation* may induce a downturn of aggregate investment by affecting the capital outlays of the declining industries and by weakening investment incentives generally'.[1] His evidence is derived from quarterly indices of United States total industrial production and real gross expenditure for industrial plant and equipment for the period 1947–58. The totals were broken down into sixteen industry groups.

There are some obvious qualifications to the acceleration principle. It does not operate while there is more than 'normal' excess capacity. Nor are all increases in demand judged permanent and hence as occasions for expansion of capacity. But in general terms investment should lead production at the upper turning points. Production should retard prior to a decline in investment. At the peaks, investment led by two quarters in 1948 and by one in 1953, but turned simultaneously in 1957. In 1948 the lead was long in duration and substantial in amplitude. Production retarded one quarter before the peak in investment. The acceleration principle would seem to be applicable but this expansion began from a position of deficient capacity. To this could be added the uncertainty whether post-war inflation could be checked without a severe depression. These determinants could have been just as important as the rate of change of production. The 1953 lead was briefer and milder than that of 1948 and was affected by shifts in output composition resulting from the Korean war, and then by a boom in civilian goods. In 1957 there was no lead although aggregate production retarded after 1955 and decreased during the first three-quarters of 1956 before rising again to its peak.

Quarterly diffusion indices, that is the percentage experiencing increases, of both production and investment were computed from the data for the sixteen component industries. The diffusion index of production led aggregate production, the downturn in the aggregate usually coming when more than half the industries were

[1] *Op. cit.*, pp. 535–536.

falling. Variations in the rate of change in the aggregate were closely correlated with variations in the diffusion index. The same held good for the investment measures. Investment diffusion lagged the peaks (and troughs) of production diffusion by one or two quarters. 'If investment in each industry were a lagged function of output in that industry and of nothing else, we would observe just such a correlation between the diffusion indexes. As aggregate output retarded, and production declined in more industries, so too with a lag would investment in more industries.'[1] But the correlation is not a perfect one. The component industries are not of equal size and they differ in capital intensity. And investment in the individual industries may not be simply a lagged function of output.

What were the findings at the industry level? In 1947–48 investment lagged in only two of the sixteen industries. However, the expansion was of abnormal character, as already noted. Investment showed a slight lead over production in 1953 but this could perhaps be attributed to autonomous factors. Where such factors were absent or of small importance, investment appeared to be a function of the level of output. At the 1957 peak, which was not complicated by war economy considerations as was the peak of 1953, investment led output in only a small minority of industries, even though production retarded prior to its peak in most industries.

Hickman's investigation, and others for that matter, might have been criticized on the score that it is really the investment decision that is related to the rate of change of production; investment outlays would lag production simply because the expenditures follow the decisions with varying periods of delay. Precise dating of a major investment decision is a difficult matter but at least appropriations should be a better indicator of the timing, although not of the amount, than the actual expenditures. Hickman was able to check on appropriations by using National Industrial Conference Board data for 500 large manufacturing companies.[2] If planned investment is measured by the backlog of unexpired appropriations, there is again a tendency for investment to lag or synchronize with output.

Given this tendency, how does aggregate contraction come about? Retardation is not uniform as between industries. The spread of individual declines may act in several ways to depress aggregate investment.[3] Investment may at times lead in some industries and

[1] *Ibid.*, p. 542.   [2] *Ibid.*, p. 550.   [3] *Ibid.*, pp. 561–564.

there may be autonomous change from outside the industrial sector. The incentive to invest in individual industries may be a function of the degree of diffusion through its influence upon expectations, including possible effects in the capital market.

Investment in stocks must also be considered. Here again Hickman employed the diffusion index technique and reported correlation between sales rate of change and the extent of diffusion.[1] Retardation in the aggregate derived from individual declines; sales and production at all levels moved with sales of final products. This suggests the conclusion that acceleration-induced investments in stocks is not a cause of the downturn although it can be a powerful influence in contraction.

Growth and Profit

Some further aspects of the complexity of investment motivation were developed by Lamfalussy.[2] His empirical investigations failed to reveal any clear relationship between the growth of the capital stock and the level, or the rate of increase, of profits. Nor did he find a clear relationship between growth of capital stock and growth of output and productivity. These findings implied criticism of theoretical attempts to treat investment as a function of such measures as income, sales, output, and profits and were in conflict with the acceleration principle.

Several basic patterns between growth and profit were distinguished in terms of a normal level of profit which represented opportunity costs together with an uncertainty premium. An absolute level was established by using the mean deviation of actual profits to provide a measure of an uncertainty premium which was added to bond yield after the latter had been adjusted for the impact of taxation.[3] However, such a measure does not get around the problem that uncertainty is bound up with expected rather than with realized values. Cyclical sensitivity of realized profits does not necessarily imply uncertainty. The important question is the relationship between the firm's planning horizon and the timing of the fluctuations.

In order to explain the salient features of the capital formation process in a mature economy such as that of Belgium in the years 1948–57, Lamfalussy sought to establish that less than normal

---

[1] *Ibid.*, pp. 551–558.
[2] A. Lamfalussy, *Investment and Growth in Mature Economies* (London: Macmillan & Co., Ltd., 1961).   [3] *Ibid.*, pp. 41–43, 69–71, 79–94.

profits need not lead to disinvestment; that the firm's capital stock may be maintained indefinitely provided the lifespan of that stock is long, the break-up value of the component capital items is substantially lower than their profit-earning value, and the firm's planning horizon is short. But beyond this, capital formation of the deepening kind may be stimulated by a fall in profits below the normal level, provided price elasticity is low and there is substantial change in the factor price ratio. Where the change in factor prices takes the form of a differential rise in labour cost relative to capital cost, substitution of capital for labour will follow—perhaps slowly—and lead to cost reduction as compared with the situation immediately following the rise in labour costs. Even if the firm has to reduce its size, the cost effects of the substitution-induced investment may achieve a net cost reduction.

In a declining market firms may favour innovations that do not require systematic and expensive research; and such innovations may be technological or organizational. To a large extent these innovations may be based upon applications of existing knowledge that has been disregarded by the firm, contrary to the assumptions usually made when specifying the firm's production function. This might be regarded as a consequence of disequilibrium. Until pressure is put upon the firm it lacks the stimulus to explore these possibilities for improvement.

Lamfalussy has argued the case for an association of continuous net investment with persistently low profits. For purposes of the present inquiry the significance of this argument is that the process of attainment of long-run equilibrium may take very many years; although it may be accelerated by rapid change in technology. His analysis brings out the importance of the conditions of supply of capital and labour. It permits emphasis upon the dual aspects of profit as incentive and as a determinant of capital supply. But clearly the motivational significance of the normal level of profit has to be established. Discussion in earlier chapters of this problem is applicable here. Uniformity of response patterns can hardly be expected and timing will be important. Is the response determined by realized profits or by expected profits? Or course, an attempt might be made to avoid this problem by assuming stability of the normal level of profit by measuring it as the average over a comparatively long period. Even this procedure will not usually be adequate. Accounting profits will not always be a satisfactory measure, nor is the risk premium concept adequate. However, the difficulties multiply rapidly if expectational elements are introduced and the analysis extended beyond the individual industry, for in that case the diffusion effects discussed by Hickman must be taken into account.

Decisions on Individual Investment Projects

The findings already dealt with have related to the firm, the industry, or the industrial sector. It is instructive to consider some decisions on individual investment projects. An American research group has reported[1] on four such decisions: accelerated renovation of equipment; new working quarters for a department with a doubtful future; selection of a consulting firm; and choosing a data processing system. To these will be added the introduction of LEO, an electronic computer, by J. Lyons & Company in England.

The case of accelerated renovation of equipment was observed in a firm which attached considerable importance to its safety record. The firm was changing over to magnetic crane controllers as the old controllers wore out. Then a fatal accident led to a general review of problems of crane safety. At a late date in this review, accelerated change over was suggested. Although the safety benefits were extremely hard to estimate and it was at no time established that a magnetic controller would have avoided the particular accident, it was decided to implement the change over as quickly as possible. After that decision had been reached, inquiries were undertaken on costs and other necessary information. Initial cost estimates were based on very limited investigations and were eventually found to be far too low. The estimated time for carrying through the change over increased from two to seven years. The effects upon the firm's other activities were recognized only gradually. After several years, lower levels of activity reduced available funds and the firm reverted to its original policy of installing the new equipment as the old controllers wore out.

The investigations carried out were initiated by an incident which had no direct bearing upon the firm's costs and revenues; they were limited to a few possible courses of action. Attention had previously been drawn to the course of action finally chosen. No precise calculations could be made of a rate of return on the capital outlay. The research group's report implies that the decision was taken

[1] R. M. Cyert, W. R. Dill, and J. G. March, 'The Role of Expectations in Business Decision Making', *Administrative Science Quarterly*, 3 (December 1958), pp. 307–340.

K

initially without regard to costs. But the management did know the equipment was recommended in technical literature and may well have known that it was being used by the firm's competitors. No consideration was given to seeking additional financial resources for the project. The policy was not one of maximization, but of feasibility; a question whether the project could be carried out without adverse effects upon existing conditions.

The second project concerned working quarters for a department with a doubtful future. The existence of the problem had been recognized for some time and there was a conflict of interest between departments. The fastest growing departments felt they could make better use of the facilities. Both restriction of the department's size and complete abandonment had been mooted. The actual search for a new site was stimulated in several ways. A local site became available; and it was planned to re-negotiate the profit-sharing agreements with the departmental managers and a new location might have served as an inducement to the manager to accept lower earnings. The search for alternative sites was exhaustive once an absolute distance limit had been imposed. The cost estimates represented a reasonably comprehensive attempt to assess the value of the property to be acquired to the firm. Where the procedure failed was in accepting the initial proposal for an outside site in lieu of curtailment of the department's activities or even its abandonment. The conflict of interest between departments seems to have barred effectively the way to full consideration of these possibilities once the other proposal had come forward. A number of independent criteria were employed to judge individual sites.

The selection of a consulting firm was part of a larger decision on the installation of an electronic data processing system. Through chance circumstances one firm was selected and it had been agreed generally that this firm would be retained, until someone suggested further inquiries. From a list of a dozen firms, one was chosen by the controller because it was widely known, older, and larger than the original firm. Again a number of criteria were employed: quality of personnel; cost of services; time; availability and scope; location. The balance did not favour clearly either firm. The decision to retain the older firm seems to have been made primarily because the staff members to whom the task was entrusted, interpreted the controller's choice of that firm from a dozen potential ones, as an indication of the preference to top management.

The selection of a data processing system aimed at more effective management control. Two systems were recommended by the consulting firm as both economically feasible and preferable to the existing methods. On the question of cost savings the consulting firm was indifferent initially. But after the management indicated a preference because it believed that one system might have greater potentialities as a general management tool, the consulting firm was able to revise its estimates of cost, giving different weights to uncertain items and showing the preferred system to have a small cost advantage.

The successful introduction of LEO, a large scale electronic computer specially adapted for commercial work, by J. Lyons & Company has been described as 'a long-term speculative investment'.[1] The sums involved were about £100,000 with annual operating costs of £26,000—comparatively small sums for a company with assets of some £40 million, which ranked forty-first in the list of large companies engaged in British industry. The saving in costs was not apparently a major factor. To some extent the outlay appears to have been induced by shortages of labour. The firm's tradition as an innovator no doubt played a part. The excess capacity of the computer might be assumed to ensure additional income from outside sources. Such an installation could be expected to contribute speed and flexibility in future operations, especially in such a highly centralized business organization. On the whole this seems to have been a voluntary decision—subject to the labour shortage influence. It could then be asked if it were the result of a deliberate search or impulsive action. The answer is not clear. But if it were the result of deliberate search, the firm could not have made any precise calculation of discounted net returns for comparison with the merits of other available projects or with a market rate of interest. Rather it would seem that it represented a satisfactory expenditure according to a number of criteria, including profits, and at the same time it was believed to hold a possibility of very substantial cost savings (profits) in the future, when more and more applications could be devised.

Some Discussion of Empirical Findings

What conclusions can be reached about the empirical findings? The use of the firm as the unit of observation may conceal some

---

[1] Pamela Haddy, 'Some Thoughts on Automation in a British Office', *Journal of Industrial Economics*, VI (February 1958), p. 168.

part of the relationship between investment outlays and profits although the changes in product-mix within a period as short as five years, as in the Meyer and Kuh investigation, might not be substantial. However, while the analytical distinction between short- and long-run is valuable, actual changes occur within some period of time and so enter into observations. Furthermore, the cross-section type of analysis does not permit measurement of changes in average behaviour or the effects of factors common to all firms. These qualifying considerations arise from the interdependence problem in its most general form.

One recurring theme in the empirical studies is that the level of demand or sales is the most important single factor in the determination of the current level of capital expenditure. Thus, it might be argued, investment occurs in response to an increase in demand that has been experienced and judged to be permanent. But to say that firms invest when there is pressure on capacity, or that there is demand pressure for some new type of good, is to state a rather obvious condition. This serves to emphasize the short-run nature of the aspects of investment behaviour that were investigated. Similarly, to say that the demand increase must be regarded as permanent, while it is an endeavour to extend the time scope of the analysis, is not enough. Under what conditions will the increase in demand be judged permanent? If this point is not pressed the analysis is once again dealing with the consequences of given expectations without seeking to find out what creates those expectations.

Firms might be regarded as marking time until they are certain that the increase in demand will be permanent. At this stage they could permit some running down of stocks, a growth of waiting lists, and resort to sub-contracting.[1] Competitive position would set limits to the amount of proof of 'permanence' that a firm would seek. In fact, capital expenditures would be a very important part of the firm's market strategy. And in all this activity the firm might be subject to restrictions on the supply of management, labour, finance, and raw materials.

By implication, this stress on the demand conditions tends to minimize the direct influence of profits upon the investment

---

[1] Sub-contracting as a source of flexibility during growth deserves more attention than it has received. Perhaps because of the different rates of return available to firms with limited money capital a large firm can make use of this type of flexibility until it can undertake the particular operation on a scale permitting minimum cost. The consequence for the condition of entry and measures of concentration need consideration.

decision. But there does seem to be something irrational about basing capital expenditures on sales rather than profits. Perhaps the attempts at classification point to an explanation of this contrast. Decisions of a stop-loss nature, those taken impulsively on the occasion of a revealed opportunity, and those taken as the result of a deliberate search, but, at the time of the decision, with the knowledge that more attractive projects might appear later on, may be bound up with sales even when they do not involve an increase in profits. To formulate the theory of investment in terms of sales seems only to make the inducement to invest a matter of technical necessity and to attach insufficient importance, at least in the short-run, to the fact that profits are the source of the internal flow of liquidity and influence capital market status and the availability of external finance. If the problem is posed as that of explaining a negative correlation between investment and profits, this short-run emphasis gives the key to one solution. Is there any reason for expecting firms to respond quickly to a change in profits? The answer depends upon the view taken of the capital budgeting procedure in the large firm and the flexibility of capital expenditure programmes. A moderate degree only of flexibility in capital expenditures which are undertaken intermittently, could lead to a process of building up financial capacity which would weaken the investment-profit relationship but strengthen the relationship between liquidity stock and investment expenditure. Viewed in this way there seems more justification for Heller's statement that 'profits emerge . . . as the key variable to which investment plans are geared. Profits supply not only investment funds but also the evidence of profitability which makes the game worth the candle.'[1]

As a result, attempts have been made to translate forecasted changes in sales into terms of profit. Perhaps the two views come down to the same thing if the firm assumes that profit margins on additional output, in both existing or new lines, will be about the same as those currently obtained.[2] This means that the firm will maintain its average rate of earnings; it is possible that the new activities will yield higher than average returns to offset expected declines in returns from existing activities. Profits are the underlying cause of capital expenditures; sales are the indicator used by

[1] W. W. Heller, 'The Anatomy of Business Decisions', *Harvard Business Review*, XXIX (March 1951), p. 98.
[2] Meyer and Kuh consider that net profits are the best available measure of the firm's profit expectations (*op. cit.*, pp. 65–66).

the firm and for statistical purposes will be a satisfactory explanatory variable. Or is it that the statistical results on the sales variable stem simply from necessary physical conditions in a fully employed and expanding economy?

The Meyer and Kuh investigation led to a residual funds theory of the investment decision. This prompts the remark that the investment decision reached in this way is no decision at all; for the theory can be inferred from a sources and uses of funds statement —with the proviso that the funds are not retained indefinitely in liquid form. Such a theory either ignores sources of funds other than undistributed profits and depreciation allowances, or else postulates a fixed relationship between retained profits and additional funds of all other types. It may imply that the firm has an optimal capital structure.

Ideas of satisfactory profit play some part in these decisions. Perhaps firms are guided by knowledge of costs of competing firms. The range of alternatives considered is often limited and stems from past events. Comparisons of alternatives are often in very approximate terms. This has implications for the assessment of the effectiveness of such policy measures as investment allowances and accelerated depreciation. If it is assumed that precise calculations of investment returns are made by firms, it is possible to explore the relative effectiveness of such measures.[1] But in practice small differences may be ignored. At least one large firm reported that it did not permit initial allowances to have any influence on its investment programmes.

What of search activity and knowledge of investment opportunities? Much of the discussion appears to give inadequate attention to the fact that activity, and hence costs, are involved when the firm seeks to gain additional knowledge of investment opportunities and to make estimates of the cost-revenue outcomes of alternative courses of action.[2] Given such estimates the maximization hypothesis provides a method of translating them into plans, and the execution of the plans can then be examined in the light of the availability of resources.[3] The report on Unilever's capital expenditure provides

[1] Cf. J. Black, 'Investment Allowances, Initial Allowances and Cheap Loans as Means of Encouraging Investment', *Review of Economic Studies*, XXVII (October 1959), pp. 44–49.

[2] Some exceptions are R. M. Cyert, Herbert Simon and Donald Trow, 'Observations of a Business Decision', *Journal of Business of the University of Chicago*, XXIX (October 1956), pp. 237–248; Haddy, *op. cit.*; Cyert, Dill, and March, *op. cit.*

[3] Cf. A. G. Hart, 'Assets, Liquidity, and Investment', *American Economic Review*, XXXIX (May 1949), Proceedings, p. 176.

an illustration. The system described is designed to facilitate the comparison of the returns upon different projects.[1] But the projects are those which local management wants to undertake and believes, in the light of past experience, the central executive will approve. This does not throw much light upon the way in which the investment decisions are reached; although again there is the possibility of interaction between expectations and perception.

Consider the question of the firm's research expenditure policy. If it is based upon estimates of costs and revenues, there is again the possibility of using the maximization hypothesis to derive plans from estimates, provided estimates and experience can be linked. If this problem is set aside, it is possible to examine the laws which govern the returns from, and the costs of industrial research and the factors which determine the theoretical maximum outlay.[2] Undoubtedly the problems of conducting research and development vary with the size of the firm and the structure of the industry.[3] But research expenditures are often judged by the firms to have been successful. What does this mean? Sometimes it means that some successful ideas have been developed in the firm since the research department was established; sometimes it rests upon the public relations skill of the manager of the research department. It would appear that a research department should co-ordinate closely its activities with those of the production and selling departments and that it should take into account the competitive position of the firm, its selling policy, and the practical limits to the size of project which the firm can undertake. Consequently the interdependence problem dominates. No clear answer can be given to the question of what determines the size of the research budget, nor, very often, to the question how research projects are selected. An interesting inquiry would be the relationship of research expenditure to the level of the firm's activities and the availability of internal finance. A

---

[1] See Norton and Wall, *op. cit.*, p. 242.

[2] Cf. J. C. Harsanyi, 'The Research Policy of the Firm', *Economic Record*, XXX (May 1954), pp. 48–60.

[3] Estimates derived from the Board of Trade Census of Production for 1955 show that expenditure on research and development as a percentage of turnover range from 19·4 for aircraft manufacture and repair down to 0·02 in the following industries: tailoring, dressmaking, etc.; boot and shoe: tobacco. (Department of Scientific and Industrial Research, *Estimates of Resources devoted to Scientific and Engineering Research and Development in British Manufacturing Industry*, 1955 (London: H.M.S.O., 1958), p. 24.) But differences in profit margins must be taken into account. For example, Food, Drink, and Tobacco has a low research expenditure in relation to turnover but also has low profit margins. Furthermore, some industries benefit more than others from research carried out by government establishments and in other countries.

neglected feature of search activity links with the nature of the firm and the concept of entrepreneurship. The activity is not confined within the firm; the opportunities may be brought to the firm's notice by other firms, by suppliers of factors, and by buyers of products. 'Not only are organizations looking for alternatives; alternatives are also looking for organizations.'[1]

Despite all these investigations it is not possible to give unequivocal answers to even basic questions about investment decisions. When and under what conditions do firms perceive that investment opportunities exist? Under what conditions do they search for them? Under what conditions are they receptive to suggestions from outside the firm? What estimates are made of the cost-revenue outcomes of various courses of action? Are the estimates adequate for a profit maximizing selection from amongst alternatives? What allowances are made for uncertainty? Do the criteria employed change with the business outlook and with changes in economic policy? Under what circumstances would investment of funds outside the firm be considered? What is the firm's investment horizon? What produces change in the investment horizon? What role do expected profits play in investment planning? How is a balance struck between the advantages of retaining profits and distributing them, so preserving the firm's capital market status? What pressures are there for the distribution of profits?

By using the satisfactory profit concept and by bearing in mind the decision-making processes within the business organization a growth model of the firm could be constructed. What would determine this satisfactory level? This question was touched upon in the previous chapter and will be taken up again in Chapter VII. To the extent that the firm plans to use additional share and debenture capital to supplement retained profit at some time in the future, it is obliged to keep its dividend policy in line with those of other firms. Stability of dividend rate is desirable because from the stock market point of view, fluctuation will be more significant as a measure of uncertainty than from the firm's own point of view. But the stock market looks not only to dividends at present but also to capital gains and growth prospects. It would react to a distribution ratio so high that it impaired the working capital of the firm. Thus given conditions in the capital market, and ignoring the impact of taxation, the firm needs sufficient profits to meet

---

[1] Cyert, Dill, and March, *op. cit.*, p. 338.

shareholders' dividend requirements and to offer at least average prospects of capital gains. The actual distribution ratio would be a matter of balancing these interests in dividends and capital gains against the interest of other sources of finance to ensure that retained and borrowed funds are sufficient to finance the firm's target rate of growth. In this context it could be asked how much space there is between the price ceiling implied by oligopoly analysis and the price floor established by the satisfactory profit approach. For the former has not taken account of the firm's need to expand its capacity with an expanding market; the latter has failed to take account of the firm's ability to take advantage of favourable market developments.

This view of investment decisions must be modified to allow for the process nature of investment activity, with its sequences and lags and interdependence between projects. It seems basically satisfactory in a growth situation. In such circumstances there might be no great difference between saying that a firm seeks to maximize profits and that it seeks to maximize its sales revenue. What if there is no expectation of growth? Then clearly the stimulus to investment must come from other sources; the emphasis shifts to the firm's capital structure and the possibilities of replacement and/or improvement. The steady or contracting market probably inhibits planning as well as financing. This suggests that there is a need for more than one theory. It has been argued already that two different theories are needed: one for periods of prosperity and the other for periods of decline. Further subdivisions according to the rate of growth or age of industry may be required. The age of an industry may be a matter of the ratio of existing demand to potential future demand, modified by some measure of the technical stability of the production processes. Furthermore, these comments do not relate to public investment nor to investment in countries which lack a developed system of business organization and capital markets. It would be interesting to explore the similarities in public investment decisions with some of the business decision-making procedures discussed in this chapter. Perhaps the differences have been over-emphasized and the similarities ignored.

Relevance for the Theory of Profit

The primary purpose of this chapter has not been to develop a complete theory of investment decisions. A number of reasons why it is unsatisfactory to postulate any simple and consistent relations between profit and investment have emerged. Firms differ in organizational qualities and financial structure. Their growth prospects and the industry structures within which they operate are unlikely to be uniform. They face different factor and product market conditions. Does this mean that profit is not an influential factor in the firm's investment decisions? While the incentive effect may be weaker than has been commonly supposed, the significance of profit as the means to growth gives it a key role. For example, a high ratio of undistributed to total profit may come with age of the business organization and that age may imply a greater interest in growth and a lesser interest in short-run profit maximization. However, if the industrial sector of the economy is growing rapidly and full employment levels have been reached, limitations of factor supplies and organizational capacity may emerge.

The role of profit in financing suggests also that the firm which is growing rapidly and planning further growth, will not need to draw a very clear-cut division between net and gross profits. Do the available statistics of profit have any greater relevance to decision-making if this aspect of profit is emphasized? The profits data which were employed in these investment studies have been derived from accounting records and are subject therefore to many of the limitations to be discussed in Chapter VI. The important question is whether accounting profits are the profits a firm might seek to maximize. This applies also to the profits from new investment. These limitations would be less important if it were possible to compare figures, computed according to consistent methods, of expected and actual profits from new investment. The divergence would be a reflection of managerial efficiency as well as of uncertainty. But such information is not readily available; accounting records of profit are mostly of an *ex post* nature.

In themselves profit statements may have only a marginal or indirect effect on the firm's investment behaviour. In the case of inefficient management, they may, for example, draw attention to deterioration of the firm's position. They may influence shareholders and potential lenders. They may generate expectations about operating results of other firms, especially of those firms in the same industry. But in general they will only summarize information that has already been brought to the notice of an efficient management through changes in liquidity or sales. This then is their value in the study of investment behaviour; they provide information that might not otherwise be available to an investigator.

Do the profit statistics need to be revised to bring them into line with theoretical concepts? They do not correspond, but neither do the profits of social accounting and they are believed to be of use. The accountant's profit category is more inclusive than theoretical 'pure' profit and, for this reason, it tends to assume a different role. Here it is necessary to recognize the importance of the institutional framework within which business firms operate. Compare two situations: the one has high profit retention ratios; in the other, all profits are distributed. In the former the retention ratios may be conventionally established; the relationship between investment and accounting profit may be obscured. In the latter case each new investment is like the initial investment which founded the firm. Banking policy, capital market opinion, and the flow of private savings become all-important. Profit, as it enters into a statement of sources and uses of funds and capital budgets, may be more significant than profit as a basis for estimates of future profits.

Aggregate retardation at economy level may be a matter of an increasing proportion of actual declines, rather than a uniform retardation of the industry units that make up the aggregate. What is the significance of this? It may apply with equal force to the individual firms that make up an industry group, and also to the individual product activities of particular firms. This is important because the 'product' of the large firm is changing continually in composition. The typical pattern appears to be that of expansion, stability, and contraction for the firm's individual products. These phases do not coincide necessarily for the individual products. The incentive to invest in individual product development may be a function of the degree of diffusion, through its influence upon expectations, including possible effects in the capital allocation sphere. Consequently, for the study of investment decisions, the firm is not the most satisfactory unit of observation, despite the centralized nature of capital budgeting procedures in the large firm. Since multi-product production is almost universal, details of profits on a product, rather than a firm, basis need to be known.

A further comment concerns the role in economic growth of organization. In Chapter II it was suggested that profit might be regarded as a rent accruing to the organization; and in this chapter organizational capacity as part of the initial stock of capital upon which investment activity builds has been stressed. This leads to the view that organization and capital are complementary. Rising income levels are to be achieved through growth of the capital stock, technological advance, and improvement of managerial technique which take place simultaneously, rather than simply by increasing the capital stock.[1] Of course, this discussion turns very largely upon the definition of capital which is employed, as information and organization could be regarded as capital. Such an emphasis upon the importance of information and organization is supported by studies of the qualities of technically progressive firms. Attention to such matters has an integral part in the development of such firms and can be regarded as a necessary condition for technological change.

Against the background of this chapter and the earlier discussion of uncertainty and alternative profit criteria an attempt will be made in Chapter VII to show the relevance of the nature of the firm and disequilibrium states for the interpretation of empirical findings on investment decisions.

[1] Cf. A. K. Cairncross, 'Reflections on the Growth of Capital and Income', *Scottish Journal of Political Economy*, VI (June 1959), pp. 99–115; Odd Äukrust, 'Investment and Economic Growth', *Productivity Measurement Review*, 16 (February 1959), pp. 35–53; R. M. Solow, 'Investment and Economic Growth: Some Comments', *Productivity Measurement Review*, 19 (November 1959), pp. 62–68.

Chapter VI

INTERPRETATION OF PROFIT STATISTICS

THE available statistics of profit are derived from accounting records so any attempt to examine propositions of economic theory in the light of empirical findings should consider how accounting measures of profit are related to the economist's profit concepts.[1] Of course, it is not possible to satisfy all critics so this chapter is merely an endeavour to clear the ground sufficiently to see whether profit measurements derived from accounting records have any relevance for the theory of profit. From the point of view of some notion of efficiency or productivity interest focuses not on the aggregate profits of the individual firms but rather on those aggregates expressed as rates in relation to turnover or some measure of capital employed. A convenient starting point is the measure of the financial productivity of the firm's activities which relates profit to the shareholders' capital investment together with accumulated undistributed profits; profit is the excess of sales revenue over total cost which includes all contractual cost payments made outside the firm together with the imputed cost of the firm's own resources.

PROFIT MEASUREMENT

The calculation of profit for a given period of time may be shown as follows.[2] Let R = sales revenue; C = currently incurred costs such as raw materials, wages and maintenance charges; D = expenditures made in earlier periods which have to be charged against the current sales revenue, for example, depreciation of plant and equipment and stocks of materials[3] purchased in earlier periods; V = equity capital input, that is, shareholders' direct investment

[1] Some items in the literature of this subject are Joe S. Bain, 'The Profit Rate as a Measure of Monopoly Power', *Quarterly Journal of Economics*, LV (February 1941), pp. 271–293 and *Industrial Organization* (New York: John Wiley & Sons, Inc., 1959), pp. 363–387; F. Sewell Bray, *The Measurement of Profit* (London: Oxford University Press, 1949); Fritz Machlup, *The Economics of Sellers' Competition* (Baltimore: The Johns Hopkins Press, 1952), pp. 217–225, 242–254; George O. May, 'Concepts of Business Income and Their Implementation', *Quarterly Journal of Economics*, LXVIII (February 1954), pp. 1–18; A. G. Pool, 'The Economic and Accounting Concepts of Profit', *Accounting Research*, IV (April 1953), pp. 144–152.

[2] The approach adopted here follows closely that of Bain. See *Industrial Organization*, pp. 363–369.

[3] The distinction between categories C and D cannot be equated with that customarily made between current costs and investment expenditures.

and accumulated undistributed profits; and $i =$ opportunity cost applicable per unit of V. The economist's profit is $R - C - D - iV$ compared with the accounting measure, $R - C - D$. Two methods of measuring profit rates are commonly used: the ratios of profit to sales and to capital employed. For the present V will be accepted as the measure of capital employed. The profit rate on sales is $R - C - D - iV \mid R$. The profit rate on capital employed is $R - C - D - iV \mid V$ which is equal to accounting rate less the opportunity cost of the capital input.

Can these relationships be used to interpret published profit figures for the economist's purposes. If the appropriate value of i is known and it is less than the accounting profit rate on capital employed, then price has exceeded full average cost. Conversely, when i is greater than the accounting profit rate on capital employed, receipts have not been sufficient to cover full average cost. That this affords a rough guide only is apparent from the case of equality of i with the profit rate which might seem to bear some relationship to a state of long-run competitive equilibrium. For equality does not in any way imply stability; it may occur merely as an incident in a process of change without any equilibrium state ever being reached. Can such profit rates be used for inter-firm comparison? Allowance must be made for differences in the ratio V/R; and in an imperfect capital market there is no reason to assume that the same value of i is applicable to all firms, even when they are in the same industry. These and other problems must now be taken up through a consideration of each of the symbols introduced above.

What are the difficulties that arise in the measurement of sales? Suppose first of all that there are two firms which sell identical products; behind equal sales revenues for these identical products may lie substantial differences in degrees of integration which will have implications for costs and hence profits. Similarly, there may be reciprocal relationships between firms which buy from and sell to each other, so that while revenue could be depressed by a concession, it might be compensated by a corresponding reduction in costs. Of course, the measure of sales revenue must be net of goods returned, and due allowance must be made where a firm's product is not sold but is hired—as may happen, for example, with shoe-making or printing machinery. It is assumed usually that sales revenue can be allocated to an accounting period. But the firm's period of production could be much longer than the accounting period with the result that serious allocation problems can exist.

This may be complicated further by progress payments made under contracts.

Costs have been divided into those currently incurred and those incurred in earlier periods. In a sense any period adopted will be artificial. Apart from this consideration it might seem comparatively straightforward to classify such expenditures as raw materials, wages, and maintenance charges as compared with, say, depreciation charges and stock purchases from earlier periods. But there is an allocation problem involved. Practice permits the capitalization and subsequent writing off of such expenses as those relating to the formation of the enterprise, litigation, and research and development in similar fashion to plant and equipment. But this treatment has not been advocated for the organizational resources of the firm. A management unit, for example, has to be created and maintained and with it a complex system of communication and decision-making. Much the same applies to the creation and maintenance of a skilled labour force. Consequently the customary view of the problem of maintaining capital intact is too limited in scope; at least when considering the individual firm, although the same question arises at the macroeconomic level. What are the consequences? In applying the normal accounting methods it would be neccessary to capitalize the relevant proportion of managerial and wages expenditures. What would be the relevant proportion? The extreme difficulty of making any appropriate allowance, in particular the importance of the expectational element, is apparent from the situation of a firm which builds up an organization for a market which in fact never eventuates. The same applies, but in lesser degree, whenever the rate of expansion fails to live up to expectations, even if in one department only of a firm.

Why is this matter of organizational resources of importance? Firstly, there is the time factor. The development of a large business undertaking with complex internal and external relationships takes considerable time: the organizational problems consequent upon mergers are a good illustration. An inadequate organization can of course spell inefficiency and may be the result of too rapid growth. But rapid growth would appear to favour rising productivity not only because the ratio of new investment to replacement investment will be rising and so giving greater scope for technical advance, but also because the growth will be bringing in new personnel and creating an atmosphere in which the perception of possibilities, in terms of methods and costs of production, marketing of existing products, and investment opportunities may be improved. And depreciation allowances may facilitate even more rapid growth. It is a matter of balancing these various gains against the diseconomies of imperfect integration within the business organization.

There has been some study of the relative importance of administrative and production activities but it has been directed towards long-run change and the relationship to size of firm.[1] But for present purposes it is fluctuations of the ratio with the growth of the individual firm that are of interest. Given the relevant statistics it would be necessary to inquire into the relationship between change in administrative expenditure and capital formation in the sense of the development of organizational resources. Organizational resources cannot be measured by the number or cost of personnel, as such a procedure would ignore the whole question of the standard of organizational performance and its relationship to stages of growth; nor can it be assumed that firms adopt the *best* organizational techniques. Further problems arise because substitution may take place between administrative and technical costs. For example, increased expenditure on supervision might lead to lower labour and materials cost.

The real difficulty is to give any precise meaning to *best* in this context. Just as the firm planning expansion of its productive capacities may face a set of long-run cost curves each corresponding to a different planning horizon, so there may be a set of organizational arrangements, each complementary to some stage of growth of the firm. To the extent that administrative cost serves as a measure of organizational capacity, that is by ruling out all types of qualitative change, the fluctuations in administrative cost could be related to the rate of growth of the firm. If these moved together there would seem to be no scope for building up excess organizational capacity in any period. But it would seem much more likely that the rate of growth of the firm would vary, with such excess capacity being developed prior to, or early in, periods of rapid growth. Alternatively, of course, organizational resources might operate as the factor which limits effectively the firm's rate of growth. The large firm will have greater opportunity to build up such excess capacity.

[1] See Seymour Melman, 'The Rise of Administrative Overhead in the Manufacturing Industries of the United States, 1899–1947', *Oxford Economic Papers*, N.S., 3 (February 1951), pp. 62–93; 'Production and Administration Cost in Relation to Size of Firm', *Applied Statistics*, III (March 1954), pp. 1–11; *Dynamic Factors in Industrial Productivity* (Oxford: Basil Blackwell, 1959), Chapter 17; E. T. Penrose, *The Theory of the Growth of the Firm* (Oxford: Basil Blackwell, 1959), pp. 202–204.

This will be a factor in the explanation of relative growth rates of large and small firms.

These remarks suggest several ways in which category C costs might be overstated in a given period and lead to understatement of current profits. The expenses of organizational development, research and production development, and creation and maintenance of an integrated and specialized labour force are examples. Periods of rapid growth would accentuate this tendency. Furthermore, such matters are relevant to the comparison of profit of rapidly growing and more slowly growing firms. If large firms grow more rapidly than small ones, their growth will have been fostered in the several ways mentioned above—really organizational development and research are part of the process of growth—and they may show a lower rate of profit than small and medium sized firms. This difference in profit, to which must be added the effect of depreciation being influenced by rate of growth, might be regarded, on the one hand, as a consequence of the different nature of the activities of the firms, or, on the other hand, as a result of the failure consistently to apply the rule of matching costs and revenue. In so far as this indicates a transfer of expenditure from category C to category D in appropriate circumstances, the distribution of such expenditure over future periods also has to be considered. This point is taken up when discussing category D costs.

What other charges are there that would enter into category C? Consider interest payments. These, unlike raw materials and wages, do not reflect current prices levels. Furthermore, their treatment depends upon the concept of capital employed. If the V concept is employed, interest charges will be included in costs; if, however, loan funds are added to equity in order to allow for gearing differences in inter-firm comparison, interest must be included in profit in order to measure the financial productivity of the total capital employed. Another item of current costs that has implications for the capital employed concept is hiring charges: a high proportion of hired to owned equipment would yield a different capital-output ratio compared with fully owned equipment which has the same capacity. Subcontract purchases also might fall in category C. These may be inflexible because of contract terms; and temporary either because they are employed to meet a peak demand, or because the firm at some later date plans to integrate such activities within its own organization. Considering the composition of category C costs, some of the components need not reflect fully changes in

L

price levels. Even if price levels do not change, firms which produce the same product may have different cost structures reflecting different factor proportions.

Category D costs comprise costs of materials bought in earlier periods, depreciation charges, and relevant parts of current expenditures in previous periods deemed to have been of a capital nature. The distribution of the amounts over time may be determined by conventional methods, say, the writing off of preliminary expenses or formation expenses over a period of five years, or of machinery over twenty years. These conventions may be related to the experience of the firms or be influenced by statutory requirements; for example, tax legislation. Ideally, however, the principle of matching costs and revenues involves a judgement of the financial productivity of the original outlays and the time distribution of the returns. The doctrine of conservatism reinforces a tendency to accelerate depreciation and firms are sometimes reluctant to scrap assets which still possess book value, even where the procedure followed in writing down their book values has been to a great extent arbitrary. What of the charges associated with redundant capacity? These point to errors in past allocations. What of the charges associated with excess capacity? These give rise to user cost which is the difference between depreciation charges for the unused plant and equipment and the corresponding charges when the plant and equipment is in use. This difference would more properly be grouped in category C. This raises the problem of normal capacity utilization, with possible inter-industry (and international) differences, attributable in part to relative factor availabilities.

EFFECTS OF CHANGES IN THE LEVEL OF PRICES

Category D costs will not reflect changes in price levels unless the firm decides upon asset revaluation. This makes it necessary to inquire what are the effects upon the measures of profit of changing price levels.[1] By way of illustration consider the following comment:

It is well known that changes in the price-level can alter the accountant's figures for cost and profit. A firm's inputs are normally charged in accounts at their

---

[1] This subject possesses an extensive literature: K. Lacey, *Profit Measurement and Price Changes* (London: Sir Isaac Pitman & Sons, Ltd., 1952); American Institute of Accountants, *Changing Concepts of Business Income* (New York: The Macmillan Company, 1952); W. T. Baxter, 'The Accountant's Contribution to the Trade Cycle', *Economica*, N.S., XXII (May 1955), pp. 99–112; *Royal Commission on the Taxation of Profits and Income, Final Report* (London: H.M.S.O., 1955); R. C. Jones, *Effects of Price Level Changes on Business Income, Capital, and Taxes* (Columbus: American Accounting Association, 1956). *Changing Concepts of Business Income* provides a useful bibliography (pp. 302–307).

acquisition price; and so—unless inputs and sale are simultaneous—the cost side of a revenue account must reflect an earlier price level than the revenue sale. When prices are rising, accounting costs tend to be low relative to replacement costs, and so profit looks large; when prices are falling, accounting cost is relatively high and profit small. Perhaps we may—rather tendentiously—use the phrase 'historic cost error' to describe the gap between accounting profit and the profit figure that would be found if inputs were charged at the replacement prices ruling at sale dates. This latter profit may be called 'corrected profit'.[1]

This argument that accounting method accentuates business fluctuations seems plausible. Alternate over- and understatement of profits is held likely to affect the amplitude of fluctuations through its influence on attitudes, on the supply of credit, and on consumption and investment decisions. In addition, taxation may have an effect upon managerial decisions.

The significance of this accounting error depends upon the combination of valuation methods and the extent of the price changes. Original and replacement cost valuation and pricing procedures will lead to the same accounting profit, provided the difference between original and replacement cost is small. Inconsistent procedures—for example, costing on an original cost basis whilst pricing on a replacement cost basis—can lead to the inflation of accounting profit through the inclusion of stock appreciation. Is it possible to assess the magnitude of the corrections called for and to obtain some idea of the relative importance of its component parts? Several such attempts have been made.

United States

For United States manufacturing companies over the period 1946–52 profits were overstated by 16 per cent, and the ratio of the understatement of capital consumption to the stock valuation adjustment was 1·36.[2] However, there is an important qualification to be added. The current value depreciation figures were compared with the allowable depreciation charges which may differ from the sums actually charged in published accounts. A more recent computation sets the excess of the figures reported for income tax purposes over the decade 1947–56 at 31 per cent.[3] This excess was the result of the depreciation and stock components together with the special amortization provisions after 1950. The inventory

---

[1] Baxter, *op. cit.*, p. 99. Presumably 'revenue sale' should read 'revenue side'.
[2] See Table 1.
[3] George Terborgh, *Corporate Profits in the Decade 1947–56* (Washington: Machinery and Allied Products Institute, 1957), p. 7.

TABLE I

RATE OF RETURN ON NET WORTH FOR
U.S. MANUFACTURING CORPORATIONS

| Year | Percentage Return | |
	As Reported	Adjusted for Price Changes
1929	8·72	8·38
1939	6·60	4·99
1940	8·94	7·96
1941	12·80	8·09
1942	10·55	7·73
1943	10·31	7·84
1944	9·73	8·09
1945	6·71	5·13
1946	10·94	5·06
1947	15·37	7·66
1948	15·25	9·75
1949	10·77	8·63
1950	14·76	7·77
1951	11·59	6·74

Source: R. C. Osborn, *Corporate Profits: War and Postwar* (Urbana: University of Illinois, 1954), p. 32.

adjustment was erratic, as it reflected price movements within the accounting period. But the depreciation adjustment changed slowly in response to cumulative price changes. The effects of the stock valuation adjustment have been described as follows:

Short-term swings in profits are generally more marked in this measure [i.e., book profits before tax unadjusted for inventory valuation] than in the series adjusted for inventory valuation . . ., because of the tendency for expansion of business activity to be accompanied by rising prices and associated inventory gains and for contraction to coincide with price declines and inventory losses. This pattern was distorted somewhat in the early post-war period—inventory gains following price decontrol carried book profits upward on an annual basis from 1945 to 1946 in the face of a decline in national income—but was clearly apparent in later years. The comparative movements of profits with and without the inventory valuation adjustment from 1945 to the first nine months of 1955 were very similar, each measure advancing by about 125 per cent.

In long-run comparisons significant differences may arise, e.g., from a secular change in inventory-sales ratios, from a curvilinear price trend, or from changes in accounting methodology.[1]

[1] H. D. Osborne and J. B. Epstein, 'Corporate Profits since World War II', *Survey of Current Business*, 36 (January 1956), p. 19.

At least in the United States the effect of secular change should have been slight. The sales-stock ratio in retail trade was stable in the period 1938–54, varying between 5·1 and 7·0.[1]

These studies have not attempted to examine inter-industry differences in depreciation adjustments. It is apparent, however, that different capital intensities and different degrees of change in the relevant price indices would exist and so lead to different percentage adjustments. Similarly with the stock valuation adjustment which was concentrated in trade and manufacturing.

Australia

For Australian companies over the period 1945–46 to 1952–53 the ratio of depreciation adjustment to stock appreciation was 0·15.[2] The depreciation adjustment grew steadily with continuing inflation while stock appreciation, although positive throughout the period, fluctuated considerably, with the result that the ratio of depreciation adjustment to stock appreciation also varies considerably. Table 3 shows both these adjustments on an industry basis. The ratio ranges from 1·37 for Gas and Electricity down to 0·07 for Vehicles.

TABLE 2

DEPRECIATION AND STOCK VALUATION ADJUSTMENTS
TO THE PROFITS OF AUSTRALIAN COMPANIES

Year	Depreciation Adjustment £Am	Stock Appreciation £Am
1945–46	—	2·7
1946–47	1	14·1
1947–48	3	39·4
1948–49	5	43·0
1949–50	7	65·4
1950–51	12	140·3
1951–52	20	135·7
1952–53	21	26·8

Source: Russell Mathews and J. McB. Grant, *Inflation and Company Finance* (Sydney: Law Book Co. of Australasia Pty. Ltd., 1958). For stock appreciation see Table V–5, p. 60; for depreciation see Table VI–6, p. 82.

[1] R. W. Campbell, 'A Comparison of Soviet and American Inventory-Output Ratios', *American Economic Review*, XLVIII (September 1958), pp. 558–559. The U.S.S.R. data show a much greater variation (3·6 to 18·0) and a considerable decline.

[2] See Tables 2 and 3.

TABLE 3

DEPRECIATION AND STOCK VALUATION ADJUSTMENTS TO
THE PROFITS OF AUSTRALIAN COMPANIES, 1945–46—1952–53

Industrial Group	Stock Appreciation £Am	Depreciation Adjustment £Am	Ratio
Rural	4·6	2·8	0·61
Mining	5·3	2·2	0·41
Engineering	93·1	13·3	0·14
Vehicles	23·0	1·7	0·07
Textiles	28·0	2·5	0·09
Clothing	20·6	1·8	0·09
Rubber, Leatherware . . .	7·8	1·7	0·22
Food, Drink, Tobacco . . .	43·0	8·1	0·19
Paper, Printing . . .	16·7	4·2	0·25
Wood Products and other manufactures	43·0	8·4	0·20
Gas and Electricity	2·2	3·0	1·37
Transport, Communication . .	5·0	5·1	0·98
Commerce, etc. . . .	170·8	13·3	0·08
Building and Construction . .	3·6	0·8	0·22
All Groups	466·7	68·9	0·15

Source: Russell Mathews and J. McB. Grant, Inflation and Company Finance (Sydney: Law Book Co. of Australasia Pty. Ltd., 1958), pp. 60, 82.

The ordering of industrial groups which emerges depends upon capital intensities and relative price changes. But within a period of this length the normal stock-sales ratios may have changed and accounting methods may have been revised to take account of the overstatement of profit. The more rapid the inflation the more likely does revision of accounting methods seem.

United Kingdom

For the United Kingdom the discrepancy between 'true' profits after maintaining capital intact and accounting profits as calculated for taxation purposes has not been in the main due to inadequate depreciation allowances, as is apparent in Table 4. The inadequacy of depreciation allowances has been most marked for public corporations, public authorities, and house owners. For companies alone, and including initial and investment allowances with the depreciation allowed for taxation purposes, the total depreciation charges were close to, and at times in excess of, depreciation estimated on the basis of replacement cost. These results diverge from those of Redfern, a partial explanation being that Redfern worked on straight line depreciation.[1] Most British companies, for purposes of taxation at least, work on a diminishing balance method, so giving more weight to recent investment and leading to higher depreciation charges in a period of rapid inflation.[2]

How important was stock appreciation? Paish states that ' . . . a really serious degree of over-estimation of profits and of over-taxation has occurred through including in profits the rise in the value of inventories due entirely to changes in price. . . . It is largely the check to the rise in prices which occurred after 1951, and the consequent disappearance of the fictitious element of stock appreciation in taxable profits, that accounts for the fall in the proportion of true profit which had had to be paid or set aside for tax, from 69 per cent. in 1951 to 59 per cent. in 1952, and 54 per cent. in 1953 and 1954.'[3]

These results may be compared with the estimates by the Central Statistical Office which has endeavoured to estimate the extent to which annual depreciation allowances of companies would have been higher had there been no initial allowances. The results are shown in Table 5. The different methods of estimating depreciation yielded

TABLE 4

UNITED KINGDOM COMPANIES' DEPRECIATION

£m

	1948	1949	1950	1951	1952	1953	1954
Annual Allowance for Tax . .	207	220	241	253	273	313	363
Initial and Investment Allowances.	95	184	232	236	109	97	142
Total Allowed for Tax . .	302	404	473	489	382	410	505
Estimated at replacement cost .	280	300	330	390	450	480	510
Annual Allowance as percentage of replacement cost estimate .	74	73	73	65	61	65	71

Source: F. W. Paish, 'Company Profits and their Distribution since the War', *District Bank Review*, 114 (June 1955), p. 13.

[1] P. Redfern, 'Net Investment in Fixed Assets in the United Kingdom, 1938–1953', *Journal of the Royal Statistical Society*, Series A (General), 118, Part 2 (1955), pp. 141–192.
[2] Cf. F. W. Paish, 'Company Profits and their Distribution since the War', *District Bank Review*, 114 (June 1955), pp. 12, 14. The straight line method has been employed by the Central Statistical Office. See Central Statistical Office, *National Income and Expenditure, 1958* (London: H.M.S.O.), p. 82.   [3] *Op. cit.*, p. 14.

TABLE 5

UNITED KINGDOM COMPANIES' DEPRECIATION

£m

	1950	1951	1952	1953	1954	1955	1956	1950–56
Annual, Initial and Investment Allowances	474	492	398	407	520	602	686	3,579
Annual Allowances	247	254	287	303	363	415	480	2,349
Annual Allowances assuming no initial allowances	282	307	357	374	434	483	544	2,781
C.S.O. estimates of capital consumption	329	376	416	455	499	567	615	3,257

Source: Second Report of the Council on Prices, Productivity and Incomes (London: H.M.S.O., August 1958), p. 38.

similar results. On an historical cost basis (adjusted annual allowances) net profits were approximately 3 per cent higher than when the C.S.O. estimates of capital consumption were employed.[1] Deduction of stock appreciation from trading profits involved a reduction of 6·8 per cent for the whole period 1950–56.

There are many important problems involved in such estimates. For example, the Central Statistical Office figures of capital consumption for the period before 1948 employed Redfern's price indices which are average values per unit, or more often per ton, as shown by the census of production or export statistics. The indices for later years are based on price data collected by the Board of Trade and used in the estimation of gross fixed capital formation at 1948 prices.[2] But technological and organizational progress may invalidate such an index method; there may be no connection between replacement cost valuation where the capital goods are measured by the ton and the figure yielded by an index number calculation, although the direction of the bias will be known. This criticism can be made also of the United States and Australian calculations. Then there is the arbitrariness of the assumptions made about length of life of assets. For these and other reasons it must be recognized that a considerable margin of error is involved in any estimates of capital consumption. This is accentuated when any attempt is made at international comparisons.

[1] Ibid., p. 39. This applied to the whole period 1950–56 and to 1956 alone.
[2] See Central Statistical Office, op. cit., p. 84.

The essential points to emerge are the changing relative importance of the depreciation and stock valuation adjustments, the latter being the more variable in a continuing inflation. International and inter-industry differences are apparent and are associated with different capital intensities, relative price changes, and stock policies. Similarly, variations at the firm level, where both investment in plant and equipment and investment in stocks become part of business strategy, should be expected. In assessing the operating results of individual firms it would be necessary to take account of labour and organizational aspects. Liquidity, too, would have to be examined. These points are rather obvious but they must be drawn within the theoretical framework in an attempt to show the relationship between the two types of definitions of profit. Evaluation of results on the basis of the conventional profit rate appears to have assumed the adequacy of managerial resources and the appropriateness of capital structure. On the question of the depreciation adjustment it is tempting, because of all these difficulties, to hold that ' . . . it seems reasonable to suppose that the answer given by the firm itself—that implied by the depreciation it charges—will, in the event, prove to have been a better forecast than that of an outsider'.[1] However, this is not really a solution. Firms might consistently charge too much or too little in the context of their own policies.

CAPITAL EMPLOYED

Before turning to the question of the influence of accounting method upon business decisions, it remains to consider the symbols V and i which represent equity capital input and its opportunity cost rate of interest. Any departure from the financial productivity approach requires a decision about what funds constitute capital.[2] Loans, bank overdraft, even trade credit, might be included depending upon the purpose of the measurement. An alternative approach is to look at the assets and ask whether they are being used in the business. Investments, some portion of liquid funds, and expenditures which though capitalized in the past are not expected to be revenue

[1] Jack Downie, *The Competitive Process* (London: Gerald Duckworth & Co., Ltd., 1958), p. 38.
[2] Cf. C. L. Parker, 'Capital Employed: The Need for a Definition of Capital Employed for use in Measuring Remuneration Earned', *Journal of Industrial Economics*, III (April 1955), pp. 134–143; I. P. Andren, 'Monopoly Investigation and Methods of Calculating the Rate of Return on Capital Employed', *Journal of Industrial Economics*, IV (October 1955), pp. 1–15; Aubrey Silberston and David Solomons, 'Monopoly Investigation and the Rate of Return on Capital Employed', *Economic Journal*, LXII (December 1952), pp. 781–801.

producing in the future might be excluded for some purposes, the decision resting partly upon the length of the time period being considered. Consider the case of trade investments. In a short period study attempting to relate monopoly in the product market to the firm's rate of profit these might be excluded even though in the short period they might be indicative of relative cost advantages in conditions of supply of raw materials. In a long period they might be related to investment opportunities and integration changes which would be clearly relevant to the firm's activities. Some of these difficulties arise because the unit of observation is the firm which may be producing a range of products with different but stable gross profit margins. In such cases it might well seem virtually impossible to apply the concept of capital employed and arrive at a measure of the assets employed in the production of a particular product.

The defects of internal measures of capital employed have led to a number of attempts to work with stock market valuations. For example, Gordon and Shapiro formulated an approach to the selection of investment opportunities on the basis of a required rate of profit which assumed that the firm sought to maximize the market value of the shareholders' equity.[1] The marginal return on investment would then be equated to the market rate of return on the company's shares plus a factor representing the rate at which the dividend is expected to grow. Similarly, Modigliani and Miller have sought to explain the valuation of firms and shares under conditions of uncertainty by assuming that the crucial test of an investment project is whether it will raise the market value of the company's shares.[2] Market valuation was also employed by Hart and Prais as a measure of size for the purpose of studying business concentration.[3] As a starting point it might be noted that share prices, while they are current prices, are volatile. Averaging can be a solution for some purposes, but it has limitations: for example, it may be inappropriate to group companies other than by some initial

---

[1] M. J. Gordon and Eli Shapiro, 'Capital Equipment Analysis: The Required Rate of Profit', *Management Science*, 3 (October 1956), pp. 102–110. See also M. J. Gordon, *The Investment, Financing and Valuation of the Corporation* (Homewood, Illinois: Richard D. Irwin, Inc., 1962).

[2] Franco Modigliani and M. H. Miller, 'The Cost of Capital, Corporation Finance and the Theory of Investment', *American Economic Review*, XLVIII (June 1958), pp. 261–297.

[3] P. E. Hart and S. J. Prais, 'The Analysis of Business Concentration: A Statistical Approach', *Journal of the Royal Statistical Society*, Series A (General), 119, Part 2 (1956), pp. 150–181; P. E. Hart, 'Business Concentration in the United Kingdom', *Journal of the Royal Statistical Society*, Series A (General), 123, Part 1 (1960), pp. 50–58.

measure of size as, for example, in the measurement of concentration. They may also be a tendency for yields on the shares of companies operating in the same 'industry' to converge, and this market phenomenon may bear no relationship to size of the individual firms.[1]

The essential features of the problem are brought out by Florence's attempt to use the stock exchange value of the shares and debentures of public companies to measure their size.[2] For the larger English public companies in the industrial and commercial and the brewery sections of the *Stock Exchange Year Book* this measure was used to compare rates of growth between 1936 and 1951 of small and very large companies. The results were compared with those obtained using the book gain in net tangible assets as the measure of size. By the first measure the smaller companies grew at about the same rate on average as the larger companies; by the second measure the larger companies grew very definitely more than the smaller companies. Florence considered this contradiction to be a logical consequence of the basis of stock exchange valuations and summed up his argument by stating that 'The increase in the market value of its stocks and shares can be a very unsatisfactory measure of growth of a firm. To some extent, indeed, it measures the opposite of growth, namely the degree to which a company divests itself of assets by paying *out* dividends, rather than building up its resources.'[3]

The primary importance of distribution policy undoubtedly holds in the short period determination of ordinary share prices, but even in the short period does not extend to the pricing of non-participating preference shares and debentures. Ordinary share prices may vary directly with dividend distribution ratios at any given time. However, when considering changes over a period of fifteen years it becomes necessary to take account of the process of growth of firms and of expectations that their growth will continue. Price appreciation over such a period is likely to be associated with the proportion of profits not distributed. Short period pricing on the stock exchange may be in large part a guessing game, with special importance attached to the current rate of dividend, but over longer

[1] Cf. F. A. Wells, 'The Relationship between Physical and Financial Comparisons of Productivity', *Inter-Firm Comparison* (Paris: European Productivity Agency of the Organization for European Economic Co-operation, 1957), p. 342.

[2] See P. Sargant Florence, 'New Measures of the Growth of Firms', *Economic Journal*, LXVII (June 1957), pp. 244–248; D. M. Lamberton, 'New Measures of the Growth of Firms: A Comment', *Economic Journal* LXVIII (September 1958), pp. 593–595.

[3] *Ibid.*, p. 247.

periods share prices probably reflect the value of expected dividends and other benefits, partially discounted at present, or expected, rates of interest. Even the stock exchange could not for long disregard the unwisdom of a distribution ratio so high that it impaired the efficiency of the firm by reducing its share of the market and its credit worthiness.

In the absence of conversion and voting rights the prices of non-participating preference shares and debentures tend to be dominated by considerations of security rather than dividends. An increased distribution to ordinary shareholders would, *ceteris paribus*, reduce security and so reduce market price. In so far as rising prices for these types of securities are associated with higher dividend distributions, this reflects expectations of continuing growth and profits which may bring greater security, or, perhaps, preferential rights to further issue of securities.

If dividend distribution policies are unlikely to account for the contradiction reported by Florence, some other explanation must be sought. The years 1936 and 1951 were considered comparable because each showed peaks in share prices rising about 13 per cent over the average of the four neighbouring years, but this condition may not be a sufficient safeguard. Price level is a factor determining change in share prices.[1] As shares at low prices tend to change more percentagewise than higher priced shares, the distribution of low and high prices as between the small and large company groups is important. The extent of subdivision of shares and bonus issues would need to be taken into account.[2] In addition, the shares of debtor firms show greater appreciation in the market during a period of inflation than do the shares of creditor firms.[3] This being so, the financial structure of the companies in the two groups would need investigation. Significant changes could occur in a period of fifteen years. It is also possible that while 1936 and 1951 were peaks about the same distance above the average of the four neighbouring years, they may not have represented fluctuations of equal amplitude about the trend of share prices. Whether these factors could account for the contradiction could only be established by thorough examination

[1] See S. Szatrowski, 'The Relationship between Price Changes and the Price Level for Common Stocks', *Journal of the American Statistical Association*, 40 (1945), pp. 467–483.

[2] It appears that in England very large companies have revalued more than smaller companies. See S. J. Prais, 'The Financial Experience of Giant Companies', *Economic Journal*, LXVII (June 1957), p. 254.

[3] See R. A. Kessel, 'Inflation-caused Wealth Redistribution: A Test of a Hypothesis', *American Economic Review*, XLVI (March 1956), pp. 128–141.

of the share price distribution and trend and the financial structure of the companies included in the sample.

So much for stock market valuations as measures of capital. On what other basis might estimates be made? Insurance valuations have been used as a measure of the current net worth of assets employed.[1] This measure is not entirely satisfactory. It is available for some assets only. But at least it is readily available. The rate of profit based on insurance figures has been found in a sample study to be always lower than that on book values, varying from below one-half to nearly two-thirds.[2] But consistency in this relationship could hardly be expected.

The remaining symbol is i, the opportunity cost applicable per unit of equity capital input. The essential features to note about i are, firstly, that it should be net of risk allowances; and secondly, that it should relate to an investment for a comparable period. Neither of these are amenable to precise measurement. There is also the closely related matter of taxation. Much of the discussion of depreciation and stock valuation adjustments has been directed to the question whether conventional accounting methods lead to excessive taxation, depletion of funds and so to increased reliance upon the capital market. This draws attention to the fact that the profit concept is usually defined as before the levying of taxes. But obviously the financial productivity view must be concerned with the profit return after tax payments. The extended discussion of the shifting of company tax does not appear to have reached definite conclusions.[3] Marginal analysis tends to support the view that such taxes could not be shifted because they have no direct effects on costs or on demand and there is little opportunity to avoid tax payments. However, rival views have been put forward. For example, it has been suggested that if some positive rate of return after taxes is a necessary cost in order to maintain and increase the economy's capital stock, 'Levying a tax on corporate net income drives a wedge, so to speak, between sales revenue and conventional long-run

[1] See, for example, T. Barna, 'The Replacement Cost of Fixed Assets in British Manufacturing Industry in 1955', *Journal of the Royal Statistical Society*, Series A (General), 120, Part I (1957), pp. 1–36.   [2] Wells, *op. cit.*, p. 343.

[3] See, for example, Nicholas Kaldor, *An Expenditure Tax* (London: George Allen & Unwin, 1955), pp. 141–172; M. A. Adelman, 'The Corporate Income Tax in the Long Run', *Journal of Political Economy*, LXV (April 1957), pp. 151–157; D. M. Soule, 'Shifting of the Corporate Income Tax: A Dynamic Analysis', *Journal of Finance*, XIV (September 1959), pp. 390–402; Martin R. Gainsbrugh and J. Frank Goston, 'Income Taxes and Inflation', and Emerson P. Schmidt, 'Taxation and Business', *Inflation. Annals of the American Academy of Political and Social Science* (Philadelphia, 1959), pp. 63–70 and 71–78 respectively.

cost, which requires that sales revenue be increased or cost of production reduced if former after-tax earnings are to be restored'.[1] A further aspect of taxation is that firms may respond by seeking to maximize profits, not by increasing sales revenue or reducing costs of production, but by minimizing taxation—assuming here that taxes are not already being included with costs. Such minimization may take place not only through evasion but also through trading in accumulated losses and successful efforts to influence tax legislation.

Accounting Method and Business Decisions

This seems an appropriate point at which to ask whether the errors of accounting method have any real significance. The details of business operations find their way into the accounting records of firms and so it is legitimate for the economist to inquire into accounting method and its influence upon business decisions. It is sometimes argued that although error occurs in accounting statements, it has little or no effect upon business decisions, in particular that it does not accentuate business fluctuations.[2] As the opposing view has been widely held for some time, it seems desirable to inquire into the logical implications of this view. Three possibilities arise: firstly, business management must be able to assess accurately and allow for the errors; or, secondly, management must make its decisions without regard to the record of the results of past operations; or, thirdly, the errors must be of such magnitude as to make no difference to decisions based upon recorded operating results. While it has been generally accepted that firms make some corrections to operating results it has seldom been suggested that operating results, as distinct from capital outlays,[3] are irrelevant. The basic problem is that at least a partial explanation of the way firms behave may be what they think are their profits both in terms of rates of return and availability of funds internally for investment.

Profit theory may have remained in a confused state but the contributions discussed in earlier chapters have at least clarified the distinction between the *ex ante* and *ex post* concepts. The former should properly be treated as part of the theory of expectations while

---

[1] Soule, *op. cit.*, pp. 394–395.

[2] See, for example, Delmas D. Ray, *Accounting and Business Fluctuations* (Gainesville, Florida: University of Florida Press, 1960).

[3] For example, Joan Robinson suggests that 'the man of deeds' is not concerned with valuing existing plant ('The Production Function and the Theory of Capital', *Review of Economic Studies* XXI (1953–54), p. 84).

any theory of *ex post* or realized profit, with which accounting is concerned, should aim at explaining the magnitude of that profit, its indirect contribution to the formation of expectations, and its significance as a means to action.

Accounting method would accentuate business fluctuations by way of investment decisions if investment is directed to the maximization of expected profits, which are based upon past profits as measured by accounting methods. Now it has been assumed frequently that past results do provide a basis for expectations. Keynes contended that producers operate upon 'the assumption that the most recently realized results will continue, except in so far as there are definite reasons for expecting a change'.[1] This view has suited the econometricians and model builders as it enables them to treat the firm's plans as related in simple ways to current conditions. Some interesting evidence in support of the view that expected values are simple extrapolations of current income is provided by business forecasts made for purposes of the United States capital-stock tax and declared-value excess profits tax repealed by the Revenue Act of 1945. These taxes had the effect of reducing tax liability the more precisely income was forecast. The data suggest that expected income changed almost in proportion to changes in current income.[2] However, even if it is granted that expectations are extrapolations of current experience, they need not be based upon profits; sales might serve equally well.

A more realistic view is that the firm does not itself know the answers to the questions that the economist asks, is unlikely to make important decisions if it believes that much additional relevant information is forthcoming, and will probably postpone decisions until events compel the adoption of some line of action. In a dynamic economy it is to be expected that the 'definite reasons for expecting a change' will be numerous so that the 'recently realized results' will be only one of a number of factors contributing to decision-making. The indirect influence of error in those results through the formation of expectations must seem normally to be slight. However, knowledge of the determinants of business expectations is limited, attention having been concentrated upon the influence of given expectations. Profit statements may assume an unwarranted objectivity

[1] J. M. Keynes, *The General Theory of Employment, Interest, and Money* (London: Macmillan & Co., Ltd., 1936), p. 51.
[2] See E. Cary Brown, 'Some Evidence on Business Expectations', *Review of Economics and Statistics*, XXXI (August 1949), pp. 236–238.

in the eyes of managerial personnel when they find it extremely difficult to quantify so many of the other factors that have to be taken into account. They may, of course, say that accounts play little part in their decisions believing that it is a flair for business decisions that is really important.

But what of the possible influence upon the means to action? Perhaps the three essentials of action to achieve business expansion are customers, staff, and funds. Funds are placed third and last, not because their availability may not be of crucial importance in many enterprises, but because the large firms that dominate in most industries today can usually manage to overcome financing problems for reasons to be mentioned below. Customers can be obtained in a variety of ways: lowering of prices, product differentiation, diversification, aggressive selling policies, business reciprocity, and takeovers. With price cutting out of favour in oligopolistic industries the earning of profit appears to be virtually a prerequisite for any of these measures in so far as additional expenses are involved. This view is reinforced in the cases of product differentiation, diversification, and aggressive selling policies, by the likelihood that departmental allocations of funds will be channelled towards those departments which are believed to have been most profitable in the past. Reciprocity may appear a useful remedy for contracting sales and reduced profits but here again, except in so far as these movements reflect a general contraction in the industry, profits can be held to be important because the other party to a reciprocal trade agreement will have a strong preference for association with a successful firm. Takeovers not involving cash can be a very simple means to expansion, subject to limits if the firm does set maximization of the market value of its shares as its objectives. But acquisition terms depend upon market valuation of shares and a positive relationship between share prices and disclosed profits seems reasonably well grounded outside of short period fluctuations. Within a short period share market fluctuations will influence the proportion of cash required in a takeover settlement.

Availability of management and technical staff appears to be a limiting factor upon the expansion or, at least, upon the rate of expansion of many firms. It would seem that unprofitable declining industries may experience more difficulty in recruiting first-grade managerial personnel than do profitable expanding industries. Ignoring the likely differences in rates of managerial remuneration, the significant point is that profitable firms in declining industries do succeed in achieving and maintaining high standards of management. This appears to be borne out by some recent investigations in the United Kingdom.[1] The possibility that profit statements can influence the supply of entrepreneurship to an industry, and the distribution of supply as between industries, should not be ruled out. There will also be an effect upon the demand for managerial personnel.

Funds are the other requirement. As was pointed out in Chapter V the association between investment and accounting profits generally appears weak. But perhaps a strong association is only to be expected if emphasis is placed on the role of accounting profit in determining the expected return to investment—an emphasis in keeping with the marginalist approach to the theory of investment decisions. If the acceleration principle operated smoothly, investment would be undertaken as capacity was exhausted; profits would be irrelevant. The extreme nature of this view has led to the introduction into models of profits as a second variable. If the residual funds approach is adopted profits assume considerable importance.

Recent investigations of the relationship between dividends and profits in the United States have shown that undistributed profits tend to absorb profit fluctuations[2] to the extent that firms fail to stabilize their profits. This lag of dividends behind profits has been explained in several ways. Lintner found that dividends and savings in the entire corporate sector, to a very close approximation, followed a stable linear regression on current profits and the previous year's dividend payments.[3] An alternative explanation is that firms have different conventional dividend rates for high, medium and low profits measured as a percentage on capital employed.[4] The undistributed profits determined in some such fashion are an

[1] See C. F. Carter and B. R. Williams, *Industry and Technical Progress* (London: Oxford University Press, 1957), Chapters 10, 12, 16.

[2] S. P. Dobrovolsky, *Corporate Income Retention, 1915–1943* (New York, National Bureau of Economic Research, Inc., 1951) and 'Economics of Corporate Internal and External Financing', *Journal of Finance*, XIII (March 1958), pp. 35–47; J. Lintner, 'The Determinants of Corporate Savings', W. W. Heller, F. M. Boddy and C. L. Nelson, eds., *Savings in the Modern Economy* (University of Minnesota Press, 1955), pp. 230–258 and 'Distribution of Incomes of Corporations among Dividends, Retained Earnings and Taxes', *American Economic Review*, XLVI (May 1956), Proceedings, pp. 97–113; P. G. Darling, 'The Influence of Expectations and Liquidity on Dividend Policy', *Journal of Political Economy*, LXV (June 1957), pp. 209–224. [3] 'The Determinants of Corporate Savings.'

[4] The distribution policies of British companies in the post-war years cannot be summarized so easily because of differential tax rates and the influence of dividend restraint. See S. J. Prais, 'Dividend Policy and Income Appropriations', Brian Tew and R. F. Henderson, eds., *Studies in Company Finance* (Cambridge at the University Press, 1959), pp. 26–41.

M

important source of funds. Their accumulation forces the firm to act, to expand existing types of activities, or, at times in 'a dither of diversification', to branch out into new fields, which may be technologically similar to existing activities thus giving possibilities of benefits through production arrangements, but may be entirely new and be based upon selling know-how and organization. Given the crucial importance of undistributed profits, it might be expected that error arising from accounting method might have a direct and not negligible effect through capital budgeting.

Two qualifications to the foregoing might be noted. Theoretically a firm has an alternative to diversification when it accumulates surplus funds, namely, to return capital to its shareholders. This would, however, conflict with the concept of the firm as a continuing entity directing its efforts to profit maximization in order to survive. It is nevertheless surprising that the interesting decisions to return capital have not been subjected to detailed study. In part, this is because ownership and taxation considerations tend to outweigh any detailed calculations of rates of return in alternative activities. The second qualification is one that tends to be overlooked in the residual funds approach: profits in any period may accumulate in cash or semi-liquid assets but they may equally well take the form of additional stocks or fixed assets acquired during that period and before the profit results have been ascertained. Because of this, it is evident that consideration of the structure of the firm's assets should not be omitted.[1]

Borrowing of one form or another is the remaining source of funds. The limit to such borrowing will be set by the amount of the firm's own resources, subject to such matters as the structure of existing liabilities and the desire to retain control through voting rights. Within these limits, the firm's ability to borrow, given the general state of the capital market, depends upon the attitudes and judgements of bankers, underwriters and investors. When the experience of periods of marked business fluctuations such as the 'thirties is considered, there seems to be little reason to believe that bankers and underwriters are not misled by exaggerated profit statements. Private investors rely to a great extent upon the advice of bankers and brokers or may be influenced by the writings of financial journalists who have often praised flotations destined to early death and condemned others destined to 'blue chip' status.

[1] See, for example, Eli Schwartz, 'Theory of the Capital Structure of the Firm', *Journal of Finance* XIV (March 1959), pp. 18–39.

However, the scope for private investment through the stock exchanges has been considerably reduced in the last three decades and institutional investors should be better informed.

Disclosed profits may enter into the determination of wages. Unless management is capable of eliminating the error it is likely to be more willing to negotiate when profits are high and rising, especially if there are labour shortages. And it seems probable that trade unions will be influenced by disclosed profits. The 'capacity to pay' principle plays a role in many systems of wage determination, and unions seem to interpret rising profits as evidence of increased capacity to pay, even though they refrain from using profits as a basis for wage claims. To do so would be dangerous; expanding economies with high employment levels still show disparate movements of profits, some firms and industries showing losses. Profits are volatile and fluctuations might be used by employers as grounds for wage reductions. Where arbitration systems operate there would seem to be further scope for disclosed profits to influence the outcome. And this influence extends widely through the variety of uses made of disclosed profits statistics by governments, governmental agencies, firms, and research workers. These have included measurement of monopoly power, competitive strength, efficiency, excess profits for taxation purposes, and prices for government contracts; regulation of the profits of public utilities; control of prices; and arrangement of cartels.

Since undistributed profits tend to absorb the movements of aggregate profits, it might be argued that there is little room for changes in profits to have any direct effects on consumption expenditures. But once more indirect effects have to be taken into account. Experience of the postwar years as well as of the 'thirties appears to indicate that consumption expenditures are influenced by holdings of liquid assets of which shares are a significant proportion. The influence of disclosed profits can thus extend to sympathetic movements in personal consumption. A similar effect on business firms may be noted. Increased values of investments may give both management as well as potential lenders an impression of liquidity.

Have recent developments in institutional arrangements and accounting techniques weakened the influence of accounting method as an accentuating factor? Institutional investment certainly works in this direction. So too does the development of professional management. But the position is not so clear when the recent developments of accounting techniques are considered. It is true that some firms have developed balance sheets in constant prices in addition to those required for statutory purposes; during prolonged periods of inflation many firms make additional allowances for asset replacement; and allowances are supposedly made for stock valuations. Here it might be asked whether small and medium sized firms often fail through unwise handling of stocks, or because they have less reserves and less borrowing capacity than the larger firms that survive. But what of the various methods, both mathematical and statistical, that have been evolved by management accountants and cost accountants to achieve practical profit maximization? It has been argued that they represent a movement towards marginal pricing techniques.[1] To the extent that this is true, such a development would seem to lead to an increased dependence upon accounting results. These changes in techniques raise an important point. Accounting method is not static, but tends to change with business conditions, for example, special stock provisions and depreciation charges, and a varying proportion of innovation expenses charged to current account instead of capital account. Consequently interest should be focused on the changing relative importance of historical and current cost accounting rather than a contrast of the two limiting cases. The initiation of these changes in techniques might be found to depend upon organizational features. Empirical investigation would probably show some interesting variations in executive behaviour, for example, as between a 'finance' oriented group and a 'production' or 'sales' oriented group. This is an aspect of the neglected subject of the firm's information system.

While accounting method has been the subject of professional dispute, company managements have nevertheless responded to such problems as changing price levels, but often in ways that have made it even more difficult to interpret accounts. Sometimes assets have been revalued. In some cases where this has been done, depreciation charges have continued to be based on the old balance sheet figures suggesting that the motivation arose from share capital considerations rather than from the need to provide additional replacement funds. Some companies have created secret reserves

[1] See James S. Earley, 'Recent Developments in Cost Accounting and the "Marginal Analysis"', *Journal of Political Economy*, LXIII (June 1955), pp. 227–242 and 'Marginal Policies of "Excellently Managed" Companies', *American Economic Review*, XLVI (March 1956) pp. 44–70; K. P. Norris, 'The Costing of Investment Decisions', *Journal of Industrial Economics*, V (March 1957), pp. 112–123; Sidney Robbins and Edward Foster, Jr., 'Profit-Planning and the Finance Function', *Journal of Finance*, XII (December 1957), pp. 451–467.

by charging additional amounts of depreciation, writing down the valuation of closing stock when determining profit, and by providing excessive amounts for liabilities. Another type of response has been to make transfers to various types of reserves, the transfers being disclosed in the accounts. Thus Imperial Chemical Industries Ltd., after making good the depreciation of the plant and providing for taxation, makes transfers to the following reserves:

Future replacement of fixed assets (building, plant and machinery) . . . this provision is necessary because depreciation is based on the cost or value in earlier years and when the time comes for replacement the new plants will cost more.
Reserve for the replacement of stocks . . . which have gone up in price and so cost more.

These are in addition to transfers to a capital reserve, a revenue reserve for strengthening of the business, and reserves for strengthening home and overseas subsidiary companies.[1] Unilever also fortifies current depreciation charges and guards against the possibility of falling prices.[2]

This dynamic aspect of accounting method also bears upon the investment decision. It is, of course, quite permissible to assume that investment plans are related to the currently accepted profit concepts. However, accounting method does have a history and the choice of methods would tend to be associated with historical development—an economy with a stable price history would probably differ from one which had experienced marked fluctuations. In so far as the different path followed generated different expectations, the precise nature of the relationship between investment plans and profit might differ. Nor is it sufficient in this context to refer to plans only; the relationship between realized investment and profit must also be considered. In the light of recent empirical studies no simple relationship would seem to exist and one is prompted to ask whether the conditions determining the choice of accounting method might not also enter into the investment decision. It seems certain that management does not always blindly follow the accountants but rather makes some adjustments to meet changing circumstances. Leaving such questions aside, assessment of cost of capital is one way in which accounting method might enter into investment decisions. One more comment which might be made about changing method is that the changes need not be

[1] Imperial Chemical Industries Limited, *Annual Report and Accounts.*
[2] Lever Brothers & Unilever Limited, *Annual Report and Accounts.* See also *The Economist,* 'Unilever Universe', CLX (June 23, 1951), p. 1519.

fully reflected in published accounts but may be primarily a matter of internal management accounting.

But what is the relevance of accounting records of cost for pricing purposes? At this point the guidance that management derives from conventional accounting records can be very easily over-emphasized by assuming that prices are purely cost determined and that past costs are indicative of future costs. Even if this assumption is made, it must be asked what are the relevant costs. If the firm faces potential competition it may, in Marshallian fashion, be more concerned when fixing prices with the costs that would be achieved by a new entrant than with any calculations of replacement costs of existing plant and equipment based on accounting records. This is especially so in an industry which is experiencing rapid technological change that accentuates the problem of finding suitable index numbers for estimating replacement costs. But it would seem that prices would be related to replacement costs. Burn, for example, argues that depreciation and capital must be measured at current replacement costs.[1] His reasoning is that any new competitor who may be attracted will have to pay current prices. Such a new competitor might use a different kind of plant; assuming the new plant was of higher productivity this would mean that the old plant had lost value by obsolescence. This then is a reason additional to changing price levels for seeking to use a current valuation.

The crucial question is what is meant by a current valuation. Is the significant figure the replacement cost of the existing firm or the entry cost of the potential entrant? Clearly these may differ. The existing firm may be adding to its capital stock with all the advantages and limitations that may involve; the potential entrant is most likely to be an existing firm from another 'industry' in which case it may possess financial, organizational, and marketing advantages as well as the opportunity of starting with a completely new plant embodying the most recent technological advances. The relationships between these two levels of cost, allowing for differences in cumulative learning effects, may point to a high or low barrier to entry.

As mentioned above, much of the discussion has proceeded on the basis that prices are cost determined. But it is important to recognize the limitations of such a pricing policy. Firms certainly

---

[1] Duncan Burn, ed., *The Structure of British Industry* (Cambridge University Press, 1958), Vol. 2, p. 426.

seek a measure of price (and profit) stability in both the short- and long-run. Discussions of price rigidity and oligopoly behaviour generally have been concerned with responses by firms to the actions of other firms but inadequate attention has been given to the speed of those responses. It would seem that this consideration is an important element of the explanation of price rigidity as the speed of potential response, given imperfect knowledge, will normally be faster for price as opposed to non-price behaviour. However, it is difficult to argue the case for a simple cost determined price policy where substantial cost changes are involved. Under such circumstances the fixed mark-up loses its rationale and demand forces intrude. Cost determined price would appear to be justified in an oligopoly situation where firms attempt to set a ruling price that is the highest that will exclude potential entrants. A variation in prime cost would lead firms to raise price. If demand conditions are stable and the change in costs is comparatively small, adding the existing profit margin to the higher average cost will give a good indication of the new entry-forestalling price. Applying the original total percentage mark-up to the new prime cost will serve almost as well.[1] It is, however, worth noting that merely keeping down price need not be sufficient to keep out competitors. Inadequate capacity and lengthening order books might be just as good as indicators of profit opportunities for the potential entrant. Keeping price down does not suffice unless capacity is expanded to keep pace with the growth of the market.

STATISTICS OF PROFITS

This discussion leaves much doubt about the strength of the link between disclosed or accounting profits and business decisions and therefore raises the question of the usefulness of statistics of profits. It is only recently that such statistics have become available.[2] From

---

[1] See Franco Modigliani, 'New Developments on the Oligopoly Front', *Journal of Political Economy*, LXVI (June 1958), p. 226.

[2] Cf. W. S. Ashley, 'The Statistical Measurement of Profit', *Economic Journal*, XX (December 1910), pp. 530–550; J. A. Schumpeter, *History of Economic Analysis* (New York: Oxford University Press, 1954), p. 895.

A useful bibliography of articles dealing primarily with the statistical measurement of profits appears in American Economic Association, *Readings in the Theory of Income Distribution* (Philadelphia: The Blakiston Company, 1946), pp. 707–709.

Some additional important contributions to the development of profit statistics have been: United States: J. E. Sterret, 'The Comparative Yield on Trade and Public Service Investment', *American Economic Review*, VI (March 1916), pp. 1–8; R. T. Bowman, *A Statistical Study of Profits* (Philadelphia: University of Pennsylvania Press, 1934); R. C. Epstein, *Industrial*

simple beginnings in the work of Sterret in the United States, and Stamp in Britain, a wide range of data on company profits has now been built up, faults of definition and sampling having been at least partially eliminated. Analyses of these data have yielded some interesting, if not always conclusive, results. Distribution policies and the relationship between investment and profit have been discussed above. Profits have been reported to be a linear function of the volume of production[1] and a stable share of aggregate income.[2] In small business there is some evidence of 'satisfactory' levels of profits.[3] The ranking of profit rates within industries shows a high degree of stability.[4] Profit rates are said to be related to size of firm.[5] Profit rates and high barriers to new competition seem to be positively associated.[6] Financial success and technical progress appear to go together.[7] Low average returns over long periods have been found to exist in some cases.[8]

These results have not been integrated with profit theory because that theory has not yet yielded hypotheses that can be subjected to empirical testing. Instability in earnings and great variability of earnings patterns are virtually the only hypotheses relating to *ex post* profits advanced for testing.[9] These could be consistent with almost any theory of profit. Unless it is possible to treat accounting profits

Profits in the United States (New York: National Bureau of Economic Research, Inc., 1934): W. L. Crum, *Corporate Size and Earning Power* (Cambridge: Harvard University Press, 1939); Osborne and Epstein, *op. cit.*

United Kingdom: J. Stamp, 'A New Index of Profits' and 'The Effect of Trade Fluctuations upon Profits before the War', *The National Capital and Other Statistical Studies* (London: P. S. King & Sons, Ltd., 1937); A. S. Carruthers, 'The Trend of Net Profits of Commercial and Industrial Enterprises, 1928–37', *Journal of the Royal Statistical Society*, 102, Part I (1939), pp. 63–80; Ronald Hope, 'Profits in British Industry from 1924 to 1935', *Oxford Economic Papers*, N.S., I (June 1949), pp. 159–181; National Institute of Economic and Social Research, *Company Income and Finance, 1949–1953* (London: National Institute of Economic and Social Research, 1956).

[1] E. H. Stern, 'Industrial Production and Profits in the United Kingdom and the United States', *Economic Journal*, LXV (September 1955), pp. 485–497.

[2] E. H. Phelps Brown and B. Weber, 'Accumulation, Productivity and Distribution in the British Economy, 1870–1938', *Economic Journal*, LXIII (June 1953), pp. 263–288.

[3] See Colin Bruce, F. A. Burchardt and E. B. Gibb, 'Small Manufacturing Businesses: A Preliminary Report on a Pilot Survey', *Bulletin of the Oxford University Institute of Statistics*, 17 (August 1955), pp. 241–282.   [4] See Downie, *op. cit.*, pp. 145–149.

[5] See W. L. Crum, *Corporate Size and Earning Power* (Cambridge: Harvard University Press, 1939); J. L. McConnell, 'Corporate Earnings by Size of Firm', *Survey of Current Business*, 25 (May 1945), pp. 6–12 and '1942 Corporate Profits by Size of Firm', *Survey of Current Business*, 26 (January 1946), pp. 10–16, 20.

[6] See Joe S. Bain, *Barriers to New Competition* (Cambridge: Harvard University Press, 1956), Chapter 7.   [7] See Carter and Williams, *op. cit.*, p. 185.

[8] See A. G. Bogue and M. B. Bogue, ' "Profits" and the Frontier Land Speculator', *Journal of Economic History*, XVII (March 1957), pp. 1–24; R. Davis, 'Earnings of Capital in the English Shipping Industry, 1670–1730', *Journal of Economic History*, XVII (September 1957), pp. 409–425.

[9] Cf. J. Fred Weston, 'The Profit Concept and Theory: a Restatement', *Journal of Political Economy*, LXII (April 1954), pp. 159–160.

as a reasonable approximation to the profits firms seek, earn, utilize, and dispose of, effort devoted to the collection and analysis of statistics of profit is misdirected and the hope of reconciling theory and facts needs must be abandoned.

These remarks may have brought out the importance of the questions raised concerning accounting statements. The only conclusion is, as might have been expected in a profit economy, that the influence of accounting method is extremely pervasive. The present state of knowledge does not warrant the assumption that it has no causal significance. Furthermore, if attention is concentrated on the cyclical aspects the timing of error may be crucial. These points may be resolved by further investigation of business decision-making. In the meantime it would be a pity to assume away such an interesting problem.

PROFITS AND EFFICIENCY

Finally, consider the statement that profit is an indicator of efficiency; that it can be used to appraise managerial performance. It is suggested frequently that profit is the business test of efficiency as compared with productivity or cost measures. Since total profit equals the margin between price and cost per unit of output multiplied by the number of units of output, profit may be increased by raising price or output or by lowering costs. Attention has been drawn already to the possibility that effort be directed towards minimizing taxation. But it is argued also that profits might be increased by exploiting the consumer. Given equal opportunities for exploitation, for firms with comparable costs, profits could be used as a measure of comparative efficiency.

Now it is true that business practice agrees with the economist's approach to the extent that costs and sales are measured in money rather than in physical units. However, the belief that profit, especially when expressed as a rate of return on equity, serves as a measure of efficiency, is too widely held. Many objections have been raised. Firstly, monopoly power is not related to managerial efficiency. This is harking back to the Veblenian idea that profits are made by hindering as well as aiding productive activity. Such a policy may well be a matter of managerial efficiency in the individual firm even though it appears as inefficiency from the social point of view. The creation and maintenance of a monopoly position is one of management's most pressing problems. Secondly, it is said that unforeseeable changes in markets that affect either revenue or costs and give rise to windfall gains (or losses) should not be attributed to management. This emphasis on fortuitous effects should not be carried too far; the firm's ability to respond to changes, even if it cannot predict them, depends upon the quality of management. The creation of a business organization possessing flexibility and capable of perceiving new market and investment opportunities and carrying out substitution in response to changes in relative factor prices is clearly a managerial task. Thirdly, there may be a systematic difference between the rate of return earned by small and large firms. Could this be judged the result of managerial inefficiency? Apart from these considerations, and also ignoring the problems of measurement of both profit and capital, the use of the current rate of profit as a measure of managerial efficiency ignores the whole question of the relationship of the firm to its environment.[1] Consideration of this relationship opens the way for considerable diversity between firms. Furthermore, this way of judging efficiency is essentially static. It fails to recognize the problems associated with different rates of growth of firms and their differing stages of organizational development. A high current rate of profit might reflect gross inefficiency of management if it is being achieved by destroying the firm's market and organization.

Concluding Remarks

Several important issues arise from the foregoing discussion. Firstly, reconsideration of the customary allocation of costs to current and capital categories is required because these procedures assume implicitly that organization, decision-making mechanisms, and flows of information are optimal. Secondly, the potential competition justification of replacement cost valuation of assets is unsatisfactory because differences in individual cost components may be offset by advantages in other directions; for example, by greater capacity for speedy decision-making or superior information. Comprehensive assessment is called for and this depends upon the firm's expectations, those expectations being conditioned by the nature of the firm. Thirdly, adoption of a 'satisfactory' profit policy introduces an element of flexibility which permits the firm to adopt valuations which are cruder, less precise than those that would be advocated from a marginalist point of view.

[1] Cf. Lady Hall and C. B. Winsten, 'The Ambiguous Notion of Efficiency', *Economic Journal*, LXIX (March 1959), p. 75.

CHAPTER VII

MARKET POSITION, PRICING AND INVESTMENT

THIS chapter presents some new developments and attempts to show that several aspects of the behaviour of the firm can best be rationalized within the fame of reference indicated in earlier chapters. These aspects include choice of resource combinations, interpretation of cost conditions, selection of profit criteria, responses to uncertainty including search for information, pricing and investment decisions, and measurement of profit. Fundamentally, this discussion aims to further the integration of pricing and investment theories, especially in regard to oligopolistic situations. In doing so it is necessary to clarify the concepts of capital, 'satisfactory' profit, and policy; to generalize the gambler indifference map treatment of the investment decision; and to modify the method of measuring profit.

'SATISFACTORY' PROFIT

It has been suggested in earlier chapters that full and normal cost procedures may be adopted when the firm is a multi-product firm operating under conditions of uncertainty. Furthermore, managerial objectives and the nature of business organization may point to a preference for growth. In two ways it is possible to 'reconcile' a growth policy with profit maximization. Firstly, if costs as estimated by the firm include excessive allowances for adverse future developments, in terms both of production possibilities and market conditions, the recorded estimates of profit may be, in a sense, unreal in that the firm will judge, on the basis of past experience, that the actual outcomes will be more favourable than the estimated ones. This being so, growth that involves such additional earnings may be preferred. Secondly, if the firm has adopted a policy of price stability and if the established price exceeds marginal cost at the current rates of output, profit maximation is consistent with maximization of sales revenue. Both these reconciliations might be regarded as possible only because the circumstances in which the firm is operating are disequilibrium states.

The first of these reconciliations is important for the concept of 'satisfactory' profit. It implies that the firm's policy may encompass not only the short-run operating flexibility of the full and normal cost approach but also a provision for growth. If growth is planned, it seems reasonable that the firm recognize the possibility of gains from technological and organizational improvements and make allowance for them in projecting current cost conditions. The reasonableness of this assumption derives from the importance of the technological change residual revealed by growth studies and from the extent of the efforts by firms themselves to initiate technological change. By reacting upon the interpretation of cost conditions this view opens the way for profit which is satisfactory but which is expected to increase; that is, the firm's aspirations may be related to a rate of change of profit rather than to a level of profit.

In order to develop further the concept of 'satisfactory' profit, use can be made of Heflebower's contribution to the study of stability in oligopoly.[1] This contribution is concerned with interfirm rivalry within an entry limit, assuming given factor price and demand conditions. Stressing the diversity amongst firms, it is argued that a state of balance, which may not be re-established following a change of conditions in the way usually required of a position of stable equilibrium, emerges in an industry in the course of its development. 'Each firm evolves into a "structural position" of value to itself. That position is a composite of its physical assets, its organization, its product lines, its location, and its relations with suppliers and customers.'[2] Equilibrium conditions may be replaced by a stability zone: 'a relationship among sellers' market shares and their respective prices and costs'.[3] Market shares, prices, and profit margins need not be the same for each firm; and because the response to a change of a given magnitude, say, in price, may be much greater than to a change of the same magnitude achieved by small steps, the stability zone concept is applicable to cases of slow structural change in an industry.

The conditions existing in many oligopolistic situations lead to a reluctance to engage in price competition, except where there is opportunity to prepare carefully for its consequences. These conditions include: inelastic short-run demand; cyclical variability of demand; a low ratio of variable cost to price; and a long planning horizon.[4] If the firm has excess capacity and its opportunity to engage in price competition is restricted, it will resort to other forms

[1] R. B. Heflebower, 'Stability in Oligopoly', *Manchester School*, XXIX (January 1961), pp. 79–93.
[2] Heflebower, *op. cit.*, p. 82.   [3] *Ibid.*, p. 80.   [4] *Ibid.*, p. 86.

of competitive action—provided marginal costs do not rise to equal price—within the stability zone to expand output and reduce or eliminate excess capacity. This concept of market position removes some of the rigidities in the behaviour of the firm as implied by the full cost approach. But more importantly it permits fuller scope for the influence of the individual firm's policy, which can encompass time preference with regard to profits, speed of response to external change, speed of decision-making, formation of expectations, and other aspects and consequences of the firm's organization and state of knowledge.

Viewing the firm as holding such a market position, what will be a 'satisfactory' profit? Assume (1) given capital market conditions, (2) given factor prices and demand conditions, and (3) optimal organization and information conditions within the firm.[1] If these three conditions are fulfilled, 'satisfactory' profit will be determined primarily by recent experience. It will depend largely upon what happens elsewhere in the economy, in a fashion similar to that in a state of competition. However, relaxation of conditions (2) and (3) makes 'satisfactory' profit dependent upon the quality of the firm's organization and information, on expected growth in demand, and on expected changes in costs. With a departure from optimal organization and information conditions, demand and cost expectations will depend greatly upon the 'quality' of the firm and bias in the estimates upon which those expectations are based may be upward or downward.

This situation can, through the rate of growth, be related to the entry-forestalling price level. Given conditions in the capital market, the higher the planned rate of growth the greater are the finance requirements of the firm which must be provided internally. So it seems a reasonable hypothesis that the gap between the actual price ruling in the industry and the entry-forestalling price will tend to narrow as the planned rate of growth increases. Changing conditions in the capital market could conceal such a tendency; and a necessary qualification arises if the firms are multi-product firms able to transfer profits from other areas of activity.

It must be added that the new developments on the oligopoly front have given an unwarranted precision to the concept of the entry-forestalling price, in large part because of the long-run

[1] Since condition (3) includes information it may presuppose a prior decision about the allocation of investment funds.

comparative statics approach that has been adopted. That price has been defined in terms of the effects expected to follow if *one* potential entrant of optimal scale actually entered the industry. These effects are a reasonable indication of the condition of entry, provided there is a clearly defined cost ranking amongst the potential entrants and that both existing firms and potential entrants have knowledge of these cost conditions. Alternatively, selection of the single entrant could be random and deter others from following, again assuming a high degree of knowledge. If these conditions are not fulfilled, a potential entrant may well take into account the possibility that other potential entrants enter the industry more or less simultaneously. Such expectations would raise the level of the entry-forestalling price; the importance of this deterrent perhaps being greater, the longer the process of entering the industry and the higher the capital-output ratio involved in the particular production (and selling) activity. And if the entry-forestalling price is defined as a percentage addition to 'competitive' price—that is, the long-run costs of a firm of optimal scale—there will be a lack of precision whenever learning effects are important, because the ranking of costs of the existing firms will be determined by the age distribution of those firms.

COLLUSION

Preservation of stability of the industry can be facilitated by collusion, overt or tacit. As implied above, stability might result from independent decisions by the individual firms. Nevertheless, 'the somewhat elastic glue of collusion . . . can reduce remaining doubt'.[1] This possibility has an important bearing upon the concept of 'satisfactory' profit because the determination of that profit, from the point of view of the individual firm, becomes subject to either an open bargaining process as in the case of the cartel, or what is tantamount to a bargaining process in cases where a co-ordinating mechanism such as price leadership operates. Alternatively, if the 'satisfactory' profit for each firm is determined prior to participation in such a bargaining process, a revision of the customary models of firm behaviour is needed. The issues involved here may be illustrated by such a revision of models of price leadership, together with some remarks on the kinked oligopoly demand curve and price flexibility.

[1] *Ibid.*, p. 93.

Price Leadership

The theoretical analysis of price leadership needs to be reconsidered in the light of some recent developments in price theory
and the accumulating evidence of statistical cost functions. The
traditional models of price leadership[1] have assumed the applicability
of a simple policy of profit maximization and cost conditions that
are in conflict with empirical findings. The rival assumptions of a
'satisfactory' profit objective and constant returns to scale above some
critical minimum output can be adopted. It is then possible to see
if these models still make price leadership inevitable and also make
it possible to identify the price leader. This procedure involves the
introduction of dynamic considerations into models that have been
essentially static.

Current uncertainties and the nature of its own organization
oblige the firm to adopt conventional procedures. The desirability
of doing so is increased under oligopolistic conditions by the
additional uncertainty associated with the response patterns of rival
firms. But there is one important respect in which uncertainty is
reduced. Responses to price changes can be prompt, although
not immediate, whereas responses to many forms of non-price
competition must inevitably be delayed. Consequently, strategy
shifts away from price, and investment, including expenditure on
managerial resources, technological improvements, and advertising,
becomes the firm's primary means of competing. A plausible result
of this is that the firm may, as one of its conventional procedures,
decide to seek some target rate of return on capital. This proposition
that the firm seeks satisfactory rather than maximum profits can be
incorporated into the models of price leadership. It becomes
necessary to introduce some other criterion in order to determine
the equilibrium position of the firm: sales revenue maximization
could serve this purpose.

The changed assumptions shift attention away from short-run
costs to long-run costs. Accumulating evidence suggests that many
firms experience constant returns to scale above some critical
minimum output. Difficult problems are involved. They extend
beyond the interpretation of the statistical evidence to the very

[1] See K. E. Boulding, *Economic Analysis*, revised edition (London: Hamish Hamilton, 1948),
pp. 580–587; G. J. Stigler, 'The Kinky Oligopoly Demand Curve and Rigid Prices', *Journal
of Political Economy*, LV (October 1947), pp. 432–449; J. W. Markham, 'The Nature and
Significance of Price Leadership', *American Economic Review*, XLI (December 1951), pp. 891–
905; Joe S. Bain, 'Price Leaders, Barometers, and Kinks', *Journal of Business of the University
of Chicago*, XXXIII (July 1960), pp. 193–203.

nature of the firm's long-run cost function. In the present context the important point is that all firms in the industry need not face identical cost curves. It will be assumed that firms operate at different cost levels for one or more of the following reasons: (1) production at different scales of output; (2) adoption of different criteria of performance; and (3) dynamic processes of adjustment within the individual firm. With respect to (3), it is customary to mention but ignore the fact that the firms are moving towards an equilibrium position.[1] The view to be taken here is that for multi-product firms whose activities are constantly changing in relation to any defined industry boundaries, equilibrium is never reached; that cost differences arising from dynamic processes of adjustment such as learning, technical development, and organizational change are permanent features of the industry situation. The ordering of firms according to cost may undergo change constantly.

Two basic models of price leadership have been presented in the literature to show price leadership as an inevitable consequence of certain assumed demand and cost conditions when the firms concerned pursue policies of profit maximization. In general this distinction has been between the case of the dominant (monopoly) firm and price leadership of the barometric kind. For several reasons variants of these models have been developed: it is possible to show that a small firm may be able to impose its price policy upon a large firm; and where open price cuts are avoided, it may be difficult to distinguish between a price leader and one of the early price followers.

(i) *The Dominant Firm*

In this case the small producers are obliged to accept the price set by the dominant firm which is assumed to maximize its profit by equating marginal cost and marginal revenue, the latter being estimated by deducting the total supply of the small firms as a group from total market demand. No significance attaches in this case to the shape of the cost curves provided all firms are producing beyond the minimum critical level. The large firm may produce at the lowest cost level of all producers, in which case the model yields the result usually attributed to it. If, however, the small firms achieve costs lower than those of the large firm, either through

---

[1] Cf. H. A. Simon and C. P. Bonini, 'The Size Distribution of Business Firms', *American Economic Review*, XLVIII (September 1958), p. 608; Manuel Gottlieb, 'On the Short-Run Cost Function', *Journal of Industrial Economics*, VIII (June 1960), p. 241.

dynamic adjustments or because the large firm is content with a satisfactory profit which is less than the maximum possible and brought about by more than minimum costs, it is possible that the small firm(s) could become the price leader(s). This possibility indicates a cause of breakdown of price leadership situations. It has been argued that the dominant firm case is of academic interest only; that it is essentially a monopolistic case. However, given the assumptions suggested above on profit objectives and cost conditions, it emerges that this type of price leadership may be of a barometric type reflecting the impact of changing technology, diversification, and processes of adjustment internal to the individual firm. This is in contrast to the usual meaning of barometric price leadership which emphasizes the responsiveness of the leader to changes in *demand* conditions.

(ii) *Firms with Different Cost Curves*

A second situation exists where there is a low cost, high capacity firm with one or more high cost, low capacity firms. Consider the duopoly case with equal shares of the market. The high capacity firm can impose its price policy upon its rival. If these firms face constant costs but at different levels the high capacity firm is still in a position to act as price leader by virtue of its lower costs although the extent of the conflict of interest, which is dependent upon the slope of the marginal revenue curve and the cost differential, may diminish. Even this source of conflict may be eliminated by relaxing the assumption of equal shares of the market. Given the demand curve for the product and the cost functions, there can be a sharing of the market that yields a price acceptable to both firms, provided the high capacity firm has costs per unit of output equal to or higher than those of the low capacity firm.

If the low capacity firm pursues a policy of satisfactory rather than maximum profits it is possible that its target rate of return be consistent with the price level that would be established by the high capacity firm. Here it is assumed that the failure to maximize profit takes the form of charging a price less than that which is consistent with maximum profit. Other possibilities would be higher than minimum costs and production volume greater or smaller than that which yields maximum profit. If the high capacity firm pursues a policy of satisfactory profit the conflict of interest between the two rivals may be accentuated. If both firms adopted such a policy, the price leader will tend to be the firm first coming

N

under pressure in relation to attainment of its objective and there is clearly no way of determining which firm will be the leader unless the target rates of return are known. The responses of the firms will depend greatly upon expectations and price adjustment will be only one of a number of courses of action open to the firms. In case (ii) the consequences of the changed assumptions are to weaken the chance of some inevitable form of price leadership and to make it impossible, in many cases, to identify the price leader.

(iii) *Firm with Small Share of the Market*

This situation has been touched upon already when considering case (i). The conclusion that the small firm can determine price rests upon the cost conditions assumed. If costs are constant and equal for both firms, each may seek the same price. However, in view of the firms' probably preference for non-price forms of competition it would seem undesirable to persevere too long with assumptions of perfect oligopoly and constant shares of the market. There remains the possibility that costs, although constant, are not the same for each firm. If this is so, the low cost firm becomes the price leader. As in case (ii) the pursuance of a policy of satisfactory profit can, as an extreme case, eliminate the conflict of interest or make it impossible to determine which firm would become the price leader without detailed knowledge of the profit targets. Expectations and normal response patterns would be of paramount importance.

Modification of the assumptions of these price leadership models in the direction of greater realism suggests there may be few situations in which price leadership by one (identifiable) firm is a continuing phenomenon which can be deduced from a knowledge of the relevant cost and revenue functions. Generally, price leadership will be of a barometric type and an alternative to overt agreement; it derives from the firms' preference for non-price forms of competition, subject to the possibilities for secret price cuts. Although this revision of the traditional models of price leadership has pointed to some of the implications of policies aimed at satisfactory profit as opposed to maximum profit, it would seem unreasonable to adhere to the assumption that the satisfactory profit is given independently of the bargaining process, if only because that bargaining process is likely to add to each firm's knowledge of its rivals' positions and create new expectations about response patterns.

The Kinked Demand Curve

A short exercise using the customary kinked demand curve shows some further bearing of a satisfactory profit policy upon pricing. The price level at which the average revenue curve of the individual firm is kinked acquires its significance in terms of the firm's market position. Small changes in the price charged by rival firms may not evoke a response if their effect is to leave profit within the zone regarded as satisfactory; and a response need not take the form of price adjustment but rather may be in the area of non-price competition. Even where price adjustment is contemplated it need not be immediate and it could be combined with non-price action at some future date. As a result the kinked demand curve is of limited usefulness for analytical purposes.

To equate the price at which the demand curve is kinked (Pk) with the entry-forestalling price (Pe) suggested by the barriers to new competition approach ignores not only the lack of precision attaching to Pe consequent upon lack of knowledge of, or differences in expectations concerning the number of potential entrants, cyclical disturbances, and growth patterns but also the possibility that Pk lies below Pe. If $Pk = Pe$, the possibility of new entry occurring may make the consequences of a unilateral price increase even more unfavourable. This will be so only if the firm recognizes the strength of potential competition; in which cause action to raise price above Pk seems even less likely than is implied in the customary kinked demand curve analysis. Consequently the upper section of the kinked demand curve may be relevant only when Pk is less than Pe, provided the firm is not prepared to tolerate new entry.[1] While Pk is less than Pe and is determined in the broad context of the firm's market position, a satisfactory profit policy could damp or eliminate responses both to changes in demand and cost conditions and changes in the policies of rival firms.

Within some critical limits, there may be a direct relationship between the industry rate of growth and the strength of price collusion. If a price fixing agreement seems likely to be threatened by secret price cutting, the participants would seem more likely to set the price initially below Pe. The weaker that threat, the better the prospects for maintaining a price approximating Pe. If the price cutting threat weakens as the rate of growth increases—and given a

---

[1] This assumption may not hold in cases where the firm prefers to diversify into other fields of activity rather than preserve its share of the market for a particular product.

preference for growth, this seems possible—actual price in collusive situations will be closer to Pe the higher the industry rate of growth.

Price Flexibility

A recent study of price flexibility will be used here for illustrative purposes.[1] Two basic assumptions of the model can be questioned. Firstly, price changes are treated as cost determined; secondly, expectations are allowed no role in price determination. Because the effect of demand changes upon profit margins is acknowledged in relation to the autocorrelation of residuals and the excess of actual over model-generated prices, these comments will be concerned primarily with the role of expectations.

The model is applicable to a single, isolated cost increase. If the change in costs is one of a series the model can be used only on the assumption of zero elasticity of cost expectations, an assumption that is unlikely to hold for price decisions that lead to the establishment of the prices incorporated in actual price series such as those for leather and shoes used in testing the model. The 'delayed' price response observed could have been a compound of adjustment to cost increases that have already occurred and to cost increases expected to occur. Expectations generated might differ as between cost components; for example, as between raw materials and wages. Substitution effects could be expected to occur. Furthermore, expectations of changes in the wage rate would generate expectations of changes in raw material prices.

Anticipation of cost increases in making price adjustments seems probable if firms are reluctant to make frequent price changes as is the case in oligopolistic situations. Such action on the part of firms seems necessary within the framework of the model if the equilibrium rate of profit is to be achieved. As the model has been presented, actual price lags behind the equilibrium price and, consequently, actual profit lags behind equilibrium profit. If, however, the firm delays its response to some cost increases and anticipates some future cost increases it becomes possible for average profit to equal equilibrium profit. The empirical findings would appear to offer some support for this interpretation of pricing behaviour. For example, the comparison of actual and model-generated price behaviour of shoe manufacturers shows that actual prices rose more quickly than model-generated prices during the period of

[1] J. V. Yance, 'A Model of Price Flexibility', *American Economic Review*, 50 (June 1960), pp. 401–418.

sustained cost increases in 1951. This was attributed to the existence of a sellers' market. Widening of margins could account for the gap; but so could pricing in anticipation of further cost increases.

The introduction of a positive or negative elasticity of cost expectations impairs the usefulness of the a measure of price flexibility used in the study. The price change this period may make up the whole or part of the difference between last period's price and the current normal price together with the whole or part of the difference between the current normal price and the normal price expected for the next period. Then

$$P_t = P_{t-1} + a\ (P^*_t - P_{t-1}) + b\ (P^*_{t+1} - P^*_t)$$

where P is actual price and P^* normal or equilibrium price. In practice the price adjustments may be intended to smooth out the effects of cost changes, actual and expected, for a number of periods. Both a and b will reflect elasticity of cost expectations which can vary as between cost components and over time.

Price flexibility will be further influenced by market position, internal organization, and profit goals. Market position influences both the formation of expectations and the firm's willingness to resort to price as opposed to non-price forms of competition. In similar fashion market position will set limits to the operation of accumulated orders and increased delivery delays as an equilibrating mechanism when full capacity is reached. Internal organization of the firm may retard the speed of response to cost changes. Where price changes are the results of joint decision-making by representatives of production, sales, and financial management, immediate response to changed conditions, either costs or demand, cannot be expected. Inter-industry differences in price flexibility may be accounted for partially in terms of differences in the typical size and organization of the firms. If the use of profit goals or targets is substituted for a strict policy of profit maximization, price flexibility might be expected to vary with the margin between currently expected profit and the profit target, inversely for a surplus and directly for a deficit. The hypothesis suggested here that prices may be changed to cover expected as well as past changes in cost could best be tested by empirical investigation of pricing decisions at the level of the individual firm. Such investigation might suggest ways of quantifying expectations. In the absence of such knowledge the best that can be done is to recognize that expectations might play an important role.

THE PRODUCTION FUNCTION AND COST CONDITIONS

A modified definition of the firm's production function has been suggested in earlier chapters. It implied the acceptance of non-optimal organization and information conditions as normal with the consequence that the optimal solution of the firm's production problem might not be achieved. When firms operate under conditions of uncertainty these conditions seem likely to be so widespread that they should be a subject of study rather than to be discussed as 'inefficiency' which is regrettable but capable of elimination. It may well be that these aspects of the firm's behaviour should remain, for the present, the subject of special supplementary studies, although conceptually it would seem possible to treat organization and information as forms of capital, as inputs in the production function.

Given the firm's market position, organization and information conditions will determine the planning horizon and the speed with which the firm seeks to change from one size to another. Since the speed with which a change in size is made will influence the cost level attained immediately, and perhaps that attained eventually, there are several ways in which the organization and information currently available to the firm may have an important bearing upon subsequent change in market structure. These arise from differences in planning horizons; differences in gestation periods of new plant as envisaged by the individual firms; and consequent changes in the ordering of costs amongst the firms in the industry. The effects of these conditions may not extend beyond the stability zone. However, differences between firms could conceivably be, or become, sufficient to form the basis for planned, major changes in market position.

If organization and information are to be regarded as inputs having the nature of capital, the possibilities for substitution and the process by which these resources 'depreciate' should be considered. Perhaps the most important form of substitution can be indicated in terms of the firm's market position. Organization and information may enable the firm to compensate for weakness in its competitive position in other respects; for example, in services provided with the product or the relationship with particular suppliers of materials or equipment. And as pointed out earlier, the firm may be faced with a choice between organizational improvement and technological improvement. These are, however, rather vague forms of substitution, made not in response to relative price changes, but rather as changes in the firm's policy. This is so because the price mechanism does not penetrate fully the area of administrative decision within the firm; and because customary methods of costing and profit measurement do not recognize the capital nature of these resources. In addition, these resources may not be subject to the normal processes of depreciation. Their value may increase with time; and dependent upon time and place their possession may confer strategic advantages as the market structure and technology of the industry alter.

INTEGRATION OF THEORIES OF PRICING AND INVESTMENT

In earlier chapters profit as a source of internal finance and as a determinant of capital supply was viewed as a link between pricing and investment decisions. The integration of theories of pricing and investment can be furthered in the course of an examination of some neglected aspects of the gambler indifference map treatment of the investment decision. Figure 6 shows a comparison of policies

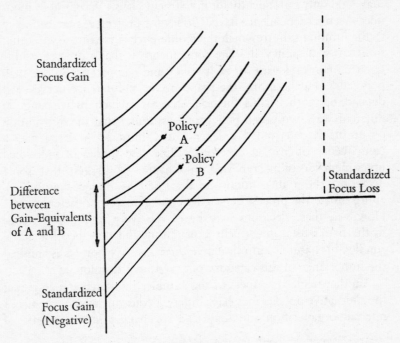

Figure 6

A and *B* in terms of standardized focus gain and focus loss, the indifference curves being asymptotic to a limit representing the entire sum of money available to be risked. These indifference curves should be regarded as bands with the consequence that differences between gain-equivalents of policies might exist and yet lack significance for the firm's decision-making. In this way seemingly irrelevant criteria might be applied during the decision process in the ways indicated by the case studies reported in Chapter V. This band interpretation of the indifference curves is of particular importance in the case of that curve passing through the point or origin because its value corresponds to the satisfactory profit the firm is seeking. In the light of earlier comments the indifference map must be viewed as changing through time; but perhaps in a systematic way as in the case where the firm's aspirations are geared to a rate of change in earnings.

Policies such as those represented by *A* and *B* can be compared by means of the gambler indifference map technique only if they are independent of each other. As suggested in Chapter V this condition may hold only infrequently for investment plans. What implications does this interdependence have? Policy (or project) *A* may be linked to the limiting sum to which the indifference curves are asymptotic; similarly with policy B. The consequence is that a different indifference map is relevant for each policy and comparison on one map is invalid. Furthermore, the shape of the indifference curves will depend upon the firm's financial structure which may change in different ways with each policy and, assuming that the distribution of profits is determined independently, must be in large part a consequence of pricing decisions.[1] The case studies of individual investment decisions reported in Chapter V suggest that some decisions, those that might be described as budget-constrained, approximate the process depicted by the gambler indifference map. However, these decisions may be of relatively minor importance in the firm's total investment expenditure and may be of a short-run flexible nature. Empirical investigations have not yet established the importance of this category of investment decision.

Another neglected aspect of the gambler indifference map is that the alternative policies may have different consequences for the firm's internal organization and may lead to changes in the criteria of

---

[1] The importance of financial structure would appear to invalidate any attempt to associate the shape of the indifference curves with conventional categories of market classifications.

performance being applied. For example, one policy could involve change in capital structure; changed participation in decision-making; and a transition from 'snatcher' to 'sticker' behaviour. A second policy could call for the establishment of a research and development department which might then become a new sectional interest in the decision-making process, placing emphasis upon the quality of technical progressiveness.

The significance of these defects in the gambler indifference map treatment of the investment decision emerges in the following ways: firstly, there is a need to integrate the theories of pricing and investment; secondly, the band interpretation of the indifference curves, the instability of the indifference map, the importance of financial structure, and possible changes in criteria of performance combine to weaken the association between profit earned and investment projects undertaken. But more importantly these considerations suggest ways in which the concept of seriability might be developed. The degree of seriability was described in Chapter III as a function of the weight of factors influencing the outcome that are repeated from one event to the next, the time interval between the events, and the financial strength of the decision-maker. It may seem that these conditions could be investigated empirically with comparative ease. But insufficient attention has been given to the nature of the events themselves, and to the nature of the decision process. What is needed is a dynamic version of the decision process envisaged in the gambler indifference map treatment, with full account taken of the organizational resources of the business firm. For example, unless it can properly be said that the decision is made at a moment of time, it should not be assumed that the decision-maker is of 'unchanging temperament', because the relative weights attaching to the various elements of the firm's policy may be changing over time. Furthermore, the experience of decision-making acquired by the organizational unit may reduce and even eliminate the seeming uniqueness of the event; and the flexibility of methods of financing, which stems in part from the interdependence of pricing and investment decisions, makes the crucialness of an event a much less precise state than the asymptote of Figure 6 suggests.

It may seem that these comments do no more than stress immeasurable factors and so reach the conclusion that any theory of decision-making must be indeterminate; for 'Theory, qua theory, contains a built-in predisposition against diversity. . . . Here diversity spells adversity, complicating theories and spoiling their precise determinateness.'[1] But recognition of this diversity is a necessary preliminary to gaining knowledge of the full range of influences from which the firm selects in simplifying the decision process.

MEASUREMENT OF PROFIT

Finally, some comments on the measurement of profit. The central modification arising from these chapters is that the nature of *capital* expenditure must be reappraised. If in order to maintain or strengthen its market position a firm may choose between organizational improvement, the introduction of new machinery, or the launching of a new product line, the expenditure to achieve that organizational improvement, the cost of the new equipment, and the development and initial advertising expenditure are equal candidates for treatment as capital expenditures. The revision of cost classifications called for is only partially achieved by conventional accounting treatments of 'goodwill'.

If the finance aspects of profit are emphasized, profit is of interest not only as a rate of return in relation to turnover or capital employed but also as an item in the firm's statement of sources and uses of funds. While shareholders remain interested in precise calculations of profit for dividend purposes, their assessment of future profits, like the assessment by the firm itself, depends a good deal upon retained profits. But from the firm's point of view there is little to be gained from drawing a clear distinction between costs and profits. For example, depreciation provisions may be just as useful as retained profits for the financing of growth. Furthermore, the firm's interest is in profits after taxes, even though it may have temporarily the use of funds reserved for tax payments. It should be noted that in emphasizing the finance aspects it is assumed not only that profits are being earned at a satisfactory rate, but also that the firm is pursuing an appropriate liquidity policy. A good deal of discussion has been directed to improvement of the quality of company balance sheets and profit and loss accounts in order to increase the efficiency of the capital market and to guide economic policy. Perhaps more attention should be given to sources and uses of funds rather than to attempts to refine methods of allocating costs in order to determine an exact figure of net profit. For this seems to be the important way in which accounting records are used in business decision-making.

[1] J. M. Clark, 'The Uses of Diversity: Competitive Bearings of Diversities in Cost and Demand Functions', *American Economic Review*, XLVIII (May 1958), Proceedings, p. 475.

CHAPTER VIII

CONCLUSION

THE $MC = MR$ formula, mainly because of its timeless equilibrium setting, has not proved adequate for the study of the behaviour of the individual firm. The theory of monopolistic or imperfect competition and the more recent developments in the theory of oligopoly have been important advances because they made room for product differentiation and for interdependence between firms. But they still have not integrated the theory of pricing and the theory of investment. Time, capital, and the nature of the business organization itself still have to be taken into account. Some of the difficulties become apparent with the realization that the marginal values to be equated are those expected and discounted. The models needed are much more complex, the number of variables greater than can be depicted in the two-dimensional, period-by-period equation of marginal costs and marginal revenue. This study has explored consequences of market imperfection, time, and the interdependence of decisions for profit maximizing behaviour in the fields of pricing and investment. Briefly, it has sought to show that the profit maximization hypothesis and the equilibrium technique of analysis have obscured the process nature of business activity. And while firms have sometimes been called organizations, the full implications of this have not been realized.

PROFIT AND PRICING

The satisfactory profit approach as developed in theories of full and normal cost pricing has emphasized that firms do not maximize short-run profits with a complete disregard for long-run considerations. Price changes are expected no longer to follow automatically and quickly from cost and demand changes. Earlier versions of these theories may have over-emphasized the rigidity of profit margins, but it is nevertheless possible that economic conditions in some periods may produce greater rigidity than in others. Consequently in more recent times, greater importance has been given to demand forces. To see this development as simply a return to marginalism, however, is to disregard the real advance that has been made. This approach has made it possible to deal with such matters as the internal structure of the business organization and its complex ties with its environment, which must be interpreted as extending far beyond the other firms in its own 'industry'. It has also paved the way for the integration of the theories of pricing and investment and for the study of the growth of the individual firm.

For what reasons may a firm be expected to seek satisfactory profit? Under conditions of uncertainty and with some measure of interdependence between firms—and this need not be entirely a matter of number of firms—competitive price cuts might lead to loss of market position. But price changes based on changes in costs will be much less likely to disturb the balance that has been achieved in the industry. Furthermore, price change is only one aspect of market strategy and its weakness is that other firms can react quickly. These remarks assume a comparatively stable industry situation, such stability having the effect of reducing uncertainty. However, the situation with new products is somewhat different, because new products can involve a greater element of uncertainty and also a greater need for profits that can be retained. In addition the firm may fear not only that high prices will attract competitors but also that buyers will react and that there may be government intervention.

Largeness of scale, diversification, and continuity of activity have necessitated the development of business organizations which for several reasons must formulate policies. First, a policy is required because of uncertainty and the costs of additional information. Second, adoption of a policy is conducive to industry stability and a consequent reduction of uncertainty. Third, the internal complexity of the large organization requires this form of decision-making. Fourth, the interests of shareholders are not sufficient to determine the goals of business activity. The internal structure of the business organization will influence its perception of market opportunities and the nature and speed of its responses to both internal and external changes. These organizational aspects combined with growth as a policy objective may help to make the growth path of the firm determinate; they may be just as important as market structure upon which the primary emphasis has been placed in the past. And in order to deal with the firm as an organization it has to be treated as the decision-making unit.

In line with discussion of the policy concept, the importance of past experience must be emphasized. For example, it might be suggested that the sales maximization model was developed and is applicable in a period of sustained growth during which marked cyclical fluctuations are absent; when growth tends to stimulate the demand for the increased output. Given separation of owner-ship and control, there is greater justification for treating the firm as the entrepreneur. Shareholders may receive even less considera-tion and priority may be given to growth. In these circumstances, although there may be substantial capital gains, the real value of shares can lag behind the growth of national product. Companies as a group may be increasing their share in national product; share-holders may be receiving a declining proportion of that share. Such a lag may well be accentuated by inflation, with its impact upon methods of financing business activity. Furthermore, changes in taxation have to be taken into account.

From the point of view of the individual firm the stability of the industry situation is much more than a matter of market share. External to the firm there are relationships with suppliers of equip-ment, materials, and capital; with sales outlets and customers, as a result of product specialization, servicing, and advertising; and with governmental agencies, labour organizations, research associations and other sources of information. On the internal side there are all the aspects of organizational structure and learning processes. Nor are external relationships and internal structure independent of each other. There will be interaction between them. For example, development of service facilities may lead to the creation or expansion of research activities.

These then are the variables that the individual firm is concerned with when it is planning survival and growth. Price is only one of a number of considerations in the problem of preserving long-run profit opportunities. The firm will produce whatever output can be sold, provided the price is satisfactory, that is, not greater than marginal cost. Diversification may occur when the price is no longer considered satisfactory. Thus in the ordinary course of events the price must be sufficient to yield a profit which covers basic interest, taxation, and the risk premium, and ensures growth finance requirements. The risk premium is dependent only partially upon profit fluctuations. It will be influenced by the stability of the industry situation. Nor will it be independent of growth prospects because in time, growth can cancel out excess capacity that may have resulted from over-expansion in earlier periods. The fact that the finance aspect is often ignored merely reflects an implicit assumption that the firm's existing policies enable it to obtain finance when it is needed.

A difficulty that arises with the satisfactory profit approach is that it might seem to imply that the rate of profit must be equalized throughout industry; and this does not seem to be borne out by observation of firms and industries. But the diversity in market position of individual firms is great. When market position is interpreted in the broad sense indicated earlier, it should not be expected that this diversity be eliminated by market forces even over a very long period of time. Uniformity of product prices may be achieved without equalization of profit rates.

Emphasis has been placed upon the applicability of theories of pricing to certain economic conditions, and upon the diversity of market positions of the individual firms. Consequently the scope of any generalizations that have been suggested has been limited; and this seems consistent with the present state of empirical knowledge. In fact there may be good reason for not seeking generalizations about all firms under any conditions, because change and diversity may be necessary conditions for the real 'equilibria' attained, and also a cause of growth of the individual firm.

THE INVESTMENT DECISION

The importance of profit for the investment decision arises primarily from its influence upon the supply of capital for growth. This is consistent with the emphasis that empirical findings have placed upon liquidity and the level of demand. But the investment decision is made by an organization and the decision is concerned usually with part only of an investment programme. Consequently, the view that bygones are bygones should not be adopted. The internal development of the organization and the evolution of its external market position play an important part in its perception of opportunities and selection of possible courses of action. The firm's policy at a moment of time can be understood only in the light of earlier events.

It was suggested that aggregate retardation at economy level may be a matter of an increasing proportion of actual declines, rather than a uniform retardation of the individual industry units that make up the aggregate. This may apply equally well to the individual firms that make up an industry group and also to the individual product activities of particular firms. A theory of fluctuations of business profits could be developed if changes in profits are resultants of movements in prices, costs, and quantities, and this diffusion aspect is incorporated. This is necessary because the 'product' of the large firm is changing continually in composition. The typical pattern for any one product appears to be a sequence of expansion, stability, and contraction. But the phases for individual products need not coincide.

Interdependence and the sequential nature of business decision-making has been emphasized because competition is a long-run matter, with investment planning as the firm's primary means of competing. The persistent behaviour patterns which make up the firm's policy can be modified more easily in the long-run. Consequently, there is need, when the relationship between investment and profitability is considered, to take account of the significance of the initial capital stock and organizational resources, the duration of the profit return, and the impact of the firm's investment upon its market position. The availability of retained profits may be far more important than precise estimation of rates of return.

There are implications for economic policy. Because returns on investment expenditures cannot be estimated precisely, monetary policy, investment allowances, and the like must operate through liquidity or through target rates of growth. Their effects may be minimized if an organizational constraint is operative already. This is not to suggest, of course, that there will not be marked differences in financial structure between firms, such differences also being important for economic policy.

THE THEORY OF PROFIT

Treatment of the firm as the given decision-making unit has led to an over-simplified view of the relationship between profit and uncertainty. The decision-making unit has to be created and maintained; and profit, defined as the income accruing to the firm, is in part the result of the firm's planning activities and organization. This part of the firm's income constitutes a return on these capital resources. Once it is recognized that the firm itself can and does change, the link between the leading types of theory of profit—uncertainty, monopoly, entrepreneurship, and disequilibrium—is apparent. To repeat a quotation from an earlier chapter, it completes 'a scheme of things in which all the various aspects and meanings of profit arise simultaneously from a single essential vision'.

It is true that this view of profit fails to escape the terminological difficulties that have beset attempts to define the boundary between

interest and profit theories. If profit is the source of interest, the
theory of profit developed in this study should prove acceptable,
in so far as 'interest theory' is then concerned for the most part with
the price of money loans. Despite this problem, the theory of profit
based upon such a model of the firm has implications for the
theoretical and empirical study of distribution in that it suggests
further categories of income classification.

This study began with the suggestion that confusion in the
theory of profit had been caused by the adoption of an outmoded
model of social and economic organization. Alternatively, it might
be said that the subtraction process which reduced profit gradually
from the income of the enterprise to the difference between expected
and realized income, has been carried too far; the observed role of
the modern large company can be understood only by abandoning
the attempt to break such organizations down into their component
parts. The firm must be seen as the entrepreneur, as the decision-
maker that may adopt a policy aimed at maximizing its rate of
growth.

In the same way as the applicability of a model of the firm will be
restricted to pricing and investment behaviour during particular
phases of growth of the firm, industry and economy, a theory of
profit should refer to the social and economic organization of a
particular period. Not all firms in the economy are organized in
the same way; nor are the salient features of the model of the firm
suggested in this study as definite in the real world as they appear
here. Nevertheless, the usefulness of a theory of profit will depend
upon the theorist's ability to perceive the emerging characteristics
of social and economic organization.

This reconsideration of the theory of profit has suggested many
subjects for empirical studies. There have now been sufficient studies
of pricing policies to establish the importance of long-run considerations. Instead of emphasizing simply the rigidity of profit margins,
the variability of individual product margins should be investigated
in relation to product combinations, organizational structure, and
to the level of activity in the industry and in the economy. It may
be that the variability rather than the rigidity of margins is the surprising feature. Because of diffusion aspects it is suggested that
changes in the level of activity in industries which are related through
factor and product markets should also be considered.

Comparative studies of changing levels of retained profits should
be undertaken on an industry and economy basis. It is desirable to

know not only the conditions under which the individual firm can increase its retention ratio, but also the process by which the ratio for the company sector as a whole can rise over a long period. Differences in profitability, rates of growth, gearing, and relationships between ownership and control, suggest that changes are unlikely to be uniform as between firms. Examination of the relationship between the trend of share prices and growth might throw light upon changes in the general level of retained profits. Ownership and control need further investigation because an arbitrary measure of voting power is no indication of operative control; and because decision-making is subject to influences which arise within the organizational structure and out of its changing relationship with its environment. There may be significant relationships between compensation and the location of decision-making power.

Further study of investment decisions is called for in order to establish the nature of the simplifying process that is involved, the extent to which firms base decisions upon single-valued estimates, the importance of the financial constraint, and the relationship between realized and expected returns. Having emphasized the importance of organizational factors, it becomes necessary to know more about the ways in which age and stability of the organizational structure influence price and investment decisions. The value of the policy concept must be ascertained by empirical studies.

The most important field of inquiry which would make direct use of accounting data would be studies of sources and uses of funds at the level of the individual firm. This would be linked closely with examination of budgetary techniques. The parallel between the satisfactory profit and the permanent income hypotheses may suggest propositions that might be subjected to empirical testing.

BIBLIOGRAPHY

THE literature on the theory of profit and profit measurement is very extensive so it seems worthwhile listing some useful bibliographies that are available.

American Economic Association. *Readings in the Theory of Income Distribution* (Philadelphia: The Blakiston Company, 1946). Classified Bibliography of Articles on National Income and Distribution, Part VI, Profit, pp. 704–709.

American Economic Association. *Readings in Price Theory* (London: George Allen and Unwin Ltd., 1953). Bibliography of Articles on Price Theory, pp. 527–561.

American Economic Association. *Readings in Industrial Organization and Public Policy* (Homewood, Illinois: Richard D. Irwin, Inc., 1958). Bibliography, pp. 393–426.

American Economic Association. *Index of Economic Journals* (Homewood, Illinois: Richard D. Irwin, Inc., 1962), Vol. I-V.

American Institute of Accountants. *Changing Concepts of Business Income* (New York: The Macmillan Company, 1952), Bibliography, pp. 147–160.

Arrow, K. J. 'Alternative Approaches to the Theory of Choice in Risk-Taking Situations', *Econometrica*, 19 (October 1951). Bibliography, pp. 435–437.

Biet, Bernard. *Théories Contemporaines du Profit* (Paris: Librarie de Médicis, 1956). Bibliographie, pp. 291–298.

Bowen, H. R. *The Business Enterprise as a Subject for Research* (New York: Social Science Research Council, 1955). Selected Bibliography, pp. 79–103.

Chamberlin, E. H. *The Theory of Monopolistic Competition*, 7th ed. (Cambridge: Harvard University Press, 1956). A Bibliography on Monopolistic Competition, pp. 277–346. This edition incorporates supplementary bibliographies which had been published in the *Quarterly Journal of Economics* in 1948 and 1956.

International Association for Research in Income and Wealth. *Bibliography on Income and Wealth* (London: Bowes & Bowes). Volumes I–VII relating to work published in the period 1937–56.

Lazarsfeld, Paul F. 'Reflections on Business', *American Journal of Sociology*, LXV (July 1959). Selected Bibliography, pp. 26–31.

March, J. G. and H. A. Simon. *Organizations* (New York: John Wiley & Sons, Inc., 1958). Bibliography, pp. 213–248.

National Bureau of Economic Research. *Research in the Capital and Securities Markets* (New York: National Bureau of Economic Research, Inc., 1954). Inventory of Recent Research, pp. 5–40.

National Bureau of Economic Research. *Research in the Capital Markets. Journal of Finance*, XIX (May 1964), Supplement, pp. 27–43.

Shackle, G. L. S. *Decision, Order and Time in Human Affairs* (Cambridge at the University Press, 1961), pp. 275–279.

UNESCO. *International Bibliography of Economics* (Paris: UNESCO). Volumes I–VIII relating to work published in the period 1952–59.

Wasserman, Paul. *Measurement and Evaluation of Organizational Performance. An Annotated Bibliography* (Ithaca, New York: Cornell University, 1959).

Wasserman, Paul with Fred S. Silander. *Decision-Making An Annotated Bibliography* (Ithaca, New York: Cornell University, 1958).

Weston, J. Fred. 'The Profit Concept and Theory: A Restatement', *Journal of Political Economy*, LXII (April 1954), pp. 152–153.

AUTHOR INDEX

SUBJECT INDEX